HOW TINY HEBRON
WON THE ILLINOIS STATE BASKETBALL CHAMPIONSHIP
AND THE HEARTS OF FANS FOREVER

SCOTT JOHNSON & JULIE KISTLER

Illinois High School Association
Bloomington, Illinois

Copyright © 2002 Scott Johnson and Julie Kistler

First printing, January, 2002.

Cataloging-in-Publication Data

Johnson, Scott (1956-) and Kistler, Julie (1956-).
Once There Were Giants / Scott Johnson & Julie Kistler — 1st ed. p. cm.

ISBN 0-9601166-5-6
1. Hebron Green Giants (Basketball team)—History. 2, Hebron (Ill.) High School. 3. Basketball—Tournaments—Illinois—History. I. Title

Printed by Multi-Ad Services, Inc., Peoria, Ill.

For ordering information, visit the IHSA Web site at www.ihsa.org/hebron.
Telephone orders: 309-663-6377
Orders by e-mail: ihsa@ihsa.org

Permissions to reprint text and photographs follow the Index at the back of the book.

To the memory of Russ Ahearn, Phil Hadley,
Don Wilbrandt, and Clayton Ihrke.

Table of Contents

chapter 1

Two Lights Shining

Two lights glow into the darkness high above the crowd at Huff Gymnasium. Only two.

They may be small, but they blaze bright red against an oversized map of Illinois. One round bulb shines in the far west, and one sits at the very top of the state, almost into Wisconsin.

They are the survivors. Over the past four days, the lights of the other fourteen competitors have wavered, blinked, and then fallen dark, one by one, until only these two — the two high schools that will meet to decide the Illinois state basketball championship — remain.

To get here, to make it through to this last game in Huff Gymnasium on this chilly March evening in 1952, each team has had to pass through a grueling, month-long elimination tournament. One loss and the season was done.

Now only a single game remains. Two lights still shine.

The light on the left side of the map, set into a wide curve of the Mississippi north of St. Louis, represents perennial power Quincy. Quincy won the state championship in 1934, and over the last eleven years, the school has appeared in the Sweet Sixteen nine times. The Blue Devils are still stinging from a last-second loss in last year's semifinals that cost them a chance at the state championship. They can't help but see this game as a golden opportunity for vindication.

With 1,035 students in three grades, Quincy Senior High School is one of the largest schools in the state outside the city of Chicago. Quincy has a pool of 480 boys to choose from, fielding three levels of basketball teams and keeping 45 players in training.

In contrast, the high school in Hebron, where the other light shines, has a total enrollment of 98. There are far more cows than people in the Alden-Hebron school district.

To make it this far, Hebron's plucky Green Giants have defeated a series of teams from much larger schools. The imposing foes they've vanquished along the way include former state champs Elgin and Champaign as well as mighty Rock Island. Each of these schools could swallow Hebron's entire student body without having to add so much as a single teacher or classroom.

Most of the people crowded into the stands at Huff Gym, squinting up at those two small lights high overhead, realize that it's an amazing, once-in-a-lifetime occurrence for a team like Hebron to get this far. No school with so few students has ever won the state basketball championship. Only a handful of schools Hebron's size have even reached the Sweet Sixteen.

Across the gym floor, Quincy enters the arena with pride and presence. If anyone belongs here, it's these blue-chip Blue Devils, with their long-standing basketball traditions, superlative facilities and coaches, and huge, faithful following. Year in and year out, Quincy fans back a winner.

Against this kind of competition, Hebron seems like the longest of long shots. This tiny school tests fate every time it takes the court. The Green Giants can't possibly win. Or can they?

As those two small lights flicker high above, it's as if the crowd holds its collective breath. Their heads tell them that Quincy will prevail. But in their hearts...

In their hearts, they're hoping against hope that the little guy can pull out a victory, one more time.

One more time.

chapter 2

Basketball Town

In 1952, Hebron, Illinois, was indistinguishable from thousands of other small towns across the American Midwest.

Although the village of Hebron was nearly a hundred years old, it had moved forward slowly from its rural beginnings. Major highways bypassed Hebron, as did major rail lines. The town sat only 55 miles as the crow flies from one of the country's great urban centers, yet Hebron seemed very much unaffected by big-city life.

Walking through its two-block-long business district in 1952, you'd find four small groceries, two restaurants, and two taverns. Not far away, the hardware and feed stores, the blacksmith, and a men's clothing and shoe store served the town's basic needs. A milk processing plant, a grain elevator, and a small water tower sat near the old Chicago and Northwestern railroad depot at the north end of town.

All very normal for that time and place. So what set Hebron apart from all the other small towns in Illinois?

For one thing, it was surrounded by cows. Lots of cows. As a matter of fact, the rolling hills around Hebron looked a lot more like Wisconsin than Illinois. That was no surprise — only a last-minute amendment approved by the U.S. Congress had sneaked Hebron and the rest of northern Illinois into the "Land of Lincoln" at all.

Just before the statehood bill passed in 1818, Illinois' northern border was moved some 41 miles north of the original line. In that instant, the state of Illinois gained some 8,000 square miles of unexpected new territory, including the lucrative lead mines of Galena, the site on Lake Michigan that would become Chicago, and the undulating glacial moraines that would sustain Hebron's settlers.

The area was settled in the 1850s and 1860s by farmers pressing west in a search for good land. The hills of McHenry County were difficult to plow, but they proved perfect for pastureland. And so, as the decades passed, more and more acreage was dedicated to dairy farming. By 1952, cows drove the economy of this town of 680 inhabitants.

But citizens did find time for other pursuits. For recreation, there was tennis and baseball in the summer, football in the fall, and basketball... Well, there was always basketball.

Always.

Hebron might have been a perfectly ordinary town in other respects, but when it came to basketball, it was a cut above. There were different theories as to why the game became so popular, but there was no doubt about it — in the 1930s, 1940s and 1950s, Hebron was a basketball town.

Some people thought it was due to a genetic predisposition for tall children among the predominantly English, German and Dutch settlers. Others guessed it might have something to do with the generous blacksmith who made hoops for the town's children. After all, where there were hoops, there would be children who wanted to toss basketballs through them.

Or perhaps it stemmed from a regular diet of beef and whole milk, leading to strong, healthy children who had energy to burn.

Whatever the reason for the initial spark of interest in basketball, there were clear indications that success bred success, that parents and older brothers passed along their own passion, one generation to the next, until basketball was everywhere you looked, from youngsters playing in driveways and haylofts to elders dissecting each and every game from a circle of chairs set up at the harness store.

In the end, it really didn't matter how it began. Whether by design or serendipity, basketball reigned supreme in Hebron.

Immersion

Basketball came to northern Illinois and thus to Hebron in the 1890s, not long after it was invented by James Naismith. But Hebron's immersion in the sport really began in 1927, when Lowry B. Crane was hired as the high school's coach and physical education instructor fresh out of the University of Chicago.

The Hebron school board took a risk when they hired Crane. After all, Lowry Crane was an urbane young man. He'd grown up in Jacksonville, Florida, and later Chicago, and was a graduate of the city's most prestigious university. Now they were dragging him all the way out to the hinterlands of McHenry County. Who could guess whether Crane would fit in or how long he might stay?

Crane had charted a course toward law school until his senior year when, following his mother's example, he decided to become a teacher instead. When it came to choosing a place to start his career, Crane saw something he liked in Hebron. The school wanted him to teach math and physics and start off coaching the junior varsity team, but fate intervened. When Hebron's varsity coach resigned prior to the start of the school year, Crane moved up directly to the top basketball position.

In his playing days, he had always been known as "Red" for his shock of striking auburn hair. A modest, unassuming man, Crane played on Englewood High School's city championship soccer team in 1923 and substituted on Nelson Norgren's University of Chicago basketball teams. But he was the first to point out that he was never a starter, much less a star, on those teams.

Now, with his soft, southern accent and easy-going manner, Crane made the case for physical education and especially for the game of basketball. After his arrival, he talked the board of education into putting hoops in the schoolyards, and he encouraged townsfolk to hang baskets on their garages. He felt strongly that building a successful physical education program as well as a first-rate basketball team depended on developing good habits at an early age.

Whether they were persuaded by his logic or his personality, Hebronites heeded his message. Soon balls were bouncing all around town. In Hebron, as in many small towns where recreational prospects were limited, basketball quickly became the game of choice.

Adults, teens, and even grade school kids played basketball in driveways and playgrounds, in all kinds of weather, at all times of the year. As Crane walked around town, it was not uncommon for young children to shout, "Look, Mr. Crane, I'm practicing. I'm going to be on the team!"

As a matter of fact, the coach could monitor the development of his program by looking right out his front window. The Judsons, an athletic family with three young boys, lived right across the street, and they seemed to love basketball.

As he found his footing in the new town, Crane remained an educator first and a coach of the old school. For him, athletics were not a means to glory, money, or adulation, but an exercise in discipline and self-awareness. His motto was *mens sana in corpore sano*, "a sound mind in a sound body." For his athletes, winning was definitely the goal, but only because winning was the end product of striving for excellence. Competing simply for the sake of glory was not acceptable to Lowry Crane.

Instead, he stressed conditioning and fundamentals. He taught teamwork and discipline. And in a few years his teams were the class of McHenry County — no small accomplishment for a town of Hebron's size. All the practice and hard work had begun to pay dividends, just as Crane had promised.

In 1935, Hebron won its first county title since 1924. No longer would "Little Old Hebron" be considered a pushover on the basketball court. Crane's teams now won more games than they lost every year and competed on an equal basis with bigger county rivals like Woodstock and Crystal Lake.

A Backhanded Boost

But beating up on local rivals and achieving statewide success were two different things. In the Illinois state tournament, where every school played for the same prize regardless of its enrollment, the deck was stacked against small schools like Hebron.

Prior to 1936, all the teams in the state started out in "district" tournaments. The district winners then advanced to sectional tournaments, and the sectional winners to the state final tournament. The numbers of teams in each tournament varied, but the basic recipe was the same: from district to sectional to state, a three-stage, winner-take-all tourney.

While Crane's teams might be able to start the district tournament with a win over a small school like Richmond or Huntley, and maybe even topple a medium-sized school like Woodstock or Crystal Lake, there was little hope of beating the really big schools further down the road.

In 1924, Hebron's most successful season up to that point, the locals won the county tournament for the first time and made it all the way to the finals of the district meet. Hebron was just a win away from the sectionals before losing to Elgin, the eventual state champion, by the score of 65-11. The city boys took the best McHenry County had to offer and basically mopped the floor with them.

But Hebron's tournament prospects, and the prospects of all small schools in Illinois, received a boost in a backhanded way in 1936.

For years the number of mismatches occurring in the district tournaments had increased, but in 1935 there were an embarrassing number of blowouts. The scores from the first round of the tournament sounded a disheartening drumbeat across the state: Olney 107, Parkersburg 13. Moline 110, Coal Valley 11. Joliet 136, Mokena 5. And on and on.

The clamor among small schools to split the tournament field by enrollment and award two, three, or even four state championships became so loud that the Illinois High School Association, which organized the state basketball tournament, realized that some action needed to be taken. The solution the association came up with was almost revolutionary, but despite its unusual approach, it generated surprisingly little protest.

Starting in 1936, the IHSA set aside the preliminary stage, the district tournaments, and reserved them for small schools only. The winners of the district tournaments advanced to a newly created level, the regional tournaments, where the big schools played their first games.

This two-tier process eliminated the worst of the early mismatches, allowing the small schools to compete on an even playing field for local bragging rights and a district tournament plaque. Of course, it also meant that to win a regional championship, they would have to play two or three more games than the big schools.

The state tournament had thus become a four-stage event: district, regional, sectional, and state, with the district level reserved for smaller schools.

The IHSA added another curiosity when it reorganized the tournament, one that created more controversy. After the shake-up, both the regional champion and runner-up advanced to the sectional tournament. This meant that the regional championship game was essentially meaningless, since both teams advanced to the next level regardless of the outcome. The important game had become the regional semifinal. Winning that semifinal game was the ticket to the sectional tournament where, it could be argued, the serious action began.

Hebron's program thrived under the new system. The school won the local "small-school" district in 1936 — the first state tournament award ever to decorate the school's walls — and then again in 1937. In 1939, Hebron swept through the district once more, and this time recorded the school's first win over its big-city rival, Elgin, in an overtime decision in the regional semifinals. Hebron was then steamrolled by Dundee, the defending state champion, in the regional championship game. But because of the curious rule that qualified two teams from each regional, Hebron made it into the sectional tournament for the first time in the school's history.

The town was thrilled that its team had made it to the next level. But the celebration was short-lived.

In the sectional, Hebron ran into a tough Rockford team, losing 39-34. The pain of that narrow defeat lessened somewhat the next week when Rockford, with an enrollment 35 times larger than Hebron's, mowed down the rest of the tournament field to win its third state championship.

In just a few short years under Lowry Crane's direction, Hebron's basketball program had risen to a completely new level, one where the small-town team played on seemingly equal footing with the biggest and best schools in the state. It was true that Hebron had yet to strike fear in the hearts of opposing coaches. But as the 1939 tournament drew to a close, Crane knew something these men did not.

There was an eighth grader across the street named Howie Judson, and he was looking more and more like a budding superstar.

Sparks

Expectations were high for the 1939-40 team, but when practice was called at the start of the season, Crane shared some bittersweet news. He'd finished his master's degree during the summer and had now been offered a position as a physics instructor at Senn High School, one of the most prestigious high schools in Chicago. For the conscientious, thoughtful coach, it represented an opportunity to better provide for his family, which now included two daughters, Barbara and Nancy.

But who would Hebron find to replace the much-loved L.B. Crane? With little time before the season began, the school plucked a graduate student named Ed Willett out of Northwestern University. Standing a full 6-foot-6, Willett had grown up in Canton, Ohio, and had starred on the basketball team at Wooster College. He'd wanted to get back into basketball after completing his undergraduate studies, but times being what they were, had opted to study chemistry instead. When the position at Hebron became open, however, Willett could not resist the temptation to coach the highly regarded team. By the time Willett arrived in Hebron, Crane had already started the team off with two victories.

Working with an enrollment of just 42 boys, the towering new coach had an unusually tall team at his command. Keith Johnson, captain of the squad, stood 6-foot-1. John Kjellstrom and Russell Voltz were both 6-4. Gordon Burgett, 6-1, and John Ryan, 5-11, rounded out the starting lineup. Freshman Howie Judson, the top reserve, was also 5-11.

Using its height to good advantage, Hebron tore through its competition at the start of the season, winning its first 20 games before falling in an upset to Crystal Lake. But that single setback was not enough to derail their hopes for success in the state tournament.

The Green and White, as the team was known, encountered virtually no competition in the district tournament, defeating three local teams in quick order. A win over Arlington Heights started the regional meet. And then Hebron went on an amazing run, almost certainly unequaled by any Illinois high school basketball team before or since.

In the regional semifinal, Hebron rallied from ten points behind to beat Elgin in overtime for the second straight year, 26-23. Dundee awaited in the next game, but Hebron's plans were upset when Burgett came down with the flu. Then, tragically, Ed Willett's sister died. While the coach returned home to Ohio for the funeral, the call went out to Lowry Crane, who drove out from Chicago to work with his old squad one last time. Dundee fell, 37-34, and Hebron had won an emotional regional championship, its first ever.

In the eight-team sectional tournament, Hebron beat Mt. Morris, 37-22, and then Freeport, 40-29, to set up an epic sectional title game.

Everyone loves an underdog, but on this night the sentimental odds were stacked against the smaller team. Rockford High School was the defending state champion and a perennial state powerhouse. It planned to close its doors that summer to reopen in the fall as two separate schools, East and West, in two brand-new buildings. Held at the local armory, this was to be the last home game ever played by a team from Rockford High School. Alumni packed the arena to say goodbye to their alma mater.

But Hebron was the spoiler, leading from start to finish and vanquishing the Rabs, 35-24.

The final toll was nothing short of amazing. In nine short days, just to qualify for the Sweet Sixteen, tiny Hebron had made a clean sweep of the elite teams of northern Illinois — Elgin, Dundee, Freeport, and Rockford — four schools responsible for 8 of the 32 state championships awarded up to that time.

It was the high school basketball equivalent of Carl Hubbell's great feat in the 1934 All-Star Game, striking out five consecutive future Hall of Famers.

No wonder the Hebron fans built a bonfire in the street.

Over 400 citizens had traveled to the game in Rockford, leaving Hebron nearly a ghost town. As soon as they heard the good news from Rockford, the few that remained piled wood, boxes, and tires in the middle of the intersection at Main Street and Prairie Avenue and set the rubble ablaze. As each new carload of fans arrived from the west, the crowd grew larger and louder, recounting again and again their team's great feats. To punctuate the event, the fire department set off its siren, causing some concern among less sports-minded locals. A farmer from across the state line in Wisconsin called the Hebron operator and asked where the fire was.

"He didn't even know there was such a thing as a Hebron basketball team," the operator related with disgust to a local reporter. "Such folks shouldn't be let run loose."

But nothing could dampen Hebron's spirits that night. As the sparks rose over the assemblage, the glow from the fire matched the glow in the hearts of the citizens of Hebron.

The Hebron High School basketball team was going to state.

Talk of the Town

Hebron's amazing streak caught the attention of sportswriters across Illinois. Irvin Lisagor, a staff writer for the *Chicago Daily News*, was the first to document the sensation, couching his account of the Hebron phenomenon in Biblical terms:

> *"So David prevailed over the Philistines with a sling and with a stone,"* whereupon he went up to Hebron and was there anointed King of Judah. This little farm community of 608 souls is preparing for a modern depiction of that Biblical event.

The reference was entirely appropriate. From the moment the small-school district stage was introduced in 1936, fans across the state had developed a deep fascination with "Little David" basketball teams. When a "district-school" David managed to topple a big-city Goliath, it merited headlines everywhere.

In 1938, one of those Davids gave hope to every other small school by advancing all the way out of a district tournament to the state championship game. Braidwood, with just 96 students, proved that the best small schools could compete with the largest schools at the highest level of competition, in spite of being relegated to preliminary district tournaments. Braidwood lost to Dundee in the championship game that year. Now Hebron appeared ready to take up where Braidwood had left off.

Lisagor probed for the reasons behind Hebron's success.

"We don't have much time to practice," Ed Willett explained. "The farm boys have to get home and do their chores. We have two town boys, though, Judson and Kjellstrom, and they're here shooting after practice, at noon, even in the mornings. They're all hearty kids, drink plenty of milk, you know, and get lots of fresh air. Lots of stamina."

The Chicago reporter joined the men of Hebron around the hot stove in Ed Kjellstrom's harness shop as they described the small-town team.

"There ain't any star," explained William Graunke, a disabled veteran. "All of 'em's stars. Clarence Judson there's got a boy who's doin' all right."

Milton Ryan, whose son John was a starting guard, offered his own account of the team's success. In the hayloft of his ancient barn, he'd cleared away the hay, attached a hoop, and set up a year-round court for the players.

"Why, I've seen ol' Clarence Judson's boy out there shooting baskets when it was so cold I couldn't even stand it. He'd come into the house, warm himself awhile and go right back."

Impressed with the testimonials on young Howie Judson, Lisagor and his photographer ambled down Maple Street to visit the Judson household. They found Howie's five-year-old twin brothers, Paul and Phil, practicing in the snow on a netless hoop. The camera clicked as the boys, clad in matching plaid jackets, knit caps, and boots, fought for a rebound. The photo ran with the story on the front page of the next day's *Daily News* sports section.

"THEY START 'EM YOUNG IN HEBRON," the caption declared.

Neither Hebron nor the Judson family had ever known such fame. Clarence Judson bought two copies of the paper and put one in a trunk for safekeeping. His wife Jessie took the other and delicately cut out the article and photos, using flour-and-water paste to glue them into the family scrapbook.

Getting There

And so the town of Hebron prepared to make the trek, en masse, down to Champaign and the University of Illinois, where the state finals were held. Some in the group lightheartedly dismissed the problems of displacing practically the whole town.

"We're going to hire a train," one rooter declared to a newsman.

But getting there, as it turned out, was only half the battle.

Clarence Judson was determined to drive some of the players to the tournament in his 1936 Chevrolet. To make the trip — 180 miles each way — he figured he'd need to buy four new tires. His wife, the ever practical Jessie, was having none of it. The family couldn't afford it, she contended, and someone else would have to drive. But on this occasion, her husband's will prevailed. After all, Clarence argued successfully, how many chances does a father get to see his son play in the state tournament?

As the Green and White entered the tournament, their stock had never been higher. There were no statewide polls in 1940 to gauge the relative strength of the state's teams, but with only a single loss and a giant-killer reputation, Hebron ranked among the favorites.

In those days, the *Champaign News-Gazette* was the bible of Illinois high school basketball and sports editor Pat Harmon was its prophet. In his column, Harmon extolled the virtues of the team with the best record in the state.

"If there is a team capable of duplicating or even improving on Braidwood's performance," Harmon wrote in his tournament preview, "it is probably Hebron, a little school of 92 students."

Hebron was by far the smallest school to qualify for the Sweet 'Sixteen that year. Its first-round opponent, Lewistown, had 355 pupils. Located in western Illinois, Lewistown had no particular reputation or previous tournament history. All in all, it seemed a good draw for Hebron.

But there were no scouts, no way of knowing what kind of team they had to face. The only consolation for Hebron coach Willett was that the Lewistown coach, George Dertinger, was surely just as much in the dark about Hebron.

For scouting purposes, only two things could be determined. Lewistown did not have a single player who was even six feet tall. And in something of a surprise, two other small schools that played in Lewistown's conference, Rushville and Beardstown, also qualified for the Sweet Sixteen. As diminutive as Lewistown's players might be, it seemed they played pretty good competition in that area of the state.

Hebron's reputation, meanwhile, preceded it to the state tournament. Intrigued by newspaper reports about the Hebron team, curious fans scoured the hotels of Champaign and Urbana, hoping to catch a glimpse of the tall team from the tiny town, but they were disappointed.

Sensing that the hubbub surrounding his team's entry in the tournament might turn into a distraction, Ed Willett had come up with a strategy for keeping his players out of the limelight. He stole a page from Braidwood's coach, Louis Bottino, who in 1938 had sequestered his players in private homes around town. Bottino's rationale? "They're small-town boys," he'd explained, "and conditions should be as nearly like they are at home as possible."

Following this example, Ed Willett chose the Middlecoff Hotel in the small town of Paxton, some 28 miles from Huff Gym, as his team's home base.

Game time was seven o'clock on Thursday, the first game of the evening session, and after a big sendoff in Hebron on Thursday morning, the team arrived in Paxton shortly after noon. Willett, Clarence Judson, and Claude Higdon, the high school principal, dropped the boys off at the hotel and then headed into Champaign to catch the afternoon session and get a look at possible future opponents.

All three games that afternoon were tight, nail-biting affairs. The game between Paris and Taylorville even spilled into overtime. And when Higdon and Judson, already running late, left the gym to retrieve the team, they ran into heavy traffic outside the arena. Once they fought their way out of town, they raced down U.S. 45 through Thomasboro, through Rantoul and Ludlow, and finally into Paxton. They grabbed the team as quickly as possible and headed straight back to Champaign.

But they got lost on their return trip. And when they finally neared Huff Gym, traffic was backed up in every direction as fans scrambled to get to the evening session. By the time the team reached the gymnasium it was a quarter to seven, with barely enough time for the players to jump into their uniforms, let alone warm up. For the biggest game in the school's history, Hebron took the floor stone cold.

Still, the players eventually managed to overcome their stiff muscles and ragged nerves and play their game. The teams were tied after the first half, but slowly Hebron began to pull away. With just four minutes to play, Hebron led, 30-23, and victory seemed assured. Seven points was a huge deficit to make up in those low-scoring days, and Lewistown had shown no facility to make the kind of shots necessary to close the gap.

And then everything fell apart.

Was the team tired from the day's long car trip, exhausted by their nerve-jangling entrance, or did Lewistown's press suddenly become impenetrable? Whatever the reason, Hebron began to turn the ball over left and right — they couldn't even get it over the ten-second line — and Lewistown found new life. The downstate team made three quick baskets and suddenly Hebron led by only a single point. After another squandered opportunity by Hebron, Lewistown scored again to take the lead at 31-30. Hebron missed a final shot, and Lewistown stalled out the last 50 seconds to seal the upset.

A disappointed Ed Willett could only be philosophical after the loss.

"I guess one can't win all the time," he told the press, "but I would like to have the fans down here see my team play the ball it can. We were clearly off tonight."

The big-city sports reporters who'd played up the Hebron story for more than two weeks wrote no more paeans that year to the miracle team from up north. The prevailing wisdom was that they made good copy, these Little Davids, but in the end, bigger schools always won the day.

Although they were disappointed in their quest, the team returned home to a heroes' welcome. Few had expected the team to win the tournament, after all. And regardless of the final outcome, the team's achievement was important. That became even clearer at a banquet held the next month in the high school gym, when the whole town turned out to pay tribute.

At the top of the bill was Henry V. Porter, assistant manager of the Illinois High School Association. From his office in Chicago, Porter had read the stories about the plucky, small-town team, and like so many others, he'd developed a soft spot in his heart for Hebron. He even drove out from the city to watch the team play one of its regional games.

Now, as he gave the main address, Porter spoke on success in sports and success in life. In closing, he recited a poem about the Hebron team that he'd written especially for the occasion. Porter honored them in verse for their never-say-die attitude, lauding the players as "basketball czars." Sentimental and sweet, his poem was high praise indeed.

Awash in tributes and testimonials, the town looked back on the year with great joy. The 1940 season was the most successful in Hebron's history, filled with so much excitement that any other town would've been happy to trade places. The future of the basketball team looked bright indeed.

Still, the sense of lost opportunity haunted many of the fans and players. Who knew if Hebron would ever get another shot at the big time?

Hebron Humor

By Henry V. Porter

Now open your eyes,
You basketball guys,
And take a squint at this team:
Russ Voltz who is tall
John Ryan who's small,
And Kjellstrom a cheerleader's dream
They are basketball czars
These Hebron stars
Who never were known to quit tryin'—
Johnson, Burgett, and Voltz,
Kjellstrom, Bigelow, and Ryan.

In the early fall
With first team call
Other fans were tearing their hair
But Hebron rejoiced,
And this sentiment voiced—
They're the answer to a harness shop prayer!
They learned as they played
The tricks of the trade
Pranced over the floor like gigolo—
Judson, Rehorst, and Ryan,
Behrens, Norgard, and Bigelow.

They picked up speed
As they fought for a lead
In that Harvard free for all.
McHenry got fussed
Eating Hebron's dust
And Woodstock they took for a fall.
Jim and John dribbled down,
Dead-eye Keith went to town,
As Man-mountain Tibbits got set.
Kjellstrom, Rehorst, and Ryan,
Peterson, Voltz, and Burgett.

They cleaned up quick
In their own bailiwick,
All opponents could see was their heels.
Crystal Lake they tried,
And took them for a ride,
Those slippery spot shot eels.

Their long shots clicked
Their flicker plays flicked—
These frisky Shorty Willett colts—
Johnson, Kjellstrom, and Ryan,
Wally, Elly, and Voltz.

In the Crystal Lake affair
Principal Marsh got gray hair
Ken Lopeman was tongue-tied and dizzy.
Two minutes to go,
Two waives in a row,
Then the Crystal Lake jinx got busy.
Back to old Hebron town
They wouldn't stay down
As Huntley and Capron were sunk
By Sam and Kelly and Les,
Kenny and Juddy and Unc.

Down the tournament trail
The Giant-Killers set sail.
Each opponent became Hebron's mutton.
Freeport was a foe,
Dundee they laid low,
And Rockford they clipped on the button.
Thus the Jim-John flash
With the Kelly-Keith dash
Rolled on with vigor and vim—
Kelly, Howie, and Keith,
John and Gordie and Jim.

In each final test
Every man gave his best—
They were one of the best in the field
We all celebrate
With players who rate
With the best Illinois can yield.
We are toasting a team
That followed a gleam
To sit near the champion's seat
Kjellstrom, Johnson, and Voltz,
Ryan, Burgett, and Pete.

chapter 3

Interlude

There were two immediate byproducts of Hebron's dream season.

For one, the sports world was now on notice. Basketball had put Hebron on the map, and the team could no longer surprise anyone. Even the larger schools began to treat the Hebron basketball program with deference, and at times shied away from scheduling games with the Green and White. After witnessing the team in action, coaches and sportswriters across the state, and especially in northern Illinois, began boosting Hebron's reputation. Woody Boyer of the *Elgin Courier-News* took note of the school's bountiful supply of tall cagers and started referring to the Hebron team in print as the "Green Giants." The moniker stuck.

But the change in the way the team was perceived by out-of-towners was perhaps not as important as the change in how it was perceived by the folks at home. The 1940 team had set a new standard. Success was now expected of the Hebron basketball five and each new team did its best to fulfill those expectations.

In its second season under Coach Ed Willett, with sophomore Howie Judson stepping into a starting role, Hebron won 29 games against only four losses. Once more Hebron tossed Elgin aside in the regional tournament and followed that victory by downing Dundee as well. Only a heart-breaking 20-18 slowdown loss to Waukegan in the sectional tournament ended hopes of a repeat trip to the state tournament.

Howie had become the leader of the squad by 1941-42, his junior year, as Hebron posted another strong season. Yet again the Green Giants bounced Elgin in the regional semifinals, and after a meaningless loss to Dundee (since both teams automatically advanced), Hebron headed for the sectional tournament. By now the sporting newspapers kept a regular watch on Hebron's progress at tournament time. Playing in the sectional tournament for the fourth season in a row, a feat never before accomplished by such a small school, the Green Giants beat Rochelle before bowing to East Rockford, 40-32.

By his senior season, Howie Judson had developed into a consummate high school athlete. He was tall and handsome and a star on the baseball field as well as on the basketball court. With such an abundance of talent, the question was not whether he would earn an athletic scholarship to college, but whether he would choose to play more than one sport.

That summer Ed Willett was lured away to coach at West Rockford High School, and in his place Hebron hired Les Harman, another Northwestern graduate, to coach the basketball team. With Judson more dominating than ever, Hebron swept through its competition. Winners of 25 games through the district tournament, Hebron beat Crystal Lake and Dundee easily to reach the regional final.

There, for the fifth straight year, Hebron met Elgin to determine which team would play in the sectional tournament. For the past four years, this critical match had occurred in the regional semifinal, and Hebron had beaten the larger school all four times. This time each school had won its semifinal handily, but a new rule eliminated the free pass for regional runners-up. In 1943, only the regional champion would advance to sectional play.

Elgin was aching for revenge after four consecutive years of humiliation at the hands of the McHenry County upstarts. For the first time in those five meetings, the game would be played in the Elgin High School gymnasium.

And this time, unbeknownst to the players and coaches, Elgin had a new weapon — literally.

Not long after the opening jump ball, one of the Hebron boys felt a sting on his arm. As the teams ran up and down the court, another Green Giant was stung, and then another. Soon there seemed to be a barrage of small, sharp objects flying from the stands. Fearing for their eyesight, the Hebron players finally complained to the referee.

The officials stopped the game to inspect the floor, where they recovered an abundant supply of heavy wire staples. They seemed to have originated from the balcony at the end of the gymnasium, and more to the point, they hurt like the dickens when they hit their mark. Several Green Giants displayed cuts on their faces and slashes on their arms and legs. A few Elgin players indicated that they, too, had been hit.

The referee ordered the public address announcer to inform the crowd that technical fouls would be called if any more staples came out of the stands. The onslaught ceased, but Elgin seemed to have gained a psychological advantage from the bizarre incident. The Maroons went on to win the game, 38-29, ending Hebron's four-year reign of upsets and Howie Judson's illustrious high school basketball career.

A few days later, Elgin school authorities identified the staple snipers — a pair of 11-year-old boys with slingshots.

At about the same time, Howie woke up seeing spots in front of his left eye. His doctor recommended a specialist for treatment, but that required the kind of money the Judson family simply did not have. The town of Hebron banded together to raise money for their high school hero with a basket social, where ladies prepared special picnic suppers to be auctioned off. With their help, Howie Judson got the funds for the medical attention he needed.

For a while rumors flew around Hebron that the staple attack had caused his injury. In fact, none of the players reported being hit in the eye. Doctors eventually determined that Howie had contracted an infectious disease called histoplasmosis, probably while working in a pigeon coop. Luckily for the young athlete, his vision responded to treatment and slowly got better through the summer.

Still, it represented a melancholy end to a tremendous high school career. Judson had become the most decorated athlete in Hebron's history. His four years had brought unparalleled success to the high school athletic teams, but fans also realized that his departure meant the end of an era. Stars like Howie Judson were few and far between.

After the season, Howie was named to the first-team All-State basketball team by the *Champaign News-Gazette*, the highest honor an Illinois schoolboy athlete could receive. To no one's surprise, after graduation he accepted a scholarship to the University of Illinois in Champaign-Urbana, electing to play two sports.

The Coach Who Couldn't Lose

While Howie Judson embarked on his college basketball and baseball careers, back home in Hebron school officials were struggling to find a way to keep the basketball program alive.

By the fall of 1943, America was fully involved in World War II, and the draft had decimated athletic programs everywhere. Late in the year, Hebron's Les Harman was called into the Navy, like so many other young men. The high school put out a search but could not locate a man to fill Harman's position.

Desperate times called for desperate measures, so the school came up with an innovative solution. Mel Stuessy, the coach down the road at St. Mary's High School in Woodstock, volunteered to run Hebron practices early in the morning while guiding his own team back at St. Mary's in the afternoon. Stuessy directed both schools' practices during the entire 1943-44 season, even though in actual games, Paul Tigard, the Hebron superintendent, sat on the bench to lead the team.

As the state tournament approached, it became obvious what was going to happen. Sharing a single coach, Hebron and St. Mary's were headed for a showdown in the district tournament finals.

After newspapers caught hold of the story, one reporter wrote Stuessy up as "the coach who couldn't lose," a tale that eventually made Ripley's "Believe It or Not." The truth, however, was that he never coached Hebron in a game situation.

When the two schools finally met in the district final, Stuessy and his St. Mary's squad knew Hebron inside and out. It was no surprise when they beat the Green Giants, 33-30.

The next year, George Simes, a player on the 1942 and 1943 squads, coached the team in practice, assisted at times by another former player, Elly Behrens, and Principal Claude Higdon. Simes worked on a farm and didn't have a teaching degree, so Tigard remained Hebron's official coach when the team suited up. Whether it was due to the tag-team coaching system or not, the 1944-45 team gained limited success.

Post-Howie, post-Harman, the Hebron program languished. In tough times, when patriotism was more important than success in sports, the lack of a cohesive basketball program was not the primary concern of either the school board or the citizenry.

When the war ended and veterans began returning home, however, Hebronites once again turned their attention to the hardwood.

Baptized in Coal

While Hebron's varsity cagers suffered without a regular coach, a new generation of players was growing up right under their noses. These grade school athletes were raised from birth on Hebron's exceptional basketball ethic, and it was clear from the outset that they were special.

They were town kids, local boys who'd played together before school, during school, and after school, in driveways around the neighborhood as well as in the old brick grade school that stood in the center of town. You could count on Howie Judson's younger brothers, Paul and Phil, already players with a front-page newspaper photo in their file, to be there. Other town boys like Bill Thayer, Clayton Ihrke, Charlie Mau, Ray Halstead, Ken and Wayne Spooner, and Don and Jim Wilbrandt entered the fray. From a farm a couple of miles out of town, Jim Bergin joined in, too.

These basketball-crazy youngsters grew up in the afterglow of the great teams of the early 1940s. They listened to tales of their predecessors' glories and wanted nothing more than to recreate them on the court.

Even in the first and second grades, they showed an uncommon attraction to the sport. Since the small upstairs gym was reserved for pupils in the higher grades, the boys were happy to spend their time playing basketball in a sooty basement room instead.

Only young men with a great devotion to the sport could've wished this bandbox into a basketball court. The room measured about 20 feet by 30 feet, with ceilings only ten feet high. Players had to arch their shots at low, odd angles just to sneak between the ceiling and the rim of the eight-foot baskets.

With the coal bin just a few feet away, the little room was always filled with a fine, black powder. When the boys gathered on the improvised court for a game during recess or after school, they inevitably ended up covered in sweat and coal dust, blackened from head to toe.

Hebron's young cubs became very familiar with how to conduct a game in hazardous quarters. A few years later, around the time they graduated to the upstairs gym, they also began playing with some of the older kids in one of the many haylofts around town. Many of the houses in town had barns, and Charlie Mau, one of the boys in the group, had one with a loft, or mow, that was set up for play. With a basket affixed at each end and an open door at center court to let in a little light, Mau's mow hosted many a game among the local players when the weather was inclement.

Up in the hayloft, the lighting varied from corner to corner, murky in some spots and downright dark in others. Sometimes, when it was overcast, the boys provided a little extra illumination by knocking out knotholes, much to the annoyance of Mrs. Mau.

The floorboards were rough and uneven, and the bounce was anything but consistent. Neither rim had a net. One was a regulation-sized hoop, but the other was smaller, barely big enough to squeeze the ball through.

And yet for all its quirks, Mau's mow provided an excellent training ground for the young athletes. Everything about the place put a premium on low dribbling, good passing, and a keen shooting eye. Over time the players honed these skills without even realizing that the loft itself was an instrument in their development.

In the driveways, lofts, and makeshift gyms, the boys formed spur-of-the-moment teams and simulated state tournament play. They played the regional tournament at one location and then the sectional at another. The state final, held on yet another court, was Champaign against Decatur, and the boys all wanted to be Jesse Clements. They'd read about Champaign's shooting star in the newspapers and heard his name again and again during the state tournament radio broadcasts.

Starting in the winter of 1944-45, the boys played on an organized grade school team made up of fifth through eighth graders in a league that played competition from Lake Geneva to Marengo to Dundee. Luckily, the skills learned in the unusual arenas applied to a regular hardwood surface as well, and the youngsters held their own against teams from much larger schools, all the while developing into a cohesive unit.

A Death in the Family

When he was home from college in the winter, Howie Judson pitched in to help coach this young team, assisting a townsman named Les Oglesby. Still a local hero, Howie was easy to spot around town in his University of Illinois letter jacket.

In 1945, a Chicago newspaper stirred up a controversy when it pointed the finger at athletes in the Big Ten who seemed to be healthy enough to play collegiate sports but somehow eluded military service. Many athletes, including Howie Judson, took the accusation personally.

Judson was classified 4-F by his doctor because of the eye condition he'd contracted after the notorious "staple game." His original doctor had told him that he could go blind if the condition should happen to flare up when he didn't have access to immediate treatment, which was exactly what might happen to a soldier or sailor far away from home. It wasn't merely a problem for Howie. It could also pose a serious liability for fellow soldiers who might depend on him. The doctor saw no choice but to classify him 4-F.

After the exposé appeared, the Draft Board called Howie in to have his eyes checked by another doctor. The new physician scoffed at such caution and immediately declared him fit for service. Howie was allowed to finish his sophomore year at Illinois, but was ordered to report to Great Lakes Naval Training Center near Chicago late in the summer.

That summer, Howie went home to Hebron to enjoy the last few weeks before boot camp began. One night in July, while he was out of town on a date, his parents took the rest of the family across town to attend the carnival that came to town every summer. When the family got home around midnight, the children immediately went upstairs to bed.

Clarence Judson and his wife, Jessie, also retired. As they sat in the room, Clarence remarked to his wife that he was experiencing a sharp pain in his chest. Suddenly he collapsed. A doctor was called, but it was too late; Clarence Judson had died almost immediately. He was just 51 years old.

The sudden, tragic death of the head of the Judson household forced the family to make many changes. They were not well-to-do, and to make ends meet, Jessie Judson began to work as a dishwasher in a local restaurant. She also took in laundry for people in town.

Howie Judson, 20 years old, was now the man of the house.

Nonetheless, he reported to Great Lakes for boot camp later that month. On his second day there, before he had even been issued his uniform, he woke up and found he had no vision at all in his left eye. His chronic eye problem had flared up again.

His superiors didn't take kindly to a second-day recruit who suddenly discovered he was blind in one eye, but Judson eventually convinced military doctors that he wasn't faking his ailment. His eye responded to treatment, but it was much worse this time. A blind spot continued to block the center of the vision in his left eye. He was in no shape to be a seaman now, and with the war gearing down anyway, he was discharged from the service after only three months of duty.

Perfect vision or not, Howie could still throw a baseball. He returned home to Hebron and the next summer played semipro ball around northern Illinois. Still only 21, Howie was a live arm with a good reputation, and the Chicago White Sox were willing to take a gamble on him. He signed with the Sox in July, 1946, traveling to meet their farm club at Waterloo, Iowa, to begin his climb toward the majors.

Never the kind of person who shied away from responsibility, Howie continued to return to Hebron every fall and winter to work at an off-season job and help raise his younger brothers and sister, Ruth Ann. Once again, he found time to help Les Oglesby coach the grade school basketball team.

Time for a Change

Hebron's varsity rebounded from the hardship of the war years under a young coach named Mart Murphy. Murphy had compiled a good record at the central Illinois town of Brimfield, where his teams won two conference championships. But Murphy's teams at Hebron did not achieve the same success as the pre-war legends, in part because a new nemesis, St. Edward's High School of Elgin, now blocked the way.

In contrast with Hebron's other district-tournament rival, St. Mary's of Woodstock, St. Edward's was considerably larger, drawing its enrollment from Catholic families in a sizable area that included St. Charles, Dundee, Algonquin, and Elgin, an area that was already steeped in a strong basketball tradition. In this case, larger proved to be better.

St. Edward's won the district in 1946, immediately serving notice that it would be a team to be reckoned with. A year later, Hebron played well enough to turn the tables on St. Edward's in the district finals and qualify for the regional tournament, but an otherwise successful season ended with an embarrassing 60-36 loss to Elgin.

In Murphy's third year at the helm, the varsity team struggled. It had been six years since Hebron last qualified for a sectional tournament, and fans of the once overachieving town grew impatient. Individually, the varsity players had talent, but the teamwork did not seem to be there.

Many saw hope on another front. The best of the promising grade schoolers, including the Judson twins, were now eighth graders, and Les Oglesby, their volunteer coach, felt quite optimistic about their chances at the high school level.

"The boys have made a good showing considering their lack of height," he told the local newspaper. "With the right help and encouragement, these boys should put Hebron on top of the heap again in basketball circles."

But the fact that young players of such great potential were headed into a high school program that seemed to lack focus and direction was unacceptable to at least one Hebron resident.

At a school board meeting in January, 1948, a prominent citizen rose to voice his displeasure with the current situation. It was Howie Judson, Hebron High School basketball star, professional baseball player, and local celebrity. In a small office inside the high school building, he stood before the board and pled his case for a change in leadership for the basketball team.

"We have a good bunch of kids coming up, and they need a capable coach," he told the board. Then he lowered the boom. "I hate to say it, but if you don't get a new coach, I'm going to move my family out of here."

The school board considered its options. Murphy was a nice man, and if he wasn't a world-beater as a basketball coach, at least his teams held their own. On the other hand, losing the Judson family would be a major embarrassment to the town of Hebron. Faced with this choice, the board wasn't inclined to call Howie's bluff.

When the idea that the Judsons might be school-shopping started to wend its way through the rumor mill, more than one coach inquired what the twins might be looking for in a basketball program. But the reality was that the family always wanted to stay in Hebron, to live in the town where their father had lived and died, to play for the same team as their older brother.

With his dire words still hanging in the air, Howie Judson took off for spring training. Back home, Hebron lost again to St. Edward's in the district finals.

That was the final straw. In March, 1948, the school board set about looking for a new head basketball coach.

chapter 4

Man with a Plan

It took less than a month for Hebron to find its man. He came with a sparkling résumé and glowing recommendations. But most importantly, he was a man who appreciated life in a small town.

Edmund Russell Ahearn was born July 9, 1912, at Kinsman, Illinois, the third boy in a family of six. His father, Tom, was the son of immigrants from County Cork; his mother, Mary, was a new arrival from Ireland. Their farm on the wide-open central Illinois prairie lay just south of Kinsman. The little town, with a handful of tree-lined streets and a lone Catholic church steeple that soared over the surrounding farm fields, barely interrupted the landscape.

The Ahearns were a sports-minded family, and the boys, Lawrence, Tommy, and Russ, grew up playing baseball in the pasture. The older boys liked to bat, so when Russ was old enough to play, he became the pitcher. He was small — just 5-foot-6 — but the little left-hander with the quick smile and sparkling eyes developed into a hard-throwing southpaw ace.

Russ attended Kinsman High School, which had an enrollment so small that it could sustain classes only through the eleventh grade. The school fielded a baseball team, but couldn't quite muster a coach. Russ jumped in to fill the role of player-manager in his junior year.

For his senior year, he picked up his bat and mitt and moved down the road to Streator, about ten miles to the west, taking up residence in a boarding house. At Streator Township High School, the lively farm boy gained a reputation as a snappy dresser and something of a ladies' man. He also acquired a nickname that he carried with him the rest of life. One evening, when young Russ looked especially dapper while ushering at the school play, a classmate christened him "Duke."

The closest Ahearn came to championship basketball in his high school days was as a fan in the Streator High gymnasium. The team's revered coach was Lowell "Pug" Dale, who as a high school junior in 1912 had single-handedly led Lebanon, Indiana, to a state championship. Dale was a character builder who stressed fundamentals. In his twelve years at Streator, Dale had not seen one losing season and had already guided the school into the Sweet Sixteen three times. But during Ahearn's year at Streator High, Dale's team had an off season and did not make it past the district tournament.

That didn't matter to young Duke, for whom basketball was just a passing fancy. Baseball was the big reason he'd moved to Streator, and he wasn't about to waste his opportunity.

Ahearn picked up eight hits in his first two games in the spring of 1930, but even though he swung the bat well, he was never really more than a singles hitter. Weighing in at just 110 pounds, Russ Ahearn found his true home on the pitcher's mound. The curveball he'd developed throwing to his older brothers in the pasture now baffled batters from Canton to Marseilles. He pitched in seven games that short spring season, striking out 10 or more batters on four occasions. In the final game of his high school career, he fanned a career-high 15 against St. Bede of Peru.

Upon graduation, Ahearn had a decision to make. At one time, he thought he might be a farmer like his father, but his Uncle Edmund, who lived with the family, discouraged that idea.

"You have to get an education, son," his uncle told him. "You don't want to be a hayseed, do you?"

When Lawrence, the eldest Ahearn brother, had reached adulthood, he'd stayed on to help with the farm. But Tommy and Russ heeded their uncle's advice and applied for college. Tommy Ahearn attended St. Viator College near Kankakee and played four years on the baseball team there. Russ headed to Illinois State Normal University, a teachers' college not far from home. His brilliance on the mound at Streator had been enough to convince the college baseball coach at Normal to offer him a scholarship.

Russ arrived at college with that scholarship and little else. In need of a job and a place to stay, he made the acquaintance of a prominent local businessman named Charles Hall, who ran the Coffee Shop restaurant in downtown Normal. The Coffee Shop was a gathering place for athletes and fans of ISNU athletics; it was also the chief outpost of the local hot-stove league. Hall, it turned out, had grown up in Normal with Clark Griffith, the former major leaguer who later became owner of the Washington Senators. Surrounded by talk of sports and fascinated by his boss's baseball connections, Ahearn felt right at home with Hall and his brother, Bob. He ended up working at the store his entire college career.

At Normal, Russ set his eyes on a teaching degree, but his primary passion was still baseball. He had a strong left arm and his slight stature was no apparent handicap, though he battled soreness in his shoulder from time to time. He started all four years, taking a regular spot in what was usually a two-man pitching rotation, and also played outfield when needed. In his junior year, he was elected captain of the team. That season, he had perhaps his best all-around performance in a game against Eureka College, when he hit his only collegiate home run and pitched five no-hit innings before leaving the game with a raw finger. The highlight of Ahearn's career at Normal came in his final season, when he notched a 10-strikeout, complete-game win over the University of Wisconsin, a Big Ten team.

But he was only the second-best left-hander on the ISNU squad. The ace of the staff was James "Pim" Goff, who also happened to be the star of the basketball and tennis squads. Throughout the season, Goff was courted by six different major league teams. When the last game of the 1934 college season went into the record books, he signed a minor league contract with the St. Louis Cardinals and hit the road for San Antonio to play for the Cards' Texas League farm club.

Focusing on Pim Goff, professional scouts apparently looked past the team's other left-handed hurler. Ahearn returned to Streator and hooked up with a pair of teams in the thriving semipro leagues of central Illinois. Within three weeks, he'd pitched two no-hitters, striking out 20 batters in one game and 16 in the other. He was out to prove the scouts wrong, and seemed to be doing a very good job of it.

A friend sent a clipping on Duke's first no-hitter to J. Louis Comiskey, president of the Chicago White Sox, who immediately summoned the southpaw for a tryout. Ahearn pitched batting practice for a few days, and pitched well, too, impressing the Sox coaching staff. But Sox manager Jimmy Dykes overruled his aides and refused to offer Ahearn a minor league contract, mostly because Dykes thought he was just too small to make it in the majors.

Although he'd been rejected by the big-timers, Russ Ahearn was a sensation in the semipro leagues that season. Fans loved to see him pitch and sportswriters were charmed by his wit. Ralph Hart of the *Streator Times-Press* liked to sit on the bench with the team and turn to Duke every now and then for a few words of wisdom.

Once, after an opposing player clouted a tremendous home run off his fastball, Ahearn told Hart he'd curve the batter to death the next time up. When he got the batter to pop up in his next at-bat, he said matter-of-factly, "What did I tell you? You just need to know how to pitch to these fellows."

The climax of the 1934 semipro season was a game between a collection of Streator All-Stars and team called the Grand Ridge Merchants. Ads for the game showcased Duke Ahearn as the featured star. When game day arrived, a crowd estimated at five to eight thousand — the biggest to see a baseball game in Streator in twenty years — converged on the park by auto, bus, and bicycle to watch the big showdown.

But Russ was not on his game that afternoon. He hit two batters and gave up seven base hits, including two to his brother, Tommy, who played for Grand Ridge. After just three innings, he left the game, which Grand Ridge went on to win, 9-2. In a postgame interview with

Ralph Hart, Ahearn was inconsolable. "I'm sorry," he said. "I tried my best, but it didn't seem to do much good. I just couldn't get going."

When compiling a scrapbook some time later, he singled out the game as the most bitter disappointment of his pitching career. "Losing makes me *very, very, very* mad and unhappy," he wrote in the margin.

Lacking several credits for his degree, he returned to Normal in the fall. He was still in town the next spring, preparing for graduation, when exciting news raced through the Coffee Shop.

The Three-I League, which had disbanded after the 1933 season, was being revived. Bloomington was going to have a team in the league again, and the Bloomers would be managed by a living legend named Burleigh Grimes. The last legal spitball pitcher in major league baseball, Grimes had decided to give up pitching and planned to build a team from scratch in less than three weeks. He brought along players from the Cardinals' farm clubs, including Ahearn's old teammate, Pim Goff.

In the twin cities of Bloomington and Normal, the call went out for general tryouts. Jumping at the chance to catch on with a brand-new team, Russ and Tommy Ahearn grabbed their mitts and headed for Fans' Field on Bloomington's south side, along with two hundred other hopefuls. Each player was given just a few tosses or swings to make an impression. But the brothers made it through the first cut and were touted by the *Bloomington Pantagraph* as strong candidates for the final 21-man roster.

When the second cuts came a week later, however, Russ and Tommy were out. Goff managed to make it through to opening day, but just a week into the season he, too, was cut from the team.

With the dream of a major league career now fading, Ahearn continued to compete in summer baseball leagues around Streator and Morris. His arm may have been overworked and his curveball might not have been good enough to strike out major league batsmen, but it was more than enough to set the local competition on its ear. He nursed a sore arm through most of the next three summers, but made a comeback in 1938, again making the Streator All-Star team.

Working Man

During this time, Duke Ahearn began his teaching career. He took jobs as a junior high school teacher and coach, first at his hometown of Kinsman and then just down the railroad tracks at Ransom High School. But opportunities for career advancement were severely limited at this remote outpost. In 1939, when he was 27 years old and still single, Ahearn resigned his teaching job at Ransom and enrolled at the University of Illinois to pursue his master's degree in education.

When he graduated two years later, Duke took a position in the athletic department at St. Patrick's High School in Kankakee, where he coached football, basketball, and baseball. It was a big step up from his previous teaching jobs in the dusty little farm towns dotting the countryside where he'd grown up. St. Patrick's had better facilities, more funds, and more students to build a real team.

By now, Russ Ahearn was also engaged to be married. For several years he had dated Marie Gotch, a vivacious girl four years his junior who'd grown up in Streator's large Slovak community. They met one Fourth of July at a dance hall north of town. He was a prominent local athlete, always ready with a joke; she was a sweet and pretty town girl who loved to laugh. Though they shared an interest in ballroom dancing and big band music, Russ chased Marie for several years before she finally agreed to marry him. Now that her beau had a good job in a big town, Marie decided it was the right time to say yes to his proposal.

Kankakee was hospitable enough to the young couple, but after just two years, Russ Ahearn made another move, pulling up his roots in central Illinois. With a baby daughter, Judy, now in tow, Russ and Marie landed thirty miles west of Chicago, in Elgin, a city best known for two things: watches and basketball.

It was the fall of 1943. Russ joined the athletic department at Elgin High School, where he was initially assigned to run the intramural programs. He knew, however, that it wouldn't be long before he took on a varsity team. One by one, Elgin's coaches were being drafted into the armed services. But Ahearn, classified 4-F because of a bad knee he'd torn up in a hunting accident, would be homebound for the duration.

By January, three Elgin coaches had already reported to basic training. By the end of that first school year, Russ had his first varsity post, as assistant coach of the baseball team.

It was a prize assignment. But despite his love of baseball, it didn't take Ahearn long to figure out that the real excitement in Elgin was on the basketball court. The Maroons' head coach was a former University of Chicago player named John A. Krafft, whose 1943 team had finished fourth in the state. Krafft's program was solid, well supported, and very exciting. After one look, Duke Ahearn wanted to be part of the action.

The next year, he got his wish, assisting Krafft with the varsity basketball squad. He couldn't have asked for a better basketball baptism.

The Maroons ended up in the state finals in Champaign for the second year in a row, and for the first time since winning back-to-back state championships in 1924 and 1925, Elgin made it all the way to the title game. There the Maroons ran into a legendary Taylorville team led by superstars Johnny Orr and Ron Bontemps and coached by Dolph Stanley. By beating Elgin, Taylorville became the first undefeated state champion in Illinois history and earned its place in the pantheon of high school basketball.

The excitement of Elgin's sensational 1944 season energized Ahearn, who did his best to absorb Krafft's methods.

John Krafft was a master of details. He ran his practices like clockwork, running drills one after the other from a schedule he kept in an ever-present brown spiral notebook. Krafft was a stern taskmaster, nononsense, all-business, as tough as they came. His players knew better than to cross him. But he understood the psychology of coaching better than anyone. Krafft was always able to get the most from his players and to determine which players he could get the most from. Krafft's uncompromising manner would be difficult for his amiable assistant to emulate, but Ahearn quickly came to see the effectiveness of the approach.

With Ahearn at his side, Krafft molded teams that were state-title contenders in each of the next four years. There was no reason for anyone to think the streak would end anytime soon. But Russ Ahearn could see time running out.

He had served Krafft for five years, an apprenticeship worth every moment spent. But Ahearn was 35 years old and eager to command his own team. He knew that wasn't going to happen at Elgin. John Krafft was ensconced as head coach — at age 42, he had a lifetime job if he wanted it — and Ahearn knew he had little chance of succeeding his mentor in the foreseeable future.

As the 1948 season came to a close, Ahearn had another reason for feeling restless. There were now two young mouths to feed: Judy was six years old and his son, Billy, was a growing boy of three. As Russ began looking for opportunities, a job opened up in Hebron.

Ahearn already knew a lot about Hebron. He had followed its basketball team closely for eight years and was well aware of Hebron's history, players, and basketball ethic. In many ways, the small town that spawned the Green Giants reminded him of his own home turf.

When he was studying for his master's degree at the University of Illinois in 1940, Russ reported paying a scalper five dollars for a ticket — "a lot of money in those days" — to watch one particular session of the state tournament. His alma mater, Streator, played the third game of that session against Granite City and a high school phenom named Andy Phillip. But a different game was the real attraction. Everyone wanted to see much-touted Hebron play against Lewistown. Like so many fans of that time, Ahearn was intrigued by the very idea of the towering team from the tiny town. He'd followed Hebron closely ever since, especially after arriving at Elgin.

Hebron was a perfect match for Russ Ahearn.

The school board offered him a position in April. It might have been looking mainly for a basketball coach, but to lure Krafft's respected protégé, the board threw in everything but the kitchen sink. At Hebron, Ahearn would be principal, athletic director, civics teacher, and coach of any other team he desired. With the money for all those positions combined, it amounted to a clear promotion over his duties at Elgin. When the offer came, he couldn't refuse.

In August, he moved his family into a house on Main Street, just a block from the school. Russ Ahearn, the rookie head coach, would soon set about the business of giving the basketball program his own stamp, in the style of his mentor, John Krafft.

A New Boy in School

As Ahearn unpacked his belongings in the same principal's office where he'd interviewed a few weeks earlier, many changes were already under way. A sweeping consolidation had brought the Hebron schools under a single administration with the schools of nearby Alden and eight one-room schoolhouses in the two townships. Hebron High School had become Alden-Hebron Community Consolidated Junior-Senior High School, a change that would take a lot of getting used to.

When school opened, Principal Ahearn busied himself welcoming students, meeting with teachers, approving class plans, and overseeing the details of the brand-new busing system. The consolidation brought 24 new high school students and a dozen or so seventh and eighth graders over from Alden. These students would be attending school in Hebron for the first time ever, meaning they'd need special orientation.

With so many other things to think about, basketball took a back seat at the start. But somewhere in the middle of that first day, an unexpected encounter brought the new coach's mind right back to the hardcourt.

Russ Ahearn turned a corner in the hall of the high school, and then stopped short. As he looked straight ahead, his eyes were level with the front pocket on the bib overalls of a 14-year-old eighth grader. The boy towered over him by nearly a foot. It didn't take long for Ahearn to size up his new student.

"Son, what's your name?" he asked, craning his head upward.

"Bill Schulz, sir," came the polite reply.

"Bill, have you ever played basketball?"

"No, sir."

But the wheels were turning. How could he turn this lanky farm boy into a basketball player?

"Why don't you take gym eighth period?" he suggested, already devising a plan. "I'm the gym teacher."

Russ Ahearn had no idea whether Bill Schulz could pass or dribble or hit the broad side of a barn with a basketball, but he felt sure the boy could be taught. After all, coaches took raw recruits and taught them the fundamentals every season.

But no coach could teach height. And when it came to height, Bill Schulz was already an overachiever.

Looking at Schulz, Ahearn knew that this young man could easily grow another six inches in the next four years. That would make him one of the tallest players — maybe *the* tallest — ever to play high school basketball in Illinois.

After a few gym class sessions, Ahearn asked Schulz to join the basketball team.

Bill didn't know much about basketball, but he was willing to try. Still, he was a farm boy, the oldest child in his family, and he would need his parents' permission before he could join the team. So the new coach asked Mr. and Mrs. Schulz for their blessing.

Fred Schulz, the boy's father, listened to the coach's request and nodded his head.

"I'll strike you a deal," the elder Schulz said. "If he tends to business on your team, works hard at practice and sticks with it, I'll let him out of his evening milking."

That brought a smile to Bill's face, even if there was no hope of escaping the morning milking.

His coach was even happier. With a potential center in his grasp, Russ Ahearn had visions of great things ahead at his new school.

At Home

That fall the Ahearn family settled into the rhythm of small-town life. For Russ, who'd grown up in the even smaller hamlet of Kinsman, it was just like old times, except that now he was one of the town's most prominent citizens. As for the children, they were still too young to want anything except a big yard with an apple tree and a blackberry patch. They got exactly that in Hebron.

For Marie, however, the move required a few adjustments. She'd grown up in Streator and then set up households with Russ in Kankakee and Elgin, all good-sized towns. Now she was about as far out in the sticks as she could be without actually living on a farm. Movie houses, streetcars, dance halls, an actual downtown — Hebron had none of these.

Yet Marie loved her new lifestyle. She worked in the post office, where she quickly learned the names and faces of everyone in town. She mixed in easily with the ladies of the town, as young mothers often do, and joined a weekly pinochle game. She learned how to use a typewriter and happily set about producing a town newsletter.

Marie and Russ did their best to make themselves a part of the community. Marie helped with makeup for community drama productions. The couple provided the record player and the records for high school dances, and often led the way on the dance floor, showing off their smooth ballroom moves.

Still, certain adjustments to small-town life had to be made. Most important was the fact that Hebron didn't have a Catholic church. So on Sundays, while the Methodists, Presbyterians, and Lutherans walked to their houses of worship, the devout Ahearn family drove five miles to Richmond to attend mass. They honked to their friends each week as they headed out of town.

Truth be told, the Ahearns didn't come from classic Hebron stock. In an area settled by immigrants from England, Germany, the Netherlands, and Scandinavia, theirs was one of the few Irish surnames. Marie Ahearn, of pure Slovak descent, was even more unusual. And when it came to politics, Russ Ahearn was a Truman Democrat, surrounded by dyed-in-the-wool Republicans.

In the end, however, none of these differences mattered. More quickly than they might have imagined, the Ahearns began to feel at home in this small world.

A Place to Play

As he learned the ropes at Alden-Hebron High School, Russ Ahearn was already contemplating some of the obstacles he'd have to overcome as basketball coach.

The first was a lack of bodies. Elgin's teams had their pick from a pool of almost 700 male students. At Hebron, he'd have fewer than 50.

And then there were the facilities. There was no gleaming, 2,000-seat gym here. Instead, he'd have to make do with a tiny basketball floor perched on the stage of an auditorium. The gym also served as a theater for dramatic productions and band concerts. It even subbed as a dance floor and general meeting area.

As a theater or concert hall, the little gym functioned well. On the main floor, three small sections of seats rose up at a shallow angle from below the edge of the stage. A small balcony provided some additional seating, bringing to about 550 the number of people who could squeeze in comfortably.

As a basketball court, however, the place left a lot to be desired. For one thing, the floor wasn't of regulation length or width. On three sides of the court, the sidelines were so close to the wall that the boys had to stay aware of their surroundings at all times. A single thin wrestling mat attached to the wall behind each basket provided scant relief for someone completing a fast break. Along the sidelines, there was practically no room for the team benches or the scorer's table.

Still, the biggest problem was the elevated stage. Players had to be very careful or they could simply fall off the west side of the court. The dramatic four-foot drop was not forgiving. A hard-nosed scramble for the ball might send a player, or two or three, sailing into the first row of spectators or crashing into the tuba in the pep band.

Creating a first-class team in this eccentric gym wasn't going to be easy. And there were other challenges awaiting the new coach as well.

Out the door, down a cement staircase and to the left, the home team's locker room occupied part of the basement under the gymnasium. The facilities were spartan at best, offering little more than a few lockers, painted Green Giant green, a bench in the center, and a bank of cabinets. The showers were warm, but the fact that there were only two shower heads ensured a race when practice was over. Games were even worse, especially since game officials showered there, too.

After considering its limitations, Ahearn decided to forgo the dank locker room for chalk talks, preferring to use his own classroom just across the hallway from the gym's main entrance.

Accentuate the Positive

If Coach Ahearn faced a mountain of challenges, he also had some advantages.

First and foremost, Hebron was a basketball town and everyone knew it. Just about any coach would've been happy to give it a shot in a town with Hebron's reputation.

Ahearn also liked the idea that, as principal and athletic director, he controlled the whole show. It didn't matter what it was — setting the playing schedule, arranging for buses, determining the amount of time spent in or out of class — it was all his to decide. He'd have no one to report to except the superintendent and the citizens of Hebron.

Another bright spot involved the class of incoming ninth graders. Based on the boys' success in grade school, the coach had high hopes for their time under his guidance. By the end of those four years, he expected to have a crackerjack team.

Finally, there was his ace in the hole, Howie Judson. Ahearn had tracked Howie's career ever since Hebron's appearance at Huff Gym in 1940, when Howie was a freshman. Now in his first season in the majors with the White Sox, Howie came to town frequently when the Sox were at home. His twin brothers were freshmen, two of the ninth graders that Coach Ahearn would be working with over the next four years, and they had learned the game at their older brother's knee. Now Howie stood ready to assist their new coach in any way he could. With his inside knowledge of Hebron's younger generation of players, his years of high school basketball experience, and his enthusiasm and willingness to pitch in, Howie was a major asset.

He also represented something close to Russ Ahearn's heart. It had always been Duke's dream to pitch in the majors. Now, right here in front of him, was someone who was living that dream.

Another man might have been awestruck or even a little jealous. Instead, Russ Ahearn genuinely liked and appreciated his new colleague. The major league pitcher and the basketball coach who had always hoped to be one quickly became close friends.

The Secret Weapon

Ahearn had one more secret weapon in plotting the success of his basketball team.

All his coaching would be for naught if he did not have support from the families of each of his team members. So Ahearn enlisted his players' parents directly, encouraging them to monitor their sons' diet, sleep habits, and extracurricular activities. His training regimen was strict. While the boys may have deviated from the plan on occasion, their mothers followed the coach's instructions to the letter.

Coach Ahearn had strong convictions about nutrition and how to develop and maintain athletic form throughout the basketball season. Some of his ideas came from John Krafft and some from a book by Adolph Rupp, the famous University of Kentucky coach who'd started his career in Illinois at Freeport High School. Ahearn even borrowed ideas from a leftover conditioning plan that Lowry Crane had left in a desk drawer at the school.

During the off-season, the players were expected to watch what they ate, keep themselves fit, and work on their skills if they expected to play the next season. Ahearn gave the players each a jump rope and told them to use it to strengthen their leg and stomach muscles. He showed them how to practice rebounding at home by placing a lid over the basket. And he encouraged them to engage in both sprinting and distance running to build stamina.

Like Krafft, Coach Ahearn expressly forbade pastry in all its forms, from Mom's apple pie to turnovers and cream puffs. Needless to say, smoking and drinking were also strictly prohibited.

"A kid who smokes knows better than to come out for basketball," he often said. "One or two such boys would ruin a good team."

That kind of misbehavior was not even a question. The players — the ones who were serious about playing — were serious about training as well. Mr. Ahearn was the boss. If they were forbidden to eat pastry, the players reasoned, then there would just be that many more cream puffs left for everyone else in Hebron.

TRAINING SUGGESTIONS FOR BASKETBALL

Diet: Wholesome, well-cooked food, such as one usually gets at home, provides a satisfactory diet during training periods. Masticate the food thoroughly and DO NOT OVEREAT AT ANY TIME! Leave the table feeling you have not overeaten.
DO NOT EAT BETWEEN MEALS. THIS MEANS NO ICE CREAM, CANDY, MALTED MILKS, ETC.

The following list is questionable foods and should be avoided during the training period:
Bread: Freshly baked breads, biscuits, pancakes, and waffles.
Beverages: Coffee, strong tea, ice liquids. Take liquids sparingly during the first hour after exercise.
Condiments: Catsup, chili sauce, spices, meat sauces, olives, and pickles.
Pastries: Heavy cake, pie, other pastries which are digested slowly.
Fruits: Berries with seeds, figs.
Fried Potatoes and Dumplings.
Vegetables: Cooked cabbage, cucumbers, heavy dressings, raw onions, radishes, turnips, most fried vegetables.
Meat and Fish: Chopped meats, most fried meats, pork (except bacon), veal, salt fish.
Two days before a game, avoid gravies and milks.

The following list is acceptable foods from which the athlete may select his menu:
Breads: dry toast, whole wheat, graham, rolls (hard), French, rye. Use butter moderately.
Beverages: Cocoa (moderately), hot water, weak tea, mild tea (moderately, avoid two days before a game), coffee (moderately, mornings only).
Cereals: All cereals may be eaten, care being taken not to use too much milk or cream.
Cheese: Soft cheese freely, others in small quantities.
Eggs: Soft boiled, poached and scrambled.
Desserts: Custards, fruit salad, ice cream, rice, raisin and tapioca puddings, apple sauce, jello, sponge cake, fresh fruits (peeled).
Fruits: Apples (baked, raw), grapefruit, oranges, pears, pineapple, raisins, dates, peaches.
Juices: Grape, grapefruit, lemon, orange, and tomato.
Meats and Fish: Bacon (crisp at breakfast), beef (beef roast, stew, steak), fowl, lamb chops, mutton chops, and fresh fish.
Preserves: Jams, jellies, marmalade.
Sugar: Use in abundant quantities at mealtime with cereals, desserts, fruit juices, honey.
Vegetables: Asparagus, carrots, celery, corn, lettuce, spinach, parsnips, peas, tomatoes, and squash. Potatoes, baked and boiled.

Mr. Ahearn -- Coach

chapter 5

Going Places

Hebron's players were used to a coach who basically threw the ball out on the floor and let them play. By contrast, Ahearn's practices were a precisely timed, well executed series of drills. The players quickly had the schedule down pat. Five minutes of free throws. Five minutes of passing drills. Five minutes of tipping drills. Five minutes of pivot plays. It was a structure Coach Ahearn had learned from John Krafft. Now that he was in charge, he did his best to emulate Krafft — only with a smile added to the mix. Still, there was no talking or horsing around allowed in Ahearn's practices, just as there had been none in Krafft's.

As Coach Ahearn saw it, the old Hebron way, with an emphasis on scrimmages, was destined to fail. There were only five or six boys on the varsity squad, so their scrimmage competition would've ended up being underclassmen who were simply too small and too green to put up much of a fight.

When it came to playing against live bodies in practice, he decided to pair the varsity players against each other in one-on-one, two-on-two, or three-on-three drills. The only time he'd pit the JV boys against the varsity squad was to practice the mechanics of a full-court press.

On a basket at the side of the court, away from the rest, Ahearn set to work on young Bill Schulz. Before he'd entered the building at the start of the school year, Schulz had barely touched a basketball and had never seen a single basketball game. There was a long, long way to go.

But the likable eighth grader turned out to be a willing pupil. After all, practicing basketball after school meant not having to milk cows and do chores back on the farm, and that was a good deal as far as Bill was concerned. The Schulz development project would take time and effort, however, and Ahearn called on Howie Judson, spending the winter in Hebron after his first season with the White Sox, to act as Bill Schulz's private tutor, quietly instructing the tall boy on the side while the rest of the team went through its paces.

Ahearn could only dream about Schulz's potential. But until Bill matured, his coach remained a little short on manpower — literally. Unlike the Hebron teams of yore, Ahearn's initial edition of the Green Giants sorely lacked height. At 5-foot-6, the coach himself looked down at a few of the players, and that was not a good sign for a basketball team.

Ray Halstead, Earl Seavall, and Bob and Dave Nichols, who were double first cousins, formed the nucleus of the 1948-49 team. Seavall was the only senior among the starters and captain of the squad.

"We don't have anyone tall enough to pick cherries without a ladder," Ahearn told one newspaperman at the start of the season. "We don't have a lot of speed, but there's plenty of hustle."

Hustle alone would have to do for his first year as coach.

But Russ Ahearn didn't expect miracles. Instead, he was already putting the pieces together for the future, planning ahead for next year and the year after that.

His first important decision was to start a freshman, only 5-foot-4, at one of the guard positions. It was a bold move, but he felt sure that Paul Judson's quick hands and ballhandling ability would make him an asset in the starting lineup.

It didn't hurt that there was a twin brother waiting in the wings.

Terrific Times Two

The Judson family must have seemed like Russ Ahearn's own personal treasure trove.

First there was Howie, a star basketball player and all-around athlete who was generous enough to jump in and do whatever he was asked whenever he was home. Howie's support added instant credibility to the program.

And then there were the twins. A coach is lucky to get one kid who's crazy about basketball, brimming over with energy and enthusiasm, with talent and a winning spirit bred in the bone.

But two of them? That was beyond luck. That was destiny.

Paul and Phil Judson were born April 10, 1934, with Paul entering the world about fifteen minutes before his brother. Their father, Clarence Judson, worked as a carpenter in Hebron, building houses and barns; mother Jessie Kolls had grown up on a farm just over the Wisconsin border, two miles north of town. When the twins were born, older brother Howie was already nine years old, and sister Ruth Ann was almost five. Paul and Phil were the last of the Judson offspring. The family lived in a roomy house on the north side of Route 173, the main east-west road through town.

Clarence had been an athletic youth, though basketball wasn't so big in his day. He preferred baseball, and that was the game he taught his oldest son. By pitching to his father, Howie developed a terrific arm. Muscular and broad-shouldered, Howie was a prototypical power pitcher, but he also played basketball, starting in grade school when Lowry Crane was still the high school coach. Howie built up his vertical leap by jumping alongside the garage, dropping a tennis ball into the eaves trough and grabbing it out again.

By the time Paul and Phil were five, Howie was a freshman in high school, already a star athlete, a natural at both baseball and basketball. The twins quickly followed in his footsteps.

When an old tree near the grade school had to be cut down, Clarence Judson, who was on the school board, salvaged the basketball hoop that was attached to it and brought it home with him. The wrought-iron hoop, one of those fashioned years before by the town blacksmith, Jim Anderson, got plenty of use after Clarence Judson nailed it to the back of the house at a height of about six feet. The twins played on it day and night, in all kinds of weather.

Even winter didn't present an obstacle. A little shoveling kept the court clear enough to dribble on, and the twins could shoot for hours on end. They saved their best shots for those moments when their mother peeked out the back door to see how they were doing. To ensure continuous play, they kept several pairs of gloves handy. When one pair got cold or wet, they'd run inside, place them on the radiator, and return with a warm pair.

Because they were twins, each boy always had a playmate. More importantly, each also had an opponent. If the boys had been shooting baskets alone, each scrambling after his own missed shots, they might have tired of basketball early on. As twins, the Judsons could always find a game of one-on-one.

When they were in fourth grade, with Howie off at the University of Illinois, the twins faced an equipment problem. Their only basketball was getting ragged, and they had no money to buy a new one. Figuring they might have a friend in Champaign, they wrote a letter to Doug Mills, the director of athletics at the university, asking if he might be able to send them a ball.

A few days later, a package arrived in the mail. Inside was a leather practice ball, retired from service at the university because it still had laces, which were being phased out. Newfangled or not, the ball was better than any the twins had, and they played with it for years.

After Clarence Judson died in 1945, Howie assumed the role of surrogate father. Howie had always taken an interest in the twins' athletic development, and when he was home from the university during the summers, he spent a lot of time playing basketball and baseball with them. When the twins were in sixth grade, he moved the old iron rim from the house to the garage and raised it to ten feet, regulation height. He wanted the twins to start learning the game as it should be played, as they'd be playing it for the rest of their lives. Howie put big X's on the backboard to show Paul and Phil exactly where to bank the ball so that it would drop it into the basket.

The twins were friendly, fun-loving kids who were no strangers to mischief. One time, they took a lead sinker and hung it above the window of a neighbor's house with a piece of fishing line. They attached another piece of line to the first, retreating behind a tree. As they pulled on and released the line, the sinker would tap against the window, causing no small amount of consternation inside the house, and no small amount of glee to the boys behind the tree.

Another time, when they were old enough to know better, they rigged up a huge slingshot in the woods behind their house, using an automobile inner tube stretched between two branches. When a freight train approached on the nearby tracks, they fired big stones at the boxcars. One conductor who took exception to the barrage jumped off the train and caught Paul. Loading him onto the caboose, the conductor took the boy "around the bend," about a mile down the track, and then let him go, giving him plenty of time to think about his transgressions on the long walk home.

Paul and Phil were as identical as twins come, especially as toddlers. As they grew older, however, subtle differences emerged.

Stood up side by side, Paul was about an inch taller than Phil; Phil usually weighed a pound or two more, though that difference didn't show. In eighth grade, Paul got a crewcut while Phil retained his longer "Princeton" hairstyle, parted on the left side. Phil said it was so the girls could run their fingers through his hair. Their haircuts and the numbers on their uniforms were the only clues people had to tell them apart.

The twins had lots of interests, but most of all they loved sports. When the lunch bell rang, they'd run about a mile home from school to eat lunch, play some more basketball, and then run back to school just in time to make it to class.

Now that dedication was beginning to pay off. They were already good defenders and ballhandlers; Howie and Les Oglesby had taught them well on the grade school team.

Despite their athletic ability, the Judson twins were still deficient in one important area. Paul stood just 5-foot-4, and Phil was a little shorter. They were beginning to wonder when they would get their growth spurt, if indeed it was coming at all. Their brother, Howie, had been almost six feet tall when he was a freshman, but there was no way to know if they would ever catch up to him.

As they began their freshman year at Alden-Hebron High School, Paul was delighted to make the varsity team. Phil would start out with the JV team and wait for his crack at a varsity role.

Out of the Gate

With Hebron's long tradition of success, Russ Ahearn had plenty of room for optimism, but his career as a head coach got off to a rocky start. In fact, his first win required something of a miracle.

After losing two close games and then getting beaten badly by St. Edward's of Elgin, the Green Giants set off to play Genoa City, a traditional rival just across the border in Wisconsin. With Hebron trailing by one point and time running out, Ahearn sent in Jim Judson, cousin of the twins and just a sophomore, with instructions to "shoot and keep shooting."

Jim was only 5-foot-3, and he'd already played a full game in the preliminary contest, so he didn't appear to pose much of a threat. But the coach considered him a good shot. At this moment in time, that was exactly what the team needed, so he took a leap of faith and put the game in young Jim Judson's hands.

Nervous and unsure, Jim gamely dribbled down the court. With only ten seconds to go, he put up a long shot from the top of the key. When it rattled through the net, the excited Hebron crowd leapt to its feet and spilled onto the floor. That was a miscalculation, since there were still a few seconds left on the clock. The referee had no choice but to signal a technical foul against the Hebron faithful. Chastened, now more anxious than ever, the fans returned to their seats. Not until Genoa City missed the free throw could Ahearn finally celebrate his first career victory.

Innocent as it was, this game proved to be a turning point in the season. From the brink of four straight losses, Hebron sailed forward, winning seven in a row.

Then they came up against Huntley in the semifinals of the McHenry County Tournament played at Woodstock. Near the end of the game, as Hebron trailed by just a basket, Ahearn inserted all three Judsons — Paul, Phil, and Jim — into his lineup. The tiny trio tied up the ball three times in the final eight seconds, forcing jump balls that, unfortunately, they were too short to win.

After the string of victories, Hebron's loss to Huntley was unexpected. Nevertheless, the team's hustle impressed George E. Sullivan, sports editor of the *Woodstock Sentinel* and dean of area scribes, and he made his way down to the floor to chat with Coach Ahearn. Sullivan had covered sports in McHenry County since 1921, including the great Hebron teams of the 1930s and 1940s. When he complimented Russ Ahearn on his coaching acumen, it meant something.

Accepting Sullivan's praise with a smile, the coach pointed out that all of his starters save one would be back next season. He invited Sullivan to keep an eye on his up-and-coming team.

Life and Death

One night just after Christmas, shocking news came to the Ahearn household.

After a successful tournament appearance in Madison, Wisconsin, Elgin High School's undefeated basketball team set out for home. Coaches and players filled several cars, forming a caravan over ice-covered roads. The line had just crossed back into Illinois when, just outside Harvard, a semi-trailer slid across the pavement, crashing into two of the vehicles.

Although the first automobile in the caravan escaped unharmed, the truck sideswiped the second car, the one driven by Elgin coach John Krafft, nearly shearing off the top. Right behind in the third vehicle was Spencer Morris, a close friend of Ahearn's, who had taken over as assistant basketball coach when Russ left for Hebron. Unable to avoid the accident, Morris smashed head-on into Krafft's car and then into the truck.

Morris was fatally injured in the crash. Several of the Elgin players received cuts and bruises of varying severity, while Krafft sustained a skull fracture that would require several months of convalescence.

As Russ Ahearn worried about his friends and mourned the loss of Spencer Morris, difficult questions haunted him. What would happen to Morris's young family? Would John Krafft pull through?

He wondered what would have happened if he'd stayed at Elgin. Almost certainly, he would've been part of the caravan of automobiles on that icy road. If he'd been driving, would the outcome have been any different? Or would he have become a victim, too, like his friends?

Russ scanned the newspapers every day for news from Elgin, faithfully clipping the articles and saving them in his desk drawer.

He couldn't help but think about the calling that he'd chosen. Teaching was a noble profession, but like any other, it included risks as well as rewards.

He had always taken his coaching responsibilities seriously, and he put winning at the top of his list. But the death of his friend made him realize that some things were simply more important than basketball.

Family, abiding faith, and the idea of making a difference in young men's lives took on even greater significance in his life.

Making Strides

That winter, Russ Ahearn's team made steady progress on the court. At the end of the season, Hebron reached the finals of the district tournament but lost again to St. Edward's, finishing the season with a 14-7 record. The Green Wave remained a major roadblock in the path of any Hebron success, but Ahearn was building a team for the future. Success, he was sure, could not be far away.

He marveled at the boys' work ethic at the start of the 1949-50 season. "I've never seen such a basketball-oriented community," he told Don Peasley, a reporter for the local *Community News*. "These kids really train."

Ahearn seemed especially enthusiastic about the young players, starting with the Judson twins, Paul and Phil. "Each grew about four inches," he said. "Both stand about 5-9 now. And I have a 6-foot-7 freshman named Bill Schulz we've been working with, and Kenley Spooner, a lad who promises to be a good shot."

Except for Paul, these players would see limited varsity playing time. But Ahearn set his sights further down the road.

Over the summer, he had acquired something he desperately needed: help. By engaging the services of Floyd Sorenson as head football coach and basketball assistant, Russ could concentrate his efforts on coaching the varsity basketball team. Sorenson took charge of the JV team and stepped in to assist Ahearn during varsity games.

The presence of an assistant coach on the bench offered some real benefits. Ahearn could now shout out thoughts and ideas to Sorenson, who would copy them down in a brown spiral notebook just like the one John Krafft had used. During timeouts and at halftime, Ahearn flipped the pages and read back the points he wanted to make. Other coaches kidded him about his extensive use of the notebooks, but he was steadfast in his belief that it made a difference.

All the starters were back except for Earl Seavall, and the addition of 6-foot-4 center Ron Elliott provided some height in the middle. Hebron was never a pushover, but this year's team seemed to start in mid-season form.

Genoa City came to Hebron's gym for the second contest of the campaign. When the teams had met the year before, Hebron needed Jim Judson's miracle shot to pull out Ahearn's first win. This time the new and improved Green Giants won by 70 points.

Hebron stumbled three times in December against good competition, but the young Green Giants learned something in each loss. When the team went on a seven-game January run, winning each game by at least 39 points, Hebron's basketball team brought a Chicago reporter to town for the first time since 1940.

"This Hebron five is so good," wrote Tommy Kouzmanoff of the *Herald-American,* "that folks in the tiny rural community of 650 are beginning to compare it with another great Hebron team that has become legend." The fact is, many in town already considered the team *better* than the vaunted 1940 squad.

Kouzmanoff's glowing article provided wonderful scrapbook material, and the parents bought up all the available copies. But team members may have spent too much time reading their press clippings. Not long after the tribute was printed, the Green Giants suffered an inexplicable loss to Marengo, a team that had won only 9 of 21 games that season.

Once again the district tournament boiled down to a competitive championship game between the Green Giants of Hebron and the Green Wave of St. Edward's. This time Hebron won the district title,

39-35, moving on to the regional and offering Ahearn a shot at an unrealized goal.

Ever since coming to Hebron, he'd been aching to best his mentor, John Krafft. After the devastating automobile accident of early 1949, Krafft had slowly recovered and taken back the reins of his team. Ahearn's goal to meet and beat his mentor seemed unrealistic — Elgin had been on an eight-year run under Krafft that no upstart school from McHenry County seemed likely to stop — but it was a goal Ahearn held close to his heart, nonetheless.

As expected, Elgin won its regional opener on Tuesday night. The next evening, Hebron arrived at the Elgin gym for its first-round game with Dundee. The high school had been closed that week because of a coal shortage, and the gym felt like an icebox. Although the crowd of over 2,000 fans generated some heat, Hebron was as cold as the gym floor, and the Green Giants fell behind 18-6 in the first period. Despite playing even the rest of the way, they could never make up the deficit. The final score was 54-43.

Once again facing an early end to his season, two games shy of his big chance at Elgin, the Hebron coach remained upbeat.

"We'll be back again next season," he promised, "and maybe the outcome will be different."

In any case, the players certainly would be different. Ahearn would lose three starters from a 23-5 team. For his third year as head coach, only Paul Judson and Ron Elliott would return. Phil Judson and his cousin, Jim Judson, had already been pegged for starting roles. The fifth position, Ahearn concluded, would go to a young man named Don Wilbrandt.

Captain Don

A town boy with roots back on the farm, Don was the son of Louis and Florence Mackert Wilbrandt. Louie was a successful businessman and member of the school board. He owned one of only two Cadillacs in town, and every year or so he liked to trade for a new one. A small town like Hebron didn't really have an upper crust, but the Wilbrandts came close.

Louie Wilbrandt was a calf-buyer, a profession that he and his four brothers had learned from their father. When all six Wilbrandts were in business at the same time, their territory covered a wide expanse of northeastern Illinois. Louie had grown up in Algonquin, where he played basketball at Dundee High School. When it came time to branch out on his own, he'd moved to Hebron to stake out new turf.

Calf-buying was a make-it-or-break-it business that required a good deal of shrewdness as well as hard work. Smart and industrious, Louie Wilbrandt was a cash-on-the-barrelhead success story. He'd rise early in the morning to listen to the day's commodity prices on the radio before making his rounds of Hebron's dairy farms, scanning each barn, looking for a gunny bag hung on a nail, a signal that a calf was for sale. Wilbrandt would pick up the calf in his arms, estimate its weight, calculate the break-even price in his head, and make his best offer. Then he'd bring the animal back to his own farm, where it would be slaughtered, dressed, and finally transported to the market on Fulton Street in Chicago.

Eventually the business outgrew the facilities on his farm. To meet the demand, Wilbrandt built a slaughtering plant on the west side of Hebron, on the road leading out of town. A few years later, when a large company offered him a price he couldn't refuse, he sold the plant for a good profit and retired. The family lived a bit longer on their farm south of town, but with no real reason to stay there, Wilbrandt moved them into Hebron, to a pretty Queen Anne style house right next to the grade school.

The couple's first child, Don, was born on January 31, 1934, with a birth defect called hemifacial microsomia. In this condition, one side of the jaw and one ear do not develop normally. In Don's case, his right ear was almost completely missing. He never suffered from the lack of hearing in the ear — he learned to compensate by moving his head from side to side — but as any child would be, he was self-conscious about the effect it had on his appearance. When his picture was taken, Don always lined up with his left side to the camera.

But Don's appearance, or the fact that he looked different from other children, never seemed to be an issue in Hebron. He was a sweet, shy boy, and his mother doted on him. No one made fun of him or pointed him out, but as he grew older the burden of looking different weighed more heavily on his mind. Sports were his outlet. Don grew up strong and quick, good at anything athletic, but especially baseball and basketball.

Don and his younger brother, Jim, were the Wilbrandts' only children. They shared many of the same interests, including sports, but with two years separating them, each had his own circle of friends. Don was in the same grade as the Judson twins, and once the Wilbrandts moved to town, the three played together constantly.

One summer the Wilbrandt boys persuaded their father to install lights to illuminate the driveway court. The Wilbrandt house quickly became a gathering place for the town boys as they played endless pick-up games.

In school, Don took on all sorts of extracurricular activities. Though he now lived in town, he remained involved in Future Farmers of America, volunteering to help the Judsons raise a calf on the farm his parents still owned. He entered the typing contest, joined the science club, worked on the staff of the school yearbook, the *Heacon*, and even performed in the school play.

But most of all, Don loved basketball. Don and the Judson twins formed the core of the Hebron Grade School team from the moment it was organized. In high school, Don was elected captain of the junior varsity squad during both his freshman and sophomore years. Even as a JV player, he'd seen considerable playing time with the varsity, usually in mop-up situations.

As his junior year dawned, Don was thrilled to get a varsity slot alongside Paul and Phil. Finally the three friends who'd grown up together on the basketball court would be able to show the world what they could do as a team.

Back on the Map

As part of his plan to turn Hebron into a state contender, Ahearn beefed up the schedule during the off-season. To start the 1950-51 season, the Green Giants would travel to Dundee right off the bat. Late in the season, they'd see West Rockford. And in the middle, at

Christmastime, Ahearn had arranged an invitation to a prestigious eight-team holiday tournament in Kankakee.

Hebron's development under Ahearn was already well document-ed in northern Illinois. But before the season began, no one realized just how good the team had become. Hebron's ability frightened oppo-nents. Everyone on the team could shoot. Everyone could score. And the Judson twins, starting on the same team for the first time in three years, clicked with each other as though they'd never been separated, with no-look passes, perfect timing, and an almost inborn sense of where to find each other. Did they have some kind of special tele-pathic communication? Or was it simply the product of endless hours of play on the driveways of Hebron?

In their first game, the Green Giants swept aside Dundee in a 35-30 "upset," though their boosters insisted they knew Hebron was the better club all along. It was only the start of a string of dazzling per-formances.

One week Paul Judson scored 25 points against St. Mary's in an easy win, and the next Phil made 27 in a similar victory over Huntley. Against Libertyville, Ron Elliott exploded for 30 points in a game Ahearn called "the greatest scoring exhibition I have seen on the local floor."

Just before Christmas, Don Wilbrandt scored 21 against Crystal Lake in the championship of the McHenry County Tournament, help-ing them to an easy win. So dominating was the Hebron squad that the All-Tournament team consisted of all five Green Giant starters.

"I never saw a club with so many shooting stars," Coach Mel Stuessy of St. Mary's said in awe. "I think they made 90 percent of their shots against us."

It was an exaggeration, but Hebron's shooting skill *was* impressive. As a team, the Green Giants averaged about 45 percent from the field, far above their opponents, and Ahearn kept the statistics to prove it.

Hebron won its first nine games in easy fashion. The early-season performance was so inspiring that George Sullivan of the *Woodstock Sentinel*, a voting member on the Associated Press poll, began cam-paigning openly for statewide recognition of the Green Giants as

Hebron prepared for its appearance at the Kankakee Holiday Tournament.

Coach Ahearn knew that Kankakee would serve as the team's introduction to the Big Time. Though Kankakee's tournament was brand-new, it was a good bet to become one of the best in the state. Little Hebron, the curiosity, would be the biggest attraction at the inaugural tournament, and Ahearn wanted to make the most of the invitation. He was especially anxious to make an impression in Kankakee, where he'd coached and played summer baseball for two years, and where his brother had starred on the St. Viator College baseball team.

On the day after Christmas, 1950, the team boarded the train at Woodstock to set out for their first big-league holiday tournament. They traveled to downtown Chicago, where they switched trains for the leg down to Kankakee. It was an adventure for Hebron's small-town boys, many of whom had never taken a journey of this distance or stayed in a hotel. For the three-day trip, the players were responsible for their own train fare and meals, and some of them quickly ran low on money. Bill Schulz ate only a candy bar on the three-hour train trip to Kankakee, but survived just fine, and he wrote home as soon as he got there to tell his parents not to worry.

The Kankakee gym was the largest the team had ever played in. Most of the schools on Hebron's schedule had bandbox gyms with just a few rows of bleachers. By contrast, the stands at Kankakee started at the floor and just seemed to keep going up, climbing both sides to the high windows on the wall — ten, twenty, thirty rows of them.

More than anything, the gym looked like a scaled-down model of Huff Gym at the University of Illinois, where the state championship games were played. Hoping his players would take inspiration from that fact, Ahearn pointed out the similarities. In terms of its three-sided seating and general atmosphere, Kankakee followed the Huff model perfectly. But one crucial detail really impressed them. High on one wall at the end of the court hung a large, flat, wooden cutout of the state of Illinois. On the map, glowing lights represented each of the teams participating in the tournament, just like the one at Huff.

Hebron's first opponent was Bradley, a town bordering Kankakee. Bradley ranked 15th in the state just before Christmas and had lost only one game, but Hebron was not awed by the Boilermakers. The Green Giants came out hot in the first half, as they always seemed to do, and led 35-22 at intermission. The only downside? Phil Judson had picked up his fourth foul seconds before the end of the half, meaning Ahearn would have to change his game plan to protect his junior star. In the third quarter, with Phil under wraps, Bradley slowly chipped away at the Green Giants.

With Hebron clinging to a one-point lead late in the game, Ahearn ordered his team to stall some time off the clock. But the Boilermakers stole the ball and sank a shot to put Bradley ahead for good. Another bucket made the final score 56-53.

Hebron won the consolation title by beating Urbana and Kankakee easily, but the Bradley loss grated on Ahearn and his players. Thirteen points ahead at halftime — 39-24 at one point in the third quarter — and still they'd lost. The team had learned an important lesson about invincibility. It didn't exist.

Hebron rolled on through the rest of the winter. Against Marengo, the Green Giants became the first northern Illinois team in anyone's memory to hit the century mark with a 100-43 win. When Ron Elliott dropped in a hook shot in the final seconds to put Hebron up to 100, the fans in the Hebron gym let loose a roar that could be heard across town.

"There wasn't anything I could do about it," Ahearn told reporters, "as the boys were in the mood and played the best game of the season."

Three days later, against Kirkland, lightning struck again in a 103-32 victory. This time Bill Schulz, who'd played in the JV game earlier in the evening, came back in for the final four minutes of the varsity contest. He wound up scoring 10 points in his short stint, as Hebron took 93 shots and made 44 of them.

Some observers were unhappy with the relentless scoring of the Hebron team. Hal Bruno, sports editor of the *DeKalb Chronicle*, wrote, "I like to see a team from a small town produce good basketball that rates with the best. But some day the shoe may be on the other foot, and Coach Ahearn and the Hebron fans may learn what is meant by 'pouring it on.'"

Ahearn defended the use of his starting five even when the team had a big lead. He argued that his varsity starters shouldn't be expected to come out of the game simply because they were far ahead and playing well. Like any other team, they needed to run their plays and practice their defense. If that meant playing hard, putting the ball through the hoop as often as possible, and fighting for every loose ball, so be it.

Besides, what choice did he have? His starters needed to build up stamina now to make it through tougher contests down the road. They'd never get where they needed to be if they had to sit down every time they were ahead. Sending tired JV players into the game for another quarter or two of action didn't make sense. He wasn't going to ask Hebron's varsity players to stall, either. Stalling was unnatural for the running, gunning Green Giant five. It had proved to be a mistake against Bradley, one that ended up costing them an important win.

That said, there were times when Ahearn simply had to call off the dogs. Early in February, Hebron traveled to Richmond for a game their coach would have preferred not to play at all.

Richmond was coached by Bert Nafziger, who'd been an assistant at Elgin at the same time Ahearn was there. Because the Rockets' program was down, they were unlikely to provide much resistance, and he hated running up the score on his old friend. As it turned out, two of Richmond's starters were ill, making things even worse. Hebron held the ball nearly the entire fourth quarter and still won by an ugly score, 70-7.

As he did after every game, Ahearn called the Chicago papers to report the result. The reporter was so astonished by the score that he asked Ahearn to repeat it and even count it out, and then bungled the numbers in the next day's headline, anyway. It read, "HEBRON ROUTS RICHMOND, 20-7."

The big game with West Rockford proved to be the perfect finale to the regular season. Entering the game, West Rockford was ranked

15th in the state, but prior to a pair of late-season losses, the team had been listed much higher.

Hebron was the first team in the list of "others receiving votes," in 16th place, thanks mostly to George Sullivan, who had taken his one-man campaign for recognition to new heights by consistently voting for Hebron in first place.

The match-up had many people scratching their heads. Where other large schools had turned and run from Ahearn's invitations, Alex Saudargas, West Rockford's coach, seemed to view Hebron as a challenge. Playing in the Big Eight, northern Illinois' premier basketball conference, West Rockford certainly didn't need the competition. The game would be a sellout, that much was certain, but all the Warrior games were well attended. He wasn't bringing in Hebron simply to boost the gate.

Whatever the motivation, Ahearn and the Hebron players were happy to see such a tough opponent.

Coach Ahearn had arranged the Hebron schedule to give his team a whole week to prepare for this game. Preparation was his strong suit, and he knew West Rockford's strategies backward and forward from his days at Elgin, a Big Eight rival. He used his full seven days, making sure the players got plenty of rest as well as drilling them on every aspect of West Rockford's game.

Several hundred fans from Hebron attended the game in Rockford, leaving only the very young and very old to hold down the fort back home. The hometowners realized the importance of playing such a respected rival. Many of them also remembered the Rockford game of 1940 — the game that capped the remarkable run to the state finals — and hoped desperately for the same result.

In the preliminary contest, Hebron won 65-60, a result that boded well for the future, with Bill Schulz scoring 27 points. Then the starting five — and only the starting five — hit the floor for warm-ups for the main event. One wag in the stands yelled out, "Where's the rest of your team?" A Hebron fan called back, "Taking a shower!" which was the absolute truth. After their JV game finished, the reserves headed to the locker room, undressed, showered, put their sweaty uniforms on, and then sat on the bench for the varsity contest. They were already warmed up and ready for action, if needed.

With no starter under 6-foot-2, West Rockford had a tall team that matched up well against Hebron. Not having a height advantage gave the Giants fits, and they fell behind, trailing 35-28 at halftime. In the second half, with Don Wilbrandt hitting shot after shot from outside, they slowly worked their way back into contention. With about a minute remaining, Phil Judson made a terrific steal at midcourt and scored a lay-up to put Hebron ahead for the first time.

West Rockford started fouling Wilbrandt in a desperate comeback attempt. Don did everything he could, making his single free throw each time he went to the line, but West Rockford continued to nip at Hebron's heels. With three seconds remaining, the Warriors had a chance to tie the game by making two free throws. When the second shot glanced off the rim, the game finally belonged to Hebron.

Wilbrandt finished the game with 27 points, including all 11 free throws he attempted, the greatest individual performance of his young varsity career. The 57-56 win over a Big Eight Conference school also represented a new pinnacle of success for Russ Ahearn as coach of the Hebron team.

Such a significant victory should have been a great going-away present for Howie Judson, who was headed for spring training after the game. Instead, he was incensed. The officiating in the final minute had set him off, and he and Louie Wilbrandt marched into the officials' locker room to confront them. They raised such a ruckus that they finally had to be escorted away from the area by school authorities.

Despite the incident, the win provided the perfect springboard for the upcoming tournament. The six-team district tournament was already being conceded to Hebron, despite the fact that its annual nemesis, St. Edward's, had only four losses.

Since their teams both had byes, Ahearn and St. Ed's coach Greg True sat together in the bleachers during the opening session of the district tournament, scouting potential opponents. As always, Ahearn wrote down his observations in his spiral notebook. This time True showed up with his own notebook in hand. The two talked basketball as Ahearn watched the action and scribbled his impressions, carefully noting the offensive and defensive strategies he thought might work against each of them. True appeared to do the same.

But when a reporter took a peek at True's notebook late in the game, he found only a single entry, dated July 20, 1950, that read, "I hoed my potatoes today — that's thirty for the day."

Perhaps if he'd had something more insightful to write, True could've come up with a magic strategy to stop the rampaging Green Giants. When the teams met in the district finals for the sixth year in a row, it was strictly no contest. Hebron led 20-3 after four minutes and coasted to a 61-36 win for its second consecutive district title.

George Sullivan of the *Sentinel* had come to be such a familiar face in Hebron that he was now sitting on the bench, right next to the coaches. "We never saw a team so fired up," he wrote. "They could hardly wait to get at the crack team from Elgin [St. Edward's]." In fact Sullivan himself may have had a little leftover adrenaline pumping when he wrote his column that evening, describing Ahearn — for perhaps the only time ever in print — as "tall."

And so it was on to the regional round. Sited at Woodstock, the regional was packed with talent once again. Always tough Elgin was the top seed, but a pair of recent losses had knocked the Maroons out of the state rankings. By contrast, Dundee, the second seed, was on a late-season surge. With just three losses, Dundee ranked No. 9 in the state. Hebron had risen to No. 12.

A routine win over Woodstock set up the expected match the next night with Dundee.

The opposing coach, Eugene de Lacey, was another northern Illinois legend. He'd led Dundee to a state championship in 1938 and his teams were always tough at tournament time. The previous year Dundee had ended Hebron's season in the regional. Now a win over the Cardunals would allow Hebron to move ahead a step or two in what was essentially a three-school race for the regional title, with Elgin and Dundee as the perennial leaders and Hebron coming up strong on the outside. Other than these three, no school had won the local regional in the last 15 years.

This time Hebron held the upper hand. Ahearn's charges came out shooting, as expected, and quickly ran up an 18-8 lead. Dundee closed within four near the end, but Phil Judson made a close shot and Jim Judson sank a free throw for the final 63-56 score.

The team had little time to celebrate, since the title game against Elgin loomed the next night. Finally, in his third year at Hebron, Coach Ahearn had his chance to face Elgin.

But Elgin was without his mentor, John Krafft, who had retired as head coach at the end of the 1950 season. Krafft had never fully recovered from the skull fracture he'd suffered in the car crash, and so, at age 44, he'd given up the reins. Bill Chesbrough, a young coach from New York who'd been hired as an assistant after the death of Spencer Morris, was now in charge.

Ahearn's desire to beat Elgin had by now become almost an obsession, even with Krafft watching from the stands instead of the bench. With Dundee conquered, with the West Rockford notch already carved on his belt, there was no one else Ahearn wanted to beat. Except Elgin.

Most of all he wanted to get the better of his old teacher. But until and unless Krafft returned to coaching, conquering Krafft's successor would have to suffice.

The Green Giants and the mighty Maroons fought evenly throughout the title game, with Elgin leading 17-13 after a quarter and 29-27 at halftime.

Hebron wasn't used to playing catch-up. Ahearn tried to keep his players focused in the locker room, but his tactics didn't seem to work. In the third period, Elgin started to pull away and led by nine points, 50-41, entering the final eight minutes.

But Paul Judson would not let the game slip away. After an exchange of free throws, Paul scored seven consecutive points, the last two on a long set shot, to pull Hebron within two at 51-49. When Jim Judson dropped in another rainbow from the top of the key to tie the game, the crowd erupted.

Hebron scrambled to get the ball back, resulting in a flurry of whistles. When the smoke cleared, both Phil Judson and Don Wilbrandt had fouled out. Ahearn had no choice but to send in his substitutes.

He turned to Bill Schulz and Ken Spooner, both sophomores. They'd seen some action during the regular season, but never in a big game with so much on the line.

Elgin's Dale McCallum hit a free throw to put the Maroons back in front, and then both Jim Judson and Schulz missed free throw attempts for Hebron. After Willard Schuldt made a lay-up for Elgin, the Maroons stalled out most of the final 2:45. With two starters out and with Paul Judson also in foul trouble, Hebron had no way to get the ball back except to pray for a turnover.

Elgin escaped with a 54-51 win, sending Hebron and Ahearn home disappointed.

"We were beaten by a great team, and our boys just didn't have the physical strength to stave off that final Elgin rally," Ahearn told a reporter after the game. He felt Hebron was sapped by playing games on three consecutive nights, while Elgin, playing in the upper bracket, had rested on a night off.

Coach Ahearn fought back tears as he recounted the events of the evening to the newspaperman. But as badly as he wanted to win, and especially to beat Elgin, he was happy for the success of the Maroon players, many of whom he had coached before he left for Hebron.

"I know these boys," he said. "They are a great bunch of kids, and I hope they can go all the way now."

Already he was looking ahead to next season, making plans, juggling new ideas for his lineup and teams to put on his schedule. He expressed frustration that he could not find opponents big enough and talented enough to test the team he knew would be his best yet. He wanted to give his players a challenge. He couldn't figure out why other coaches didn't feel the same way.

He'd gotten Joliet to agree to a game, and Waukegan and Oak Park looked certain. On the other hand, Dundee, stinging from the loss in November, and West Rockford, still trying to figure out what had hit them in February, had flat-out refused. The Green Giants were ready and willing to travel, but few were willing to host them.

Ahearn's real quarry still eluded him. Elgin appeared in no hurry to schedule a regular-season game against a former coach with a talented, hungry team.

In a quiet moment, Ahearn admitted, "We'd love to play in that wonderful EHS gym." He knew the odds were against it.

The only way the Maroons were going to play Hebron was if luck, fate, and the IHSA threw them together in the state tournament.

INSTRUCTIONS TO THE BASKETBALL TEAM

Remember -- you do not have to go out for basketball. If you decide that you are going out for the team I shall expect you, in order to have as good a team as possible, to:

1. Keep your school work up to the satisfaction of all teachers and to check with them on your status weekly. If you can't keep eligible you are not smart enough to play on the team.

2. Get at least nine hours of sleep nightly.

3. If you can't be gentlemen around teachers, the school, students, and the community, do not go out for the team. We have plenty who will.

4. Your teammates will not tolerate any one on the squad who uses tobacco or alcohol in any form _anytime_. You can't give 100% if you do these things.

5. If you have any injuries or sore spots or are not feeling up to par, see the coach.

6. You should be on time at every practice -- dress fast.

7. While on the floor we expect no distractions or wasting time -- hustle all the time.

8. Remember -- A star does not make the team -- A team makes the star.

9. You have the finest equipment money can buy -- let's take good care of it.

10. Let's act like real men on trips.

11. Treat opponents and officials courteously, but play to win -- Remember -- in Hebron we play that way.

12. Keep off your feet as much as possible -- to keep life in your legs -- especially the day of the game.

13. Watch your training diet infinitely. You can get out of condition in 1 or 2 days if you neglect your training schedule.

14. If you don't follow these thirteen points at anytime during the season -- please turn in your suit, let somebody else have it and root for the team as a spectator -- we'll think more of you.

Mr. Ahearn -- Coach

Be in at 9:30 P.M. on weeknights.

Dates on weekends only!

chapter 6

Summer of '51

The pain of the loss to Elgin faded somewhat with the spring, especially for the players who were not staring graduation in the face.

Two weeks after Hebron was eliminated, three of the juniors got their first look at the state tournament in Champaign. With tickets Russ Ahearn had acquired as Hebron's principal, Louie Wilbrandt took his son Don and the Judson twins down to Champaign for a day's worth of first-round action at Huff Gym. The young men marveled at the size of the arena — bigger than anything they'd ever seen — and left town with aspirations of playing there themselves sometime soon.

Ahearn made the trip to Champaign the next day with a few pals to watch the weekend games. In good spirits, he began to talk up his prospects for the next year with colleagues and reporters. Yes, he was losing sparkplug Jim Judson and Ron Elliott, who had provided such a steady presence in the middle. But he'd have three first-class starters back and some excellent replacements for the pair he'd lost.

"Next year will have to be our year," Ahearn told one newsman.

While their coach planned, the boys continued playing basketball in the gym or on the driveways when they could. Ahearn did not coach them during the off-season. IHSA rules didn't allow it, and besides, the baseball season was rapidly approaching.

Although basketball was undoubtedly first in the hearts of Hebronites, baseball came a close second. After all, Howie Judson was the town's most famous person — a genuine major leaguer, even if he wasn't a star.

Once the weather got hot, there was always a baseball game going on somewhere. In the evenings, the teenagers frequently congregated at the high school, with enough kids to field two complete teams.

Quite a few of the Hebron basketball players played on the high school baseball team that Russ Ahearn coached in the spring. Ken Spooner was the first baseman, Jim Wilbrandt filled the second base spot, and Jim Judson took third. JV team members Joe Schmidt and Jim Bergin played in the outfield.

The Judson twins played baseball, too. Phil was an excellent catcher and the team's slugger, while Paul played shortstop. Both could pitch in a pinch, but neither appeared ready to follow Howie's footsteps to the mound.

Instead, Don Wilbrandt was the team's ace, and he had quite a season in 1951. In April, he threw a no-hitter against Richmond. Then in his next start, against Capron, he came within one out of a perfect game. Hebron's pitching was better than its hitting, however, and the team finished in the middle of the pack in league competition.

Soon the high school baseball season, squeezed into two short months in the spring, gave way to town ball, the great amateur pastime of the summer. Howie had played on the town team until he turned pro, and now many of the high school players joined as well. Even Russ Ahearn, 38 years old with a rusty left arm, made some appearances on the mound for the Hebron towners.

Still, the coach never let basketball stray far from his mind. His team had shown far too much promise to let the frivolities of summer distract him from his true purpose. Ahearn would have his best team yet — he was sure of that — with players who had spent their entire high school careers under his system, mixing fundamentals and discipline in practice with innovation and improvisation on the court.

Even with so few players to work with, there was still some speculation about next season's lineup. Paul and Phil Judson and Don Wilbrandt, the three incoming seniors, would be back, of course, but two new starters would have to be chosen from the players who'd labored on the JV squad. Bill Thayer, another senior, had shown a lot of ability, as had Kenley Spooner, a junior. Both had done well in brief varsity appearances during the season. But Spooner was a stronger outside shooter, and with plenty of players who could drive to the basket, Ahearn decided Spooner would be the perfect complement to his offense. Though he didn't announce it, the coach had already made up his mind about the starting guard position.

Hot Shot

Kenley Spooner was a vintage Hebronite.

His father, Harold, grew up in Hebron and played basketball for the high school team in the 1920s. Around town, Harold Spooner was best known for his fertile mind and creative skills. He owned the first automobile in Hebron with a radio, a crystal set he built and installed himself. When it came to mechanical matters, Harold took after his own father, Mark, who was one of the first auto dealers in Hebron and who now served as Hebron's mayor.

After he graduated from high school, Harold studied at the Art Institute in Chicago and worked for many years as a commercial artist. Eventually his love of gadgets caught up with him, and he decided to strike out on his own in radio repair, setting up a small shop next to his father's service station. There he repaired radios for dozens of dealers in the Hebron area. It was a good business, though his customers often complained that he didn't charge enough.

Harold married Floreice Welbon, a town girl who worked at the local drug store, and on April 12, 1935, the couple had their first child, Kenley. His mother had taken a liking to the name after reading it in a book while she was pregnant. A second son, Wayne, was born two years later.

Like so many in Hebron, Harold loved to watch basketball at the high school gym, and he took his young boys to the games religiously. Those were the heady days of the original "Green Giants," and young

Kenley nurtured dreams of suiting up and playing for the big team one day. When Kenley was still just four or five, his father cut the bottom out of a cottage cheese carton and tacked it above the door in the back room of the house. With a tennis ball in hand, the boy would practice his dribbling and shooting for hours on end, pretending to be Howie Judson.

World War II interrupted the Spooners' blissful existence. Harold Spooner took a position with Philco Radio Corporation and ended up touring the world. Brilliant in electronics, he was assigned to teach aviators the intricacies of loran, the Navy's new long-distance navigational system. Spooner was gone for months at a time, visiting naval posts in the U.S. and the Pacific Theater, always with a briefcase handcuffed to his wrist.

When he returned from the war, Harold put a backboard and hoop on the garage for his growing sons to practice their basketball skills. A nearby streetlight provided enough illumination for them to see the court, and the Spooner driveway became one of many stops for the kids who worked their way around town looking for a good game.

Ron Elliott, two years older and very interested in basketball, lived next door. Bill Thayer, a year older than Kenley and always up for a game, lived across the street. Just behind the Spooners, a short jaunt through the yard of the house where coach Lowry Crane had once lived, stood the Judson place. And behind the Spooners and to the left, you'd find Charlie and Bob Mau, whose family hayloft provided a dry, if not always warm or bright, refuge from the elements.

Kenley and Wayne Spooner grew up in the eye of Hebron's basketball hurricane.

Every one of these houses had a basketball court, and each court had its own cracks, curbs, and corners. Players who liked to dribble and drive ignored these pitfalls at their peril. But of all the boys who played on all these courts, Ken Spooner had the one weapon that flew right over these earthbound problems: a long, arching set shot.

With so many older, taller players around, he'd learned to shoot long shots out of necessity. Other players drove to the basket or jostled inside for short pivot shots, but Kenley found it easier to knock down 20- or 25-footers. Whenever he couldn't find anyone to get up a game,

Kenley would take the ball and shoot, over and over, from the farthest reaches of the court, from straight on, from all angles, memorizing each position, anticipating what it would be like to shoot from each spot in actual competition.

He was as accurate a long shooter as anyone around Hebron had ever seen. If left open for a second, especially behind a screen, he was unstoppable. He'd set up with one foot slightly in front of the other, position the ball in front of his face, and then flick his arm forward to launch the ball toward the goal.

His long-distance talent translated into a starting position on Les Oglesby's grade school team. Kenley played alongside older boys — the Judson twins and Don Wilbrandt included — and was named captain of the squad in 1948 when he was the only seventh grader on the team.

When he moved up to high school, Ken played on the junior varsity his first two years, patiently honing his talents, although he managed to get into a few games each year as a reserve. In his sophomore season he started one varsity game when the Judson twins were ill, scoring seven points against St. Edward's and drawing high marks from his coach.

Ken Spooner's patience had now paid off. In the fall of 1951, he would start for the Hebron Green Giants.

Summer Fun

Besides sports, there weren't a lot of distractions around Hebron in the summertime. A few of the players worked on farms and some in factories in Harvard or Woodstock. Coach Ahearn and the Judson twins found jobs in Woodstock at Auto-Lite Corporation, which made chrome automobile accessories.

Hebron lacked a theater, but not movies. On weekends, as dusk fell, they'd set up a projector and a screen right in the middle of Prairie Avenue to show old films, complete with popcorn and candy. The black-and-white movies, like *The Clutching Hand* thriller series that the boys loved, were free to everyone, but color films cost a quarter. The little picture show in the street could be buggy and hot, but not any hotter than staying home on a summer night without air conditioning.

Sometimes the players drove or even rode their bikes up to Lake Geneva, Wisconsin, a popular tourist spot about ten miles north, where they could swim. Other times, they'd simply entertain themselves by waving at the city girls in their snazzy cars, headed to and from the lake. If they got the chance, the boys might even flirt with the girls in one of the restaurants downtown.

Few of the players had steady girlfriends. Sports took up too much of their time, and their coach discouraged dating, anyway. During the season, Mr. Ahearn's edict was "No dating except on Saturday night."

That gave Ken Spooner pause. How were they supposed to date on Saturday nights when they had a *game* every Saturday night?

But Ahearn remained unmoved. "Being a ladies' man is a full-time job and so is basketball," he told them, "so make your decision now."

Because the girls in town knew that the basketball players could be only part-time boyfriends, they tended to shy away from dating them. At least that's how the boys explained it to themselves.

Nevertheless, when prom rolled around the players usually managed to get dates. For the junior prom, Phil Judson had a girl from his class lined up but no car to take her in. Always thinking ahead, Phil persuaded Don Wilbrandt to double-date with him — and bring his father's famous black Cadillac — so that they would have transportation.

Paul Judson came up with a different solution. He used the coach's car. Of all the players, Paul had grown especially close to Russ Ahearn. That summer Paul occasionally borrowed the Ahearn family auto when he had a date and no wheels. When the evening was over and Paul drove back into the garage, he'd notice the side door pull shut and the lights go off inside the house, which meant that the coach was keeping an eye out, as watchful as any parent. But Paul always brought the car back safe, sound, and on time, and Coach Ahearn continued to allow him car privileges.

Even though the boys enjoyed baseball and managed an occasional date, summer was mostly about basketball. They practiced their skills in all kinds of weather on the driveway courts. They also honed their game at the high school. The gym there was always open to them

— as long as they remembered to turn out the lights and close the door behind them.

When the boys weren't shooting hoops, they'd often drop by Ken and John Lopeman's place for a game of pool. Father and son ran the town grocery and were two of Hebron's most avid fans. Their house was right next door to the Wilbrandts', and on many a rainy summer day their pool table provided good, clean fun for the players. Lopeman let them come and go as they pleased, leaving his doors unlocked, as did just about everyone else in Hebron.

In June, the local post of the American Legion sent the Judson twins to Springfield to attend the annual Boys State leadership conference. Thousands of boys from around the state gathered for the jamboree that year. At one point during the conference, someone nudged the Judsons and pointed out a tall, dark-haired boy at the other end of the hall, whispering, "That's Bruce Brothers from Quincy."

Brothers was already a household name in some parts of Illinois. Among his accomplishments, he'd led Quincy to a third-place finish in the 1951 state basketball tournament. But the Judsons hadn't seen Quincy play at Champaign and had no idea who Brothers was. They looked at each other and shrugged their shoulders.

Hot Stove League

As autumn leaves began to fall, basketball talk heated up all over Hebron. The hot-stovers had no official meeting place, but the most animated discussions took place in the back room of Lopeman's Grocery.

Ken Lopeman, the acknowledged expert on Hebron's basketball fortunes, had followed the team since the days of Lowry Crane. He even splurged on an eight-millimeter movie camera and took short shots of some of the game action to show to the players. Of course, they loved to watch themselves on film, and the clips became a regular treat. Even without the game films, Lopeman was almost an unofficial member of the team, since his store was on the front lines in enforcing Coach Ahearn's strict no-candy rule. But the coach said gum was acceptable, so Lopeman gave out free packs to any players who wanted them.

Down the street, Joe Fabri entertained more basketball talk in his barber shop. When Ahearn mentioned that his team could use light T-shirt warm-ups in addition to the heavier jacket warm-ups they already had, Fabri and other merchants got to work with a plan to get something ready for the team before tournament time. Fabri was proud that he'd signed up to provide a new warm-up for his favorite player, Phil Judson.

Ed Kjellstrom, whose son John had been a star on the 1940 team, remained a faithful Green Giant booster. He'd long since phased out the harness portion of his shop, but he still sold clothing and other dry goods when he wasn't talking basketball. Hank Freeman, the auctioneer, Joe Horeled, the oil man, Walter Gabel, the druggist, Gene Losee, the factory owner, and John Sime, the banker, were among those who kept the hot-stove league in full swing throughout the fall months.

Naturally, they thought a lot of Hebron's chances for the upcoming season. Certainly the record from the previous year, with 28 wins and just 2 losses, was enough to bear out such optimism.

But there were still many question marks. And the biggest one, literally and figuratively, was a 6-foot-10½, 17-year-old center who had started only one varsity game in his career.

High Hopes

Bill Schulz, the final starter in Russ Ahearn's lineup, grew up only four miles away from the Judsons, Wilbrandts, and Spooners, but he may as well have come from a different planet.

His father, Fred Schulz, had left Germany with his parents in 1923, at the age of 18, when the surge in the popularity of the Nazi Party presaged another war. Once in the United States, the family settled in southern Wisconsin, in dairy country. Fred Schulz was a dairy farmer, and the regular rhythms of milking and feeding dominated his daily life. When he courted Helen DeVries, a dairy farmer's daughter from near Hebron, she promised to marry him, but only if she never had to milk another cow. He gave his word, and the pair settled on a farm north of Alden, near the state-line hamlet of Big Foot.

Their first child was born there on November 11, 1934, and given his father's full name. He was the third male in the family to carry the name Fred William Schulz. But the baby soon acquired nicknames as well. His grandfather was Old Fritz and his father was Young Fritz, so they started calling the boy Little Fritz. Outside the family, he was known as Bill.

The Schulz farm lacked electricity until 1936, when lines were finally strung through the countryside outside Alden. Fred Schulz put the new juice to work with an electric milking machine. Helen bought herself an iron and a Frigidaire.

When Bill started first grade, he walked to a one-room schoolhouse about a mile down the road. In addition to giving instruction in reading, writing, and arithmetic to pupils in grades one through eight, the teacher also had to arrive early to stoke the furnace and clear the snow in the wintertime. When things really got cold, there was simply not enough coal to heat the drafty room. If the water in the bubbler at the back of the room ever froze, it was a sure bet that the teacher and her pupils, who normally sat by row according to grade, would all have to crowd around the stove at the front of the room just to stay warm.

The schoolchildren walked to school every day, in rain, wind, or snow, with no question of a ride. It was the older kids' job to keep the younger ones moving. In the winter, a quick pace was the only way to stave off the bite of the howling wind. In the fall and spring, it was the best way to escape the bite of the surly farm geese that chased the children down the road.

Bill was the first child, but the Schulz family quickly grew larger. John was next in line, and then Ken, Jim, Russ, and finally, Marybeth. Aside from the family, farm life was a solitary existence. During the summer, a week would often go by without seeing anyone from the outside world.

When Bill was in fourth grade the family moved to a larger farm down the road, on a high moraine overlooking a branch of Nippersink Creek. The children loved it because it had a perfect sledding hill angling down to the stream. Fred and Helen Schulz cared for around fifty cattle there in a large milking barn.

The Schulz family worked hard and had little money, but food was never scarce. There was always milk, of course, and the family slaughtered its own cattle and could depend on a steady supply of beef. In the summer they grew fruit and vegetables, storing apples and potatoes in the cellar for the winter. Bill was a good eater, too. He enjoyed his mother's hamburgers and mashed potatoes, which she made with the jackets on. And, following the advice of the time, he ate an apple every day.

The Schulzes were a tall family. Fred Schulz was six feet tall and Helen was 5-10; their fathers had each hit six feet as well. But from an early age something about Bill indicated he was going to top them all. By sixth grade he had passed his mother. By the time he was a seventh grader, Little Fritz was looking down at Young Fritz.

At the new farm Bill attended class at Kingsley School, about two miles away, but still within walking distance. It was about that time that the postwar drive for school consolidation hit McHenry County. One-room schoolhouses were viewed as inefficient relics of rural life, relics that couldn't hope to provide instruction in the variety of subjects a modern student required. With the stroke of a pen, Bill found himself transported out of his bucolic surroundings and into the bustling town of Hebron, as a student at Alden-Hebron Community Consolidated Junior-Senior High School.

The change meant a different way of life for farm children like Bill. Most of them could no longer walk to school and had to ride buses instead. They got to know students from other farm areas and from the towns, too. But the change of schools affected Bill Schulz more than any other student.

When Russ Ahearn bumped into the gangly teenager in the bib overalls for the first time, he looked at the boy's height and immediately thought about basketball. Bill didn't know a thing about basketball; it was certainly not something he would have taken up if he'd stayed in Alden. But as he got to know the game, he really began to like it. He enjoyed the friendship of the players and being part of a team. He also liked not having to milk the cows in the evening.

Still, the after-school practices presented a transportation problem for the Schulzes. Busy with the cows, Fred Schulz had no time to ferry his son back and forth to basketball, so he bought a 1930 Model A Ford for Bill to drive. In the mornings he'd chug down Main Street toward the school, making sure to honk his horn — *Ah-OO-gah!* — at Judy Ahearn, the coach's daughter, as she walked to the grade school.

Until he got to the high school in Hebron, Bill had never considered becoming anything but a dairy farmer. He had intended to quit school when he was 16 and learn the ropes from his father. But as Bill improved his skills, he discovered that playing basketball might be a way to further his education. His father had always stressed the importance of education, but Fred Schulz had never dreamed of sending his son to college. Now Bill realized that with basketball on his side, he might be able to earn his own way.

Just a few years earlier, he probably wouldn't have been given the opportunity. No coach in his right mind would have wasted his time trying to teach the game to such a gangly boy. "Giants" weren't considered basketball material. According to common wisdom, they lacked the coordination and stamina to be successful players. Coaches expected smaller, more agile players to run circles around them.

George Mikan changed all that. As a youngster growing up in Joliet, Mikan had been an awkward, ungainly beanpole, barely able to run down the court or lift the ball into the basket. By 1946, Coach Ray Meyer of DePaul University had transformed the 6-foot-9 Mikan into college basketball's premier player and the game's first superstar. In the post-Mikan era, extreme height was no longer shunned by basketball coaches. Now it was coveted.

With visions of George Mikan in his head, Russ Ahearn set into motion the plan to make Bill Schulz into a real player. Bill worked hard, first in gym class with Russ Ahearn and then during practice, to adapt to his new role. The coach wrote down specific rules for him to follow, stressing proper conditioning and diet as well as decorum both on and off the court. Bill did his best to follow them.

Although he was an integral part of the Hebron basketball team, in some ways Bill remained an outsider. He never participated in the informal pick-up games around town and never visited the other players in their homes. With practice and farm work, there simply wasn't time. Outside of school and practice, he stayed in his own world, four miles away, far from the playgrounds and porches of Hebron.

Bill Schulz had played in a handful of varsity games as a freshman and a few more as a sophomore. All in all, he'd scored 75 points for the varsity team. Now, after just three years of practice, he would be a starter on one of the best high school basketball teams in Illinois.

RECOMMENDATIONS FOR BILL SCHULZ

The very minimum if he wants to become a polished ball player by Nov. 1951.

1. Jump rope -- 5 minutes per day -- jump on toes.

2. 50 pushups -- done on fingers -- 10 at a time.

3. 100 jumping jacks -- 20 at a time -- for coordination.

4. Drag dribble -- 5 minutes for footwork.

5. Ball handling -- ball around body between legs.

6. Rebound for 5 minutes with rim covered.

7. Shoot like a forward from side & in front. 2 handed high (kiss style).

8. Right and left pivot shots -- 5 minutes.

9. Get down and take starts like a sprinter, say to yourself on your mark, get set, go, & see how fast you can get away -- Run at top speed for about 50 yards -- 10 times a day -- 3 or 4 sprints at a time.

10. Hang around our regulars from last year -- Paul Judson, Phil Judson, & Don Wilbrandt, Bill Thayer & Ken Spooner -- Learn to think the way they do -- adopt their splendid habits.

11. Continue to be a splendid gentleman & win the sportsmanship award when you are a senior or junior.

12. Do not imitate any players of the past -- They were individuals -- so are you -- Be yourself & help your brothers to learn the game.

13. Shoot an unlimited time every day -- Be a scorer.

14. Squeeze a ball in either hand.

15. Matching exercise with another center 5 minutes.

16. Come up to the gymnasium any day this summer & shoot in the gym or any evening from 6:30 on.

17. Eat good solid foods.

18. Convince your brother that he'll be a good player when he is a junior & senior.

19. Start drive / step with either foot -- take big step back & shoot.

20. Observe all training rules.

21. Get a lot of sleep.

22. Set your scoring aim at a 20 point average next year.

Mr. Ahearn -- Coach

chapter 7

The Season Begins

As the new basketball season began, there were few vestiges of the schedule Russ Ahearn had inherited three years earlier. It was a line-up that even the largest schools in the state would have had difficulty with, and for good reason. Ahearn was not content merely to compete. Instead, he intended to compete for the state championship.

Since Hebron was not a member of a basketball conference, Ahearn had the flexibility to schedule any opponents he pleased. Only a few traditional small-school rivals remained: Maple Park; the McHenry County foes of Harvard and Marengo; and St. Edward's, Hebron's almost-certain opponent for the district championship.

Bypassing some of the old rivalries presented a political problem for Superintendent Paul Tigard. He had to explain to his colleagues at Richmond and Huntley and St. Mary's why their schools were no longer worthy of a place on Hebron's schedule. Fans of those schools would have welcomed a chance to watch the Green Giants play, even if their players were less than thrilled with the prospect of getting shellacked.

But now was the time for Ahearn to look beyond the ego-building boost of lopsided victories, to focus on challenging his team enough to make it through the long haul.

There were large schools galore on his schedule, and practically all of the games would be played on the road. Ahearn reasoned that playing in larger gyms would get his players accustomed to the atmosphere of the big games in the regional, sectional, and state final tournaments. And he was more specific than that.

If Hebron made it to the sectional, it would probably be at Waukegan. So the coach scheduled a game there in late February to check the place out and, with luck, beat the local team as well. Besides another trip to the tough Kankakee Holiday Tournament, he also scheduled games at Lake Forest, Oak Park, DeKalb, and Barrington, schools with many times Hebron's enrollment.

In a surprise move, Joliet, a member of the Big Eight Conference and state champions in 1937, agreed to come to Hebron to play in December. Joliet played its home games in an enormous field house that held over 3,000 people. The visit to Hebron's bandbox gym, with all of its eccentricities, could only be a shock for the Steelmen.

For the first time, the Hebron faithful could buy season tickets with reserved seat numbers on them so that they wouldn't have to arrive hours before the game to be assured of a space. But there was little else about the home schedule to please local fans. There were a paltry seven home games on the card. After the Green Giants hosted Joliet and St. Edward's on consecutive nights in early December, the rest of their home games promised to be cakewalks.

If they wanted to watch this edition of the Green Giants, Hebronites would have to become very familiar with the highways and byways of northern Illinois.

As the football season wound down, Ahearn whetted everyone's appetite for the upcoming season, sending off a missive to George Sullivan through the high school's student sportswriter, Tom Kuecker.

"It is difficult to say how good or how poor a team we'll have at this time," the coach said in his letter.

With a three-year coaching record of 79 wins and 17 losses, three returning starters, and a very tall center ready to step into the lineup,

Ahearn's statement must have elicited more than a few groans from the readership of Sullivan's "Put and Take" sports column.

Putting it Together

Ahearn had his own seniors now, boys he'd been coaching since they were freshmen, a good crop of players who could run the court, shoot, and rebound like nobody's business. Just about everything was coming together as the coach had hoped.

First of all, he had a new assistant to replace Floyd Sorenson. His name was Phil Hadley, and he was a new college grad fresh out of LaCrosse State Teachers' College in Wisconsin. A native of Oconomowoc, Hadley was a handsome, muscular fellow with wavy red hair, a football man with an easy-going manner. The kids loved working with him. He'd coached Hebron's six-man football team in the fall, and now he'd get to be part of the real excitement as Ahearn's basketball assistant. Hadley didn't know a lot about coaching basketball, but he'd learn soon enough, helping the head coach put the team through its paces in practice as well as guiding the junior varsity team in the preliminary contests.

In addition, Howie Judson was back as Ahearn's unofficial assistant and full-time confidante. Judson had finished his best season yet in the majors — five wins and six losses with fourteen starts — but he was back in town by early October after the Yankees ran away with the pennant again. Ahearn sought Howie's counsel often as they discussed strategy for the coming season. The two mapped out a fourth-year lesson plan for Howie and his star pupil, Bill Schulz. Schulz was even taller this season — 6-10½, or so the coach proudly claimed — but Bill was also thin as a rail, weighing less than 200 pounds. He would need all of Judson's savvy and then some to overcome the burlier centers he'd encounter down the road.

As he had in previous years, Schulz worked with Howie Judson a few times a week on the side basket. Howie had played center in high school and still knew all the moves — heck, he still *had* all the moves. Even though Schulz had improved tremendously in their three years of work and towered over him by several inches, Howie could still show the big kid a thing or two in a one-on-one match-up. Howie worked on a whole range of shots with Schulz, but not a hook shot. Ahearn didn't believe high school players could master it, even though Howie had possessed a deadly half-hook in his day.

Even without the hook, Bill Schulz had plenty he could use to his advantage. He was surprisingly fast given his height, plus he was left-handed, which tended to confuse defenders.

Ahearn had no reservations about starting either Schulz or the other junior, Ken Spooner. Spooner stood about 5-foot-11, above average for a guard, and he could shoot the ball with radar accuracy from just about anywhere on the floor. Spooner didn't drive to the basket often, but that wasn't his job. Instead, he was in the game to shoot the set shot whenever he got an open look. If Hebron couldn't get a fast break, and especially if the other team was packed into a zone defense, the Green Giant offense was designed to set screens for Spooner, to allow his long shots to rain down over the zone.

Ahearn had such confidence in Spooner's range that he frequently told his guard, "Kenny, anywhere on the floor, you shoot." Spooner shot from 20, 25, even 30 feet out on the floor without hesitation, especially if he had a good look at the basket and a teammate setting a screen.

The seniors, Don Wilbrandt and the Judson twins, gave Ahearn no cause for concern. They were veterans of the 1950-51 season and each had proven his ability.

Wilbrandt, the star of last year's big upset at West Rockford, was always ready to play. At 5-foot-11, he occupied a forward position on the left side opposite Phil Judson. Wilbrandt was a threat both inside and out. He could drive to the basket and rebound with taller players, and he was never afraid to shoot. He'd unleash long shots, running jumpers, pivot shots, and lay-ups. His only weakness was that he fouled out a lot, nine times in the last nineteen games of the previous season. He'd need to control those aggressive tendencies if Hebron was to make it through the season with only five regular players.

And of course, there were the twins. Unless you had time to scrutinize their haircuts, the twins were virtually indistinguishable on the court. By contrast, their roles were quite different.

Paul, now 6-foot-3 and a four-year starter, was the unquestioned team leader, the guard who brought the ball down the floor on a fast break, who made things happen with a quick pass or drive to the basket. He was a good shot, but most of all he was quick. With cat-like hands on defense, he turned innumerable steals into fast-break lay-ups. His height was also a major asset at his position — Paul loomed over most of the guards he matched up with.

Phil was still an inch shorter than his brother at 6-foot-2, but what he lacked in height, he made up for in hustle and aggressiveness. He was just as quick as Paul, and from his forward position that quickness translated into blitzkrieg breaks to the basket, where he was often on the receiving end of blazing baseball passes from his brother. On more than one occasion, one of the twins would make a pass that seemed headed straight for the sidelines, when the other would appear out of nowhere to snatch it out of the air. Usually it ended in a score. Every time it elicited oohs and aahs from the crowd.

Phil's game included one other feature — rebounding. He soared above taller players, displaying a real nose for the ball.

Both Judsons were excellent free throw shooters. Every year, they battled each other for the trophy Coach Ahearn awarded to the player with the best percentage from the charity stripe.

In addition to his starting five, Ahearn had some encouraging prospects on the junior varsity team. They'd all grown up around town, playing basketball together, imitating the older players, eager for a shot at the big time. There was Jim Wilbrandt, a sophomore, brother of Don; his good friend, Clayton Ihrke, also a sophomore; Jim Bergin, a junior, a farm boy who lived just east of town; Joe Schmidt, a tall junior; and Lynn Judson, a sophomore, brother of Jim, and cousin of the twins.

Against all those positives, the coach had one big problem to overcome. He'd been counting on Bill Thayer to be the sixth man. Now a senior, Thayer would be the only substitute available who did not play in the preliminary game. But Thayer and the coach did not always see eye to eye. Ahearn was upset when his potential sixth man decided to play football in the fall. The coach preferred that he concentrate on basketball instead. But Thayer didn't see any point in giving up football when he'd been passed over for the final guard position in favor of his neighbor, Ken Spooner. Upset by the decision, Thayer decided not to go out for the basketball team at all. His friends tried to change his mind, but he could not be persuaded.

That meant that Ahearn would have only five rested players for the varsity contests, but five would simply have to do. The rest of his players — twelve freshmen, sophomores, and juniors — still needed the seasoning that the JV games provided. Once the state tournament started, the coach wouldn't have to worry about the preliminary games, and all the players on the bench would be rested. He hoped they would be ready as well.

Ahearn had two other cards in his deck. First, he looked to Dr. Alex Leschuck, a local physician who acted as the team's trainer. He took care of any aches and pains and recommended treatment when a player pulled a muscle or sprained an ankle. Leschuck also saw to it that the team took the proper vitamins, as Ahearn was a firm believer in proper nutrition.

Finally, in an unofficial role as public relations man, Coach Ahearn depended on George Sullivan of the *Woodstock Sentinel*. Sullivan got the word out about Hebron better than anyone else, and his "Put and Take" sports column included a lot more than scores and schedules. He gave readers across McHenry County the inside scoop on what the coach, players and fans were talking about around town, in practice, and even on the bench. His readers got a close-up and personal view of a team that, if people's predictions were right, just might make history.

Practice Makes Perfect

Practice for another season opened in November with the annual photo shoot. Don Peasley of the local *Community News* came by from Woodstock to take photographs of the team and interview the coach and players about the upcoming season. He'd been on the McHenry County beat for five years, and during that time he'd developed a special interest in the Hebron team.

As always, Peasley set the team up in a variety of poses. The players wore the same uniforms they'd been issued when they started with the team — in the case of the seniors, three years before — consisting of a home jersey of white or an away jersey of green, with matching satin trunks. The only thing missing from the shirt was the school's name, the result of a decision the coach made when he started at Alden-Hebron. With the consolidation still in its infancy, he'd opted to drop the name "Hebron" rather than add "Alden" to their uniforms. So when the players took the floor, they wore numbers only. Finally, like all the best teams, Hebron wore Converse Chuck Taylor sneakers. This year they chose white instead of green.

Once the photos were out of the way, it was all business. Ahearn insisted on being the only one to talk in practice, but the presence of the new assistant, Phil Hadley, lightened things up a bit. He was just a few years older than the boys, still full of youthful spirit, and he could joke with the best of them. Hadley could play basketball, too. With his football player's arms and chest, he proved an interesting challenge for the Hebron players, who ranged from thin to thinner to thinnest.

As always, Ahearn's practices were about fundamentals. In composition they never changed. Five minutes — maybe ten, if the coach was really feeling wild — of the same drills, one after the other, day after day, week after week. These drills were designed to hone the skills he believed were necessary for the development of a complete ballplayer. Never mind the long shots. That was something the players could practice in their driveways on their own time. Dribbling, passing, rebounding, tipping, faking, shifting your feet — these were the skills that his team worked on in practice.

"This is standard procedure for us," the coach told one reporter, "and it pays off. Paul Judson is playing his fourth year of varsity ball this season and he still goes through the 30-minute daily sessions the same as the other boys."

After the drills, they'd practice up to a dozen standard play situations, again in five-minute sessions: zone offense, man-to-man press, guard across, the revolve. Finally, after 50 free throws, practice was over. The workouts lasted almost three hours at the beginning of the season, getting somewhat shorter as the winter went by. Absolutely none of that time was wasted.

Hebron's offense was based on a fundamental philosophy — if you have the ball, look to the basket, and if you can score, score. The Green Giants tried to fast break on nearly every play, putting the defense on its heels and opening up holes for a lay-up or a running push shot. Only tip-top conditioning allowed such a strategy to work, so Ahearn encouraged his players to run as much as possible. Some of them participated in cross country races during the fall. All of them ran, as hard as they could, a mile down the road and then back at the start of physical education class. They did the same if they wanted to shoot baskets after school. Russ Ahearn was unconcerned by the idea that his five starters might have to play an entire game without a rest. In fact, he anticipated games where they'd have to.

Hebron's defense, especially its press, was as deadly as its offense. The Judson twins had such quick hands that they could catch the ball at the bottom of an opponent's dribble, flip it up in the air, and be down the court before the other player knew what hit him. Quickness and conditioning played a role in all of Hebron's strategies. The game plan was to put the opponent away as quickly as possible.

The JV team took part in the same drills, but only on rare occasions were they allowed to scrimmage with the varsity. When they did, it was hardly a fair fight.

As the season wore on, the starters tried to set ever more difficult goals for themselves. In the beginning, each player tried to keep his man from scoring. Eventually it evolved into each player keeping his man from shooting, and finally from even touching the ball. Needless to say, this treatment was neither fun nor instructive for the junior varsity players. As a result, Ahearn used scrimmages sparingly.

The Leaning Tower of Hebron

Hebron opened its season in late November with predictably easy wins over Maple Park and McHenry. The home game against Joliet promised to be a test, however, and Hebron passed it with flying colors. Even though they had a bad shooting night, hitting only 19 of their 73 shots, the Green Giants held Joliet at bay all game and coasted to a 51-43 win. More importantly, Bill Schulz was impressive.

"The Leaning Tower of Hebron," as the *Elgin Courier-News* had taken to calling him, scored 18 points and showed he could get down the floor to play defense as well.

It was the same story the next evening against St. Edward's. Greg True's team played even with Hebron for two quarters. But in the second half, Schulz got hot and finished the game with 27 points on 13-of-19 shooting. The 66-36 final score sent a disheartening message to Hebron's main rivals for the district tournament title.

The next week, the Hebron Express stayed on schedule. After an exhibition win over a team of Hebron alumni and a resounding defeat of Lake Forest, Hebron was 5-0 heading into the McHenry County Tournament, a three-day affair they were expected to win easily.

The only question on many minds was how high the team would rank in the first polls of the season. Hebron had inched into the top 15 at the end of the 1950-51 season. Fans expected more after this hot start, but they needn't have worried. Poll voters remembered the little team that could. The Tuesday editions of newspapers around the state showed Hebron coming in at No. 8 in the Associated Press writers' poll and No. 3 in the United Press coaches' poll.

Quincy, a traditional powerhouse that had finished third the previous season, ranked No. 1 in both.

The Best in the County

The McHenry County Tournament was a rite of passage for basketball players in this part of northern Illinois. For more than 30 years, high school teams had met at one of the county gymnasiums to vie for local bragging rights. Through World Wars and even the Great Depression, the tournament had thrived. Its greatest nemesis, in fact, was the weather.

December in northern Illinois can be brutal, and December of 1951 was as brutal as they come. The temperature was ten below zero and headed downward when play opened on a Saturday night at Woodstock.

One of the tournament's quirks was the lack of seeding. Names of entrants were pulled from a hat and placed on the bracket exactly as they were drawn. "Let the chips fall where they may" was the motto, since better teams were not given any special path to the championship.

This time Crystal Lake fans cursed their luck. The Tigers had won all six games they'd played and were strong enough to draw several votes in the wire service polls. But in this version of the McHenry County Tourney, Crystal Lake found itself pitted against powerful Hebron. It was a first-class first-round match-up. Russ Ahearn and Crystal Lake coach Max Brady would have to prepare for it as if it were the championship game.

The fans did, too. The Hebron-Crystal Lake clash was the most sought-after ticket in tournament history. Officials delayed the start of the game to accommodate the crowd, but there were no complaints from anyone who made it inside. Everyone was simply glad to be in attendance at the best game of the young season, a game that would be the first of at least two and possibly three meetings between the area's premier teams.

As the showdown got under way, the chill outside matched the play inside. Neither team was on its game. Paul Judson started strong for Hebron, but the rest of the starters had trouble hitting the mark. Schulz had to retire early, fighting the effects of a flu bug he'd been battling all week. Despite an off night, Hebron pulled away. The Green Giants led 45-22 by the end of the third quarter, and although the substitutes let some of that lead fritter away, Hebron took an easy 56-39 decision.

There was no question now who owned bragging rights in McHenry County, even though the tournament itself still had two rounds to go.

Over the next two nights, Hebron locked up the championship trophy with convincing victories over McHenry and Woodstock, scoring 85 in the first game and 77 in the second. The team had found its groove. With any of the starters capable of connecting from anywhere on the court, opposing teams were having trouble holding the score down. Putting all five players in double figures was Hebron's goal, and as often as not, the Green Giants succeeded.

A blizzard the next week wiped out Hebron's game at DeKalb, keeping everyone homebound. The players were disappointed that they'd have to go eight days between games. Mother Nature was having her way, and Christmas of 1951 dawned snowy and bitterly cold. But in Hebron, the warm glow of the basketball team's success helped keep spirits bright.

A Bigger Pond

Hebron's biggest test to date, the Kankakee Holiday Tournament, lay just ahead. In its second year, the tournament offered an outstanding field. The host school was a contender, with an up-and-coming team and a big junior center named Harv Schmidt. Danville, a new entry, was ranked No. 3 in the state in the latest UP poll, and featured another flashy center, Ron Rigoni. And of course there was Hebron, now ranked No. 4, with its own flash and dash.

Of the more than forty tournaments played across Illinois during the holiday break, the Kankakee meet was one of the most important. Sportswriters near and far touted the various strengths of each of the eight teams entered. One reporter for the *Kankakee Daily Journal* remembered the play of the Judson twins from the previous year, noting that they were fan favorites. On the subject of Bill Schulz, however, the writer expressed doubt that a first-year starter could make much of an impact. "Unless he's improved tremendously," he wrote, "he might be the weak link against strong competition."

The Kankakee folks seemed to know plenty about Hebron, despite its remoteness. The Green Giants had not played outside their own region of the state since the previous year's holiday tournament, when they were still relative unknowns. This time, as the team emptied out of their cars after the long, icy trek, reporters and photographers met them at the hotel and clamored to get a fresh angle on the Hebron story.

Luckily, the Green Giants did not disappoint their newfound fans. South Shore, their first opponent, was no challenge. The Tars were the tournament's defending champions, but they'd been wracked by graduation. Undermanned and outplayed, they ended up as easy pickings for the Green Giants. Hebron pelted the basket with abandon, taking 85 shots and making 32, compiling an 80-42 win. Hebron's speed, shooting, and finesse all impressed the crowd, and Schulz's 23 points, on 10-of-17 shooting, offered proof that he was no weak link after all.

The home team, Kankakee, didn't offer a lot of resistance in the next game, either. The Kays hung with Hebron for a half, but when Harv Schmidt got into foul trouble and had to take a seat, the Green Giants went to work, eventually winning by 17 points. That set up the long-awaited match with Danville.

According to the pundits, Danville would be Hebron's first true test. Not only were Danville's Maroons a downstate power, a big school with even bigger aspirations, but their coach had a first-class pedigree. Art Mathisen had been the star center on the famous "Whiz Kids" squad at the University of Illinois in the early 1940s. The tall, slender Mathisen and the diminutive Ahearn made an interesting study in contrasts as they shook hands before the game.

Games like this presented a challenge not only to the Hebron players but also to the coaches, who needed to be on top of every defensive and offensive opportunity, every trip down the floor. All of them would need to do their jobs perfectly to beat Danville.

Although Danville had five solid players, the key was Rigoni, a scoring machine with a deadly hook shot. The game plan called for Schulz to start out guarding Rigoni. If Schulz ran into trouble keeping his man in check, Ahearn would look to one of the Judsons to help out.

The teams played even through the first half, which finished tied at 25-all. Ahearn was in his element. He realized this was the biggest game of his career so far, and he coached with unmatched fervor, calling out rapid-fire notes to Phil Hadley, who faithfully recorded them in the notebook.

Exactly like so many games before, Hebron's speed and conditioning wore down the other team in the second half. Schulz managed to keep Rigoni under wraps, blocking several shots while scoring 18 himself. Paul Judson finished with 16, Phil with 14, and Don Wilbrandt with 12 in another demonstration of the balance that had become standard operating procedure for the Green Giants.

In the end, Hebron coasted to a 67-54 win. This was a victory that could not be ignored. An intersectional clash, played against a top team on the road in front of a huge crowd, and Hebron had come through with flying colors. The players took it all in stride. After raising their coach up to their shoulders and carrying him to the dressing room, they showed no outward evidence of excitement or celebration.

Ahearn, however, was ecstatic with the victory, his biggest yet. He held on to the trophy like a new toy as he talked to reporters after the game, sketching out the season ahead. Two tournaments, two trophies — now Ahearn looked forward to skating on through the rest of the regular season and straight into the state tournament.

People were starting to believe him. Hebron had handily defeated the best team on its regular-season schedule. The Green Giants were 12-0 and there was no reason why the team could not make it to the start of the state tournament with an undefeated record. That vision played in more than a few heads as the team set out from Kankakee, smiles on their faces, trophy in their arms, toting a bushel of apples that an admiring fan had given them for the journey home.

Top of the Charts

On the heels of the win at Kankakee, the media circus began in earnest. A shakeup in the polls was inevitable, since the state's top-ranked team, Quincy, had traveled to the Centralia tournament and lost to the home team. But to the surprise of just about everyone, when the polls came out the next week, Hebron — impossibly tiny Hebron — had leapfrogged over undefeated West Rockford and Mt. Vernon to be ranked No. 1 in the state by both the AP and the UP. With an enrollment of just 98 students, Hebron was the smallest school ever to occupy the top position.

Around town, sportswriters began beating down doors looking for interviews. The Chicago dailies picked up the scent again, sending out writers and photographers to document the latest episode in the Hebron saga. Ahearn worked the press like a pro, frequently flashing his trademark wit. His ability to turn a phrase only added to the affection the public felt for the small-town team.

When Bud Nangle of the *Chicago Daily News* asked him whether there was any pressure on the team, Ahearn replied, "The only fellow who puts on the heat is the school's maintenance engineer, Ray Scholl, and he has a license."

The next game on the chart, a big-time match-up at Oak Park, was one of Ahearn's most brilliant additions to the Green Giant schedule. It was tiny Hebron versus giant Oak Park, and the big-city press played up the David-and-Goliath angle to the hilt. Fans were eager to see if the slick suburban squad, ranked No. 13 in the state in the latest UP poll, would be able to send the milk-town boys packing.

It was also the best chance all winter for basketball fans from Chicago — the city of Nat "Sweetwater" Clifton and Bob Gruening, of George Mikan and Johnny Kerr — to see Hebron in action. Most of Hebron's games were played far from the city, but the village of Oak Park was just past the Chicago city limits. Oak Park played its home games in a massive field house, and word soon got around that there just might be tickets available. Throughout the week, the phones rang off the hook in the office of the Oak Park athletic director as Chicago fans tried to secure seats.

When Friday night came and Hebron's contingent pulled into the parking lot after the long drive, the players and coaches were amazed at the rows upon rows of cars and constant stream of fans flooding the entrance. Once inside the field house, they eyed the assembling crowd with astonishment. The junior varsity game was almost an hour away, and already the stands were packed.

Inside the field house, Oak Park's playing floor sat atop a cinder track. To prevent players from accidentally tracking cinders onto the floor, a suspended net enclosed the court, separating it from the stands. The scene was reminiscent of a bygone era when many basketball courts were surrounded by metal cages, a temporary contrivance whose lasting legacy to the game was the term "cager." For those fans who had never attended a game at Oak Park, the odd netted contraption only added to the circus atmosphere. The only thing missing was a flying trapeze.

The fans grew more boisterous as the opening game progressed. When the final gun sounded, Hebron's JV team retreated to the showers to cool down before the marquee match-up, while Oak Park's team

— a dozen strong on the varsity — took the floor to a roar of applause. The much-anticipated event was under way.

Down in the locker room, Ahearn held his varsity players back. There were only five of them, after all, and with such a small number it wouldn't take long to get warmed up. Out in the field house, Oak Park went through its paces at one end of the court while the crowd stomped and shouted, anxious for some action on the Hebron side. They'd heard all about these Green Giants and how amazing they were. So where in the world were they?

As a coach, Ahearn was all business, but some of it was undoubtedly show business. When the cheering finally hit a crescendo, he sent out his seven-year-old son, Billy, dressed in a miniature Hebron uniform with the number 0, to lead the charge from the locker room. Billy was followed closely by the towering Bill Schulz, the Judsons, Wilbrandt, and Spooner, in that order. From tiny Billy Ahearn to tall Bill Schulz, with only four other players bringing up the rear — the abbreviated parade provided a startling image in the huge gym.

"I think you forgot some of your players!" someone shouted from the stands, as everyone laughed. Despite all the publicity, Hebron's lack of numbers never really hit home without seeing the team in person.

But the crowd loved it. Hebron managed to be a sideshow attraction and the main event, all rolled into one.

Finally the battle of the giants tipped off. Oak Park featured a center named Jim Duncan, who competed with Bill Schulz for the honor of tallest player in the state. Both were touted at 6-10½. It was an unprecedented meeting. No one had ever seen two boys this big face off on a high school basketball court.

The nervous excitement seemed to rub off on the players, as neither team played well in the first quarter. But in the second period Hebron slowly pulled away, as Phil Judson, who had lost almost ten pounds after battling the flu all week, ran circles around the slower Oak Park team. But as good as he was at driving and shooting, it was his rebounding that awed the spectators. At 6-foot-2, he was not tall for a forward, but he had great vertical leap and an uncanny knack for being in the right place at the right time.

Phil ended up the leading scorer for Hebron with 15 points. In the duel of the centers, Duncan, a senior, outscored Schulz, a junior, 15 to 11. But with five Green Giants scoring in double figures, Hebron won easily, 63-55.

As always, Ahearn was gracious after the game. "Oak Park provided the stiffest test we've had yet," he said, leaving the underlying impression that no team had really given Hebron a stiff test so far.

And yet, there was no disputing the psychological impact of winning back-to-back games played before crowds of up to 4,000 fans each, against two of the best teams around.

"We're awfully happy about this," was all the coach could say.

Late that evening, switchboards began to light up at newspapers around northern Illinois. The Associated Press and *Chicago Tribune* sports desks fielded dozens of inquiries about the game. At the *Woodstock Sentinel*, the phones rang like election night. For every fan who got through, many more received busy signals. One frustrated fan finally called the police looking for the score.

Hebron-mania had begun.

Shooting Stars

Interest in Hebron's unusual team reached even beyond state lines. Frank Reichstein, a sportswriter for the *Beloit Daily News*, forty miles away and across the border into Wisconsin, jumped on the bandwagon with both feet. For Reichstein and fans in Beloit, it was more than a casual interest.

In many ways, Beloit College was the Hebron of the intercollegiate ranks. It had one of the best small college basketball programs in the country, and its teams held their own against universities many times Beloit's size. In 1951, the Buccaneers stormed into Chicago Stadium and beat the stuffing out of DePaul, 94-60, cementing their reputation. At the end of the season they were invited to play in the National Invitation Tournament in New York, at a time when an NIT bid really meant something.

Beloit's coach was Dolph Stanley — the same Dolph Stanley whose Taylorville squad had defeated Elgin for the Illinois state championship in 1944. Stanley and Ahearn had met for the first time at that tournament and now they were back in contact. More than anything, Stanley wanted the Judson twins to play college ball at Beloit. In fact, he'd have been happy to bring over the entire Hebron five, lock, stock, and barrel, and dress them in Beloit blue and gold.

In his columns, Reichstein beat the drums for the Beloit College program and offered an innocent suggestion. Since Hebron's gym held only 550 people, and far more than that wanted to see the team play, why not transfer one of the three remaining home games on the schedule to Beloit College's large gymnasium? That way everyone in southern Wisconsin could watch the miracle team play and compare them to the local brand of basketball team.

Of course, doing so would have posed a problem for the patient Hebron fans who'd already put up with a reduced home schedule. Reichstein's idea fell on deaf ears, but the Hebron team did accept an invitation to attend Beloit's game against Xavier, which turned out to be a welcome diversion for the players.

In Hebron's next game, Harvard didn't appear to pose much of a threat, but Ahearn found a way to get his boys up for the contest, anyway. Walt Kirk, a former All-State player from Mt. Vernon who'd played with Howie Judson at the University of Illinois, was the coach at Harvard. He'd been quoted as saying that "Hebron will never score 100 points on us." As idle boasts go, Kirk wasn't too far out on a limb. Nevertheless, Ahearn used the statement to motivate his team. Instead of asking for points from his players, however, he turned the challenge on its head.

"Let's show them what kind of defense *we* can play," he told his team.

Hebron came out in a full-court press. At the end of the first quarter, the Green Giants led 31-2, and by halftime it was 54-10. Hebron *could* play defense. The subs played most of the second half, but in the end Coach Kirk got his wish — the final score was 96-32.

Ahearn got some good news the next week. The players had coaxed Bill Thayer to rejoin the team as its sixth man and the coach welcomed him back. Thayer would be a full-time member of the varsity squad. He'd give Ahearn a bona fide, *rested* substitute he could use if any of the starters got into foul trouble.

Thayer saw his first action of the season and scored his first basket in the Friday night rematch against St. Edward's. St. Edward's coach Greg True was reportedly "going all out" to stop Hebron, but the game played out in a fashion depressingly similar to the first meeting. Tied at halftime, St. Edward's watched its string of good fortune unravel quickly in the second half. It was big Bill Schulz who once again made the difference, hitting 10 of 18 field goal attempts in a 71-53 win.

Hebron had won fourteen in a row, and it was beginning to look like they might just run the table. With the exception of Barrington, every team on Hebron's remaining schedule was clearly beatable or had already been beaten by the Green Giants. There were precious few roadblocks ahead as the team traveled to Marengo, league leaders of the SWANI Conference, for a Tuesday night contest.

That night Ahearn invited George Sullivan of the *Woodstock Sentinel* to sit on the bench and join the team discussions in the locker room before the game. As Sullivan took notes, Ahearn urged his team to find ways to improve even when the opponent didn't offer much resistance. "We need to start picking up our tempo," he told his team, "and play tough all the time. Beat them now, in the first half. Don't wait until the end of the game."

Sullivan noticed something else. As usual, the gym was packed an hour before game time with basketball fans from far and wide. But in talking to people on the other side of the gym, the ones wearing Marengo shirts and sweaters, he found that an amazing number of them were rooting for Hebron.

At least the disloyal fans were not disappointed. Taking Ahearn's admonition to heart, Hebron scored 10 points in the first ninety seconds of the game.

During a break in the action, one of the referees ambled over to the bench and caught Ahearn's attention. "Russ," he said, "if you keep this up, I'm going to get a chair and just sit down at the other end."

The Green Giants continued the onslaught, scoring 20 points before Marengo put a ball through the basket. Hebron led 32-4 by the time the gun mercifully ended the first quarter.

Ahearn pulled Paul Judson aside at the break and confided in him. "Paul," he said, "you're going to come out first. You can handle it. We have to start getting ready for the state tournament now, and I want Thayer to get some time to play."

Thayer went in for Judson, and later subbed for Spooner and Wilbrandt as well, finishing the game with four points. Despite playing only about half the game, Paul Judson finished with 28 points, just three off his career high.

Hebron won in a blowout, 77-34, and Ahearn was relieved that the win had been so easy. Max Brady had been one of the officials, and Brady's Crystal Lake Tigers were next on Hebron's schedule. Russ Ahearn was glad he didn't have to reveal any trade secrets on this evening.

chapter 8

Lessons Learned

The January 19 rematch with Crystal Lake was the biggest sporting event to hit McHenry County in many years. Never before had two such highly touted teams come from this neck of the woods. Hebron, still No. 1 in the polls, had won 15 straight; Crystal Lake was 13-2, with its only losses coming to Hebron and Elgin.

From his office at the *Woodstock Sentinel*, George Sullivan continued to operate as an unofficial public relations man for the Hebron team. Besieged by ticket information and requests, Sullivan described in his column how he answered one frustrated ticker-seeker from Antioch.

"We gave him the remainder of the Hebron schedule," Sullivan wrote, "and said, 'Brother, these are the dates, the rest is up to you.'"

The hype was well and good, but as always, Russ Ahearn was interested in keeping his team on an even keel. All season long the team had operated with three seniors sharing the role of captain. Now he decided it might promote team unity to choose a single captain. The players voted among themselves and selected Don Wilbrandt. It was a logical pick. Don had also been the captain of their junior varsity team two years before, and the team was happy to honor him with that responsibility again.

None of the players needed any introduction to the Crystal Lake team. They had met many times over the years and many knew each other off the court as well. The Hebron team was also quite familiar with the gym at Crystal Lake High School, a stage gym similar to Hebron's, but with a regulation-size floor.

Seating would be hard to come by, however. The spectators, about 1,100 in all, would have to shoehorn themselves into a gym designed to seat only 875.

Ahearn talked with Sullivan before the game and expressed his usual reservations about the competition ahead. "They'll be tough on their own floor and our boys are going to have to play their best ball to win," he said.

But Hebron had beaten Crystal Lake easily in their first meeting and few fans expected anything different as the players took their places on the court.

The teams traded punches throughout the first half, and at half-time, Hebron led by just two, 39-37. But something strange happened in the second half. The Green Giants' usual second-half drive didn't materialize. Or more correctly, Crystal Lake simply refused to crumble. Fritz Schneider, the Tigers' senior forward, was having a career night, hitting impossible shots from all over the floor. At the end of three periods, Hebron's lead was down to one.

The game rolled on into the fourth quarter, whistles blowing left and right. Several players from each team were in foul trouble, but still Crystal Lake hung tough. Schneider hit another shot, putting the Tigers in the lead as the fouls continued to pile up. With three minutes left to play, Crystal Lake had expanded its lead to five, 65-60, but Schneider and two other starters, John Sayles and Tom Giek, had already left the game. Hebron's Phil Judson had also fouled out.

Hebron held the advantage, with four starters still on the floor to only two for Crystal Lake, and the Green Giants peppered the hoop furiously. But there was simply not enough time. When the gun sounded, the upset was complete: Crystal Lake 71, Hebron 68.

The scorekeeper totaled his book. Fritz Schneider had made 14 of 27 shots from the field and six free throws for a total of 34 points. Crystal Lake was the first team all season to score more than 55 points against Hebron's defense.

"We just didn't play well enough to win," a disappointed Russ Ahearn said after the game. "Crystal Lake just outplayed us this time."

When the phones started ringing at the *Woodstock Sentinel* that night, many of the callers seemed stunned to hear the outcome of the game. "The People's Choice" had lost? Maybe that meant the fairy tale was over.

Back in Hebron, the news was met with mixed emotions. Some observers thought the loss might be a blessing in disguise. Didn't the coach always say, "Don't let your head get too big for your hat"? This would be a reminder to the players that other teams weren't just going to roll over and play dead.

But there were other fans who noticed an eerie similarity between the events of 1952 and 1940. Hadn't the 1940 team also gone undefeated most of the year? Hadn't that team attracted attention from newspapers from miles around? Hadn't that team subsequently been upset by Crystal Lake, its only regular-season loss?

Yes, yes, and yes. And look what happened to them.

All for One

The coach was stuck in the middle, helping his team keep the Crystal Lake game in perspective as well as fielding questions and advice from fans and townspeople. Ahearn hated to lose, but publicly at least, he made peace with the loss.

"The defeat was good for our team," he told one reporter. "The pressure was building up terrifically."

And the pressure had begun to show. Ahearn's players had always been an extraordinarily high-spirited and close-knit bunch. But as the season wore on, he noticed subtle changes in their attitudes.

The lack of strong competition in the varsity contests had caused a breakdown in team play on more than one occasion. Since winning was almost a foregone conclusion, the players sometimes lost themselves in the pursuit of individual statistics or playing time.

When faced with charges that he ran up the score, the coach had reacted by substituting his weary junior varsity players, sometimes as early as the second quarter. But the varsity squad members were irritated that the younger players got to play more than four quarters in one night while they had to cool their heels on the bench. In response, some of the starters began to slow down the game, just to keep the score close enough so that they could stay on the floor.

The coach had also begun to hear bickering among the boys. "You don't look for the open man!" "You're not passing the ball to me!" "You shoot too much!" These were all symptomatic of players who had forgotten about team goals and were thinking about individual accomplishments instead.

It was all part of Russ Ahearn's job. He had get the most out of his players individually, keep them all happy, and yet remind them that they would never reach their potential if they didn't, first and foremost, stick together as a team. As he puzzled out how to juggle all of this, he also had to meet the press. As usual, he put on a chipper face.

"Our boys bounced back in practice Monday full of pep and new determination," he told one reporter. "I am sure they realize now it will take plenty of hard work to get back up on top again."

Privately, he could only hope that the boys had learned an important lesson. They had to know now that they could lose anytime, anywhere, if they didn't play together.

As expected, Hebron gave up its No. 1 ranking in the polls, but for the most part the voters were very forgiving. The writers in the AP poll dropped the Green Giants to No. 3, while the coaches for UP nudged them down to No. 2. West Rockford occupied the top spot in both polls. The Warriors were the only undefeated team in the state except for DePue, which ranked far down the list.

Dependable George Sullivan continued to boost the local teams, giving Hebron its only No. 1 vote and also listing Crystal Lake at No. 2 on his ballot.

The Green Giants now entered the weakest part of its schedule, dispatching their next six opponents with little effort. Most of these teams folded up their tents soon after the opening tip. Only the Cadets of Marmion put up a fight, falling 60-55 in a rematch just two weeks after they'd lost by 51 points on Hebron's court.

There were still lessons to be learned, however. At DeKalb, despite an easy 70-40 victory, a few of the Hebron players were unhappy with the officiating and voiced their displeasure. Since they were used to referees who let them play, they had a hard time understanding why even minor contact was being whistled.

One of the referees approached the team after the game. Frank Falzone had officiated at the state tournament the previous year and was scheduled to work again at Champaign in March. Falzone gave the Hebron players some friendly advice.

"Boys," he said, "get used to it, because that's the way they call them at state."

Howie's Farewell

The Waukegan game on February 16 caught the interest of fans in another section of the state: the far northern suburbs of Chicago. As newspapers in the region once again played up Hebron's anticipated match-up with an old-line athletic power from the suburbs, Waukegan High School made preparations for the heightened attention. Athletic Director Leo Singer ordered temporary bleachers installed at the ends of the court to accommodate all the fans who wanted seats, and it still wasn't enough. He sold over 3,500 tickets for the event before deciding he couldn't squeeze any more seats into the school's gymnasium.

And if the unending publicity and anticipated crowd didn't make the game auspicious enough, it was special to the Hebron team for another reason. It was the last game that Howie Judson would be able to attend.

Judson's heart and soul was invested in Hebron's success. As the tournament drew near, he'd tried to convince Frank Lane, general manager of the White Sox, to allow him to postpone reporting to training camp in southern California until after Hebron was eliminated from the state tournament. Lane knew enough about Hebron's chances to realize that if he made that pact with Howie, he might not see his pitcher until spring training was nearly over. But Howie was stubborn.

Lane finally had to plead with John Sime, a banker from Hebron, to deliver the message that Howie was jeopardizing a $10,000-a-year job. "I don't care how you do it," Lane told Sime, "but get him out to California."

In the end, Lane got his way. But it took assurances from Ken Lopeman and Louie Wilbrandt that they would each faithfully send telegrams after every game before Howie grudgingly agreed to go.

For fans in northern Illinois, the Waukegan game was just the latest in a series of barnstorming adventures for the tiny Hebron team. The Green Giants struck a chord with the public, that was certain, and now even local officials got into the act. Waukegan mayor Monte Householder invited his Hebron counterpart, Mark Spooner, and two village board members, Joe Horeled and Stan Cornue, to his home before the game. In a time-honored tradition, the mayors made a friendly wager on the outcome, with the loser promising to buy the winner a new hat.

It was a sucker bet. Despite having 20 times as many students as Hebron, Waukegan was no match for the Green Giants, who won the game easily, 61-46. The Judson twins did most of the damage, contributing a total of 32 points as the Green Giants put the game away early. Ken Spooner, who seemed to enjoy the sight lines in the Waukegan gym, made five field goals and ended up with 11 points.

After the game, Waukegan High School hosted a sock hop in the gymnasium. As the Judson boys made their way back up to the gym after showering, they noticed the dance and decided there couldn't be any harm in joining in for a few minutes. The rest of the team gathered at the bus, waiting for Paul and Phil to join them. When the twins still hadn't shown up after several minutes, the team sent out a search party. Howie Judson finally tracked them down on the dance floor. As they made their way out of the gym, he scolded them for their lack of common sense.

Howie had kept his own counsel during the season, preferring to let Russ Ahearn do the coaching. But that night, in the kitchen of the Judson home, he let his brothers have it. "You guys think you're so good," he said. "Well, you'll never get to the state tournament if you don't get serious."

In the back of his mind were memories of a team in 1940, another team that had thought it was pretty good.

Howie didn't have to remind his brothers how that season turned out.

Playing Together

After the big Waukegan victory, the pollsters returned Hebron to No. 1 in the next Tuesday's newspapers. Hebron's wins over DeKalb and Waukegan had been workmanlike and not especially impressive, but they were 30- and 15-point wins nonetheless.

The same could not be said for Collinsville, which had wrested the No. 1 spot from West Rockford two weeks before. Collinsville had survived two close calls against East St. Louis and Wood River, but those skimpy wins didn't impress the voters in the polls. Enough of the pollsters switched their allegiance to put the Green Giants back on top.

Russ Ahearn was less concerned with the rankings than with his team's next opponent, Barrington, which came second only to Elgin on his most-wanted list. After all, Les Harman, the former Hebron coach, was in charge of the Broncos, and he'd vowed that Barrington would give the Green Giants a good run.

Harman's claim wasn't pure smoke, either — he had some strong stats to back up his words. Coming into the game, Barrington had won 19 of 21 contests. The Broncos now stood as the newly crowned champions of the Northwest Suburban Conference. A tall team with four starters over six feet, they had the potential to make trouble, especially when all was not well inside the Green Giant locker room.

The jealousies that had first come to the surface in the loss at Crystal Lake were now at full boil, and Coach Ahearn knew he had to put a stop to them. The more time he had to spend patching up petty disagreements, however, the less time he could devote to the strategy and nitty-gritty details he loved.

It was also exactly the wrong time for this kind of intrasquad squabble. With the district tournament just a week away, the boys needed to be bearing down, working out the last kinks in their system. The best teams, the teams that won it all, paced themselves so that they hit the tournament in full stride. Instead, Ahearn found his team lurching forward, unsteady and off-balance.

The coach sat his team down, and in the calm voice he always used with his players, let them know exactly where they stood.

"You fellows have a lot more ability as a team than we are showing," he began, "and it is my duty as a coach to get you working together."

He shook his head. "You let Howie go away to spring training, and he really felt bad when he left. He knows and I know that you will never get anywhere in tournament play unless you start playing together. You are good kids. You can go a long way if you just shake hands and from now on say it's Don and Phil and Paul and Bill and Ken."

Now that he had their attention, the coach drove home his point. "We need to work with *all* the players. At Waukegan the ball was on the right side of the floor seven-eighths of the time. Scouts notice things like that."

But he didn't want to dwell on what they had done wrong. So Ahearn turned his focus to the next game they faced, the big Barrington match-up.

"Les Harman walked out of the Waukegan game with a big, confident grin on his face," he told them, "and can you blame him? He said two years ago that he was going to Champaign. He probably has his reservations by now."

He frowned. He paused. Then Russ Ahearn continued, his words low and intent. "I want every man *on* our team playing *for* the team. From now on it's the *team* that wins. The coach doesn't win the game or any individual player — it's the team. So let's get back into the tournament spirit like we did in the county tournament and at Kankakee."

He set down his spiral notebook and looked straight into his players' eyes.

"I'm proud to be the coach at Hebron," he said softly. "Shouldn't you feel proud to have the real privilege of playing on this team?"

Hebron's players absorbed Ahearn's words, contemplated them, and acted them out with a vengeance. Barrington never had a chance.

When the game started, balls flew into the Hebron basket early and often. All five starters scored in double figures. And when the final gun sounded, Hebron had humiliated Barrington, 83-39.

A week later the Green Giants wrapped up their greatest regular season ever by crushing Belvidere, 84-54.

The coach had proven his point. From now on it would be all for one and one for all.

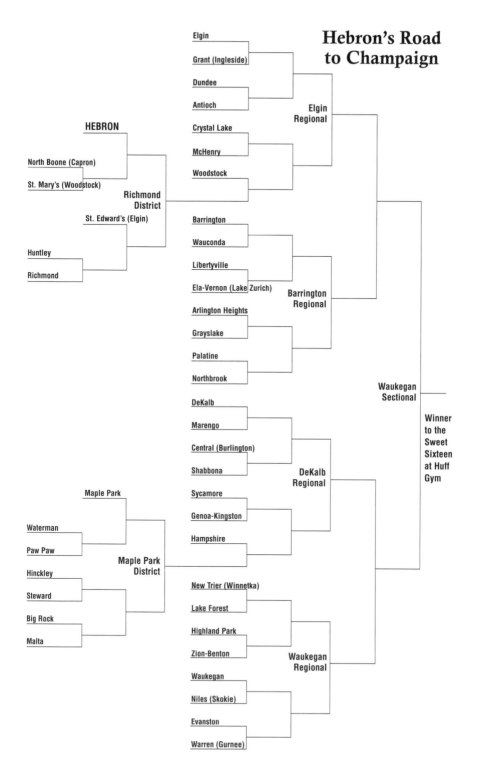

Hebron's Road to Champaign

Elgin
Grant (Ingleside)
Dundee
Antioch

Elgin Regional

Crystal Lake
McHenry
Woodstock

HEBRON

North Boone (Capron)
St. Mary's (Woodstock)

Richmond District

St. Edward's (Elgin)

Huntley
Richmond

Barrington
Wauconda
Libertyville
Ela-Vernon (Lake Zurich)

Barrington Regional

Arlington Heights
Grayslake
Palatine
Northbrook

DeKalb
Marengo
Central (Burlington)
Shabbona

DeKalb Regional

Sycamore
Genoa-Kingston
Hampshire

Maple Park

Waterman
Paw Paw

Maple Park District

Hinckley
Steward
Big Rock
Malta

New Trier (Winnetka)
Lake Forest
Highland Park
Zion-Benton

Waukegan Regional

Waukegan
Niles (Skokie)
Evanston
Warren (Gurnee)

Waukegan Sectional

Winner to the Sweet Sixteen at Huff Gym

chapter 9

Tournament Trail

In practice the next Monday, he assembled his state tournament squad. There were the five starters, of course, plus sixth-man Bill Thayer, and the four junior varsity players — Jim Wilbrandt, Clayton Ihrke, Joe Schmidt, and Jim Bergin — who'd seen the most action in varsity contests.

"I salute the Green Giants of Hebron," the coach began quietly, scanning the faces of his team. "You are the finest gentlemen I have ever coached, and you will always live in my memory. We've had a great season and I congratulate you."

After taking a few moments to recap the season, he moved on to the matter at hand.

"Our games are like chapters in a book, and all good books have conflicts," he told them. "We have had our petty little differences, too. But deep down, I know not one boy is going to let down the thousands of fans in our state. They are all pulling for you."

Continuing to challenge them, he added, "Each character in our book can contribute his share to our team. When the going gets the toughest, your character will show up. So hike up your belts for four real tough weeks, because you know that nothing good has ever come without a struggle."

Then the coach tried to bring the tasks that still remained into sharp focus.

"Determination, scrap, and loyalty to all of your teammates will win for you," he explained. "We want competitors and team men on our team. I am not interested in what you did last year, or in newspaper clippings that tell you how good you are, so speak now if you have any mental reservations."

No one said a word.

Pleased with their resolve, Ahearn gave his team some goals to think about.

"Number one," he began. "Be the second team from Hebron to go to Champaign. Number two: Be the first high school team in Illinois to play on television. Number three: Be the first team in the history of basketball in the state of Illinois to win the district, regional, sectional, and the state tournaments."

After just a second to let the enormity of these goals sink in, the coach said, "If you fellows realize how deserving you are, after four years of real hard work, fine training, and clean living, you'll strive to achieve the greatest dream of your life. You have a good chance if you hustle every second for your team."

This team had flown higher than any Hebron team before it. It had hit a few low spots, too. But with the state tournament soon upon them, Russ Ahearn was certain the Green Giants were ready to take on the world.

Eleven Games

Hebron's first game in the district was on Thursday, February 28, against St. Mary's of Woodstock. When the squad got off the bus at Richmond that evening, Russ Ahearn lined up his charges in the locker room. There the coach addressed the players briefly, one last time, before sending them into the first of what he hoped would be a long series of tourney games. At the end of his talk, he brandished a piece of chalk and turned to the blackboard, where he scrawled a big numeral 11 and circled it for effect.

"Eleven games, boys," the coach reminded them. "Win the next eleven games and you will be state champions."

And with that on their minds, the Hebron Green Giants took the floor for the 1952 state tournament.

For the first time, the team made its entrance sporting the snazzy T-shirt warm-ups the Hebron merchants had promised would be ready at tournament time. Now fans didn't need a scorecard to tell the players apart — these warm-ups had the players' last names right on the back. Of course, that didn't help differentiate the Judsons or the Wilbrandts. Regardless of that minor detail, when the Green Giants took the floor they looked ready to play.

Unfortunately, everyone else in the district tournament looked quite afraid to play Hebron.

The Green Giants' first opponent, St. Mary's, concerned itself only with keeping the final margin down to a respectable figure. The Irish stalled throughout the game, and despite trailing by almost 30 points in the fourth quarter, were content to hold the ball without even attempting to penetrate Hebron's defense. The Green Giants casually crouched on the floor or chatted with St. Mary's forwards as the clock ticked away. In the end, Hebron walked away with a 45-16 decision.

In the district championship the next night, St. Edward's was a more formidable foe, but one with basically the same idea. The Green Wave held the ball for almost five minutes before taking their first shot, holding Hebron to a 10-5 halftime lead. In the end, however, the Green Giants' overwhelming height and a little ball control of their own led to a 35-23 victory.

As Don Peasley set up for a photograph of the champions in the Richmond locker room, the players grabbed their coach and hoisted him up on their shoulders, hoping to show how much they appreciated his guidance. Ahearn's motivational speech and their success surviving the slowdown — as a team — had made an impact.

Two games down, nine to go, and now the serious work began.

In the Spotlight

The district tournament had been little more than a speed bump for the Green Giants. The regional tournament, on the other hand, presented them with a legitimate hurdle. Three other strong teams were entered in the meet, and given the right conditions, it seemed any one of them could knock Hebron off.

The irony was that Hebron, the state's No. 1-ranked team, was seeded last in the regional. The district tournament winner was automatically seeded No. 8, regardless of its actual strength, since the brackets were traditionally prepared far before the district winner was determined.

That left the top seed in the regional for the host school, Elgin. The Maroons came into the tournament with a 19-4 record, ranked No. 16 in the state in the most recent Associated Press writers' poll. Elgin had a reputation for toughness on its home court that would be hard to overcome. But there was also the small matter of unfinished business.

The loss that ended Hebron's tournament hopes in 1951 was still fresh on everyone's mind.

Elsewhere in the regional, Dundee and Crystal Lake stood right behind Elgin in the AP poll. Dundee had romped through the season with a 20-3 record, and its star player, Bob Allen, was basking in the glow of a four-page treatment in *Sports* magazine, a national publication.

Crystal Lake, meanwhile, had closed out its 21-5 regular season with a huge 115-46 win over Woodstock. But the biggest feather in Crystal Lake's cap, by far, was its win over Hebron in January. No one had forgotten that one.

Hebron would open in the last quarterfinal game against the No. 4 seed, as all district winners did. That meant the Green Giants would play a late game on Wednesday, March 5, against Woodstock. If they won, they'd look at another late game Thursday, presumably against Crystal Lake. If they made it to the championship on Friday night, they would almost certainly face Dundee or Elgin.

It was a tough gantlet for any team to run. Ahearn hoped that his emphasis on physical conditioning and the experience his players had picked up at Kankakee had prepared them for the grind of tournament competition.

All eyes were on the regional at Elgin. In his annual tournament roundup, Mark Peterman, a retired basketball coach who had won state championships at Canton and Springfield, gave his readers the lowdown on each of the 60 regional tournaments around the state, including Elgin.

"All year the teams elsewhere in the state have been glad they didn't have to play Hebron," he wrote. "Now they're glad they're not entered here. That's only false security — if your team is good enough, you'll get your chance at Hebron later."

But Jack Prowell of the *Champaign News-Gazette* signaled a warning to Hebron's legion of fans.

"The No. 1 regional in the state, without question, is at Elgin. That's a four-star headliner. Hebron, the hope of the small schools in the state, faces plenty of trouble before it can advance from this tournament."

As expected, Woodstock provided little competition in the opening game of the regional. Hebron led 28-8 after the first quarter. With no preliminary game to give his bench a workout, Ahearn had the luxury of substituting freely, and the bench contributed heavily to the final score of 95-45. Phil Judson led the team with 24 points, but Clayton Ihrke contributed nine, Bill Thayer six, Jim Wilbrandt five, and Joe Schmidt three. Only Jim Bergin failed to get on the scoreboard. It was a nice way to start the regional, and the coach was able to rest his starters for the decidedly tougher test with Crystal Lake the next night.

Crystal Lake concerned Coach Ahearn. Sure, Hebron had beaten the team easily in December, and the subsequent loss was probably a fluke. At least that's what everyone told him. But the Tigers were hot, and they had already proven that they were the kind of team that could give Hebron trouble if the stars were right and the shots were falling.

Most of all, Ahearn worried about Fritz Schneider. In January, the Crystal Lake forward and his torrid shooting had ruined Hebron's perfect season. Now Schneider was on a roll again. If his ability from outside wasn't enough of a threat, he was also on a streak at the line — he'd hit 26 consecutive free throws.

Ahearn's goal of a rematch with Elgin was so close he could taste it. The only thing standing in his way was Crystal Lake, with the possibility that Schneider might come up with one more great night. In

Coach Ahearn's mind, the matter was clear. Crystal Lake and Schneider could not be allowed to repeat the upset.

There was such an interest in the games at Elgin that by pre-arrangement, the gym, which held about 2,200 spectators, was cleared after the first game, with a new $1 ticket required for entry to the second. Both contests were easy sellouts, and since the whole first-game crowd had to march out before the next one could come in, the place bustled like Grand Central Station. In addition, several reporters and about a dozen college coaches, eager to scout players on all four of the competing teams, jammed the gym. Dolph Stanley was there from Beloit College, as were Forrest Anderson of Bradley University and Tex Winter of Marquette.

Elgin won the first game, beating Dundee, 60-40, to gain a berth in the championship the next night. That left Hebron and Crystal Lake in the second game. The teams warmed up as the second capacity crowd of the evening settled in.

The rubber match was everything the papers had advertised. Both teams were a little nervous at the outset, but the pace picked up in the second quarter and neither team could pull away. Schulz and Wilbrandt carried the scoring load for Hebron, while once again Fritz Schneider kept Crystal Lake in the game. Hebron held a narrow 27-24 lead as the teams left the floor at halftime.

The twins came out hot in the second half and still Hebron could not put the Tigers away. Then, in a heartbeat, the Green Giants got the break they needed, as Ken Spooner scored on a pair of his patented long shots and a free throw for his only points of the game. Suddenly Hebron led, 41-33.

Down by eight, the Tigers were forced out of their zone defense, and Hebron had no trouble finishing off the game against Crystal Lake's man-to-man. The final score was 61-46, the victory neatly avenging the Green Giants' only defeat of the season.

With Elgin looming on the horizon, events had now come full circle. Russ Ahearn had been aiming for the Maroons since before he could remember. And in his mind he'd been replaying the loss to Elgin ever since the Maroons ended Hebron's season exactly one year before.

Now, finally, Hebron would meet the lion in its own den.

Is It True What They Say About Hebron?

by Frank Reichstein
Beloit Daily News

ELGIN—It's true what they say about Hebron, all right.

The Green Giants are the best bunch of basketball kids in northern Illinois and southern Wisconsin. The Giants proved it with a 61-46 thumping of Crystal Lake at this mad regional center Thursday night before 2,200 mad basketball fans.

Little Coach Russ Ahearn's kids are a deadly bunch of opportunists who seldom wind up on the short end of a scramble for a loose ball, who drive in for a lay-up with the reckless abandon that one seldom sees out of college ranks, and who will steal the numbers off your jersey, if you don't watch out.

Hebron is a cocky, confident outfit. The Giants were even a little overconfident against Crystal Lake, the only team to defeat them this season. Yet they were good enough to afford the overconfidence that usually wrecks prep outfits.

And that Schulz! Everybody knows about his 6-10½ size. He dunks them in easily. He got 19 points last night, 12 of them lay-ups over the helpless heads of Crystal Lake defenders. Coach Ahearn says Schulz is a good defensive man, too. It's true. Large William shadows opponents under the hoop, his back slightly arched, and his big hands extended tenderly over the ballhandler. Schulz is most valuable for the shots the ballhandlers *don't* take. It's understandable why they chose to toss out to mates away from the hoop.

The Judson twins, Phil and Paul, are enough to make Beloit's Coach Dolph Stanley lick his chops during any given performance. Dolph was there last night, too. We liked Phil especially, but inasmuch as the Judsons are twins, we'd never separate them on any team we'd pick. They act like twins in team play. But Phil likes to bull his way past defenders with the subtle action of a meat cleaver. It's get out of the way, or pick up your own arms and legs after Phil goes by.

All of which sounds like rough basketball. It is. There's much more contact in Illinois prep basketball, and we loved it. Scrambles on the floor for loose balls are allowed to be just that, until arms and legs are hopelessly tangled.

Imperturbable Ahearn is often surprised at what he sees. Once Brother Phil fired a pass through the arms of Crystal Lake defenders, apparently at the blank wall behind the basket. Brother Paul appeared in the "hole" precisely at the right time, and it was two points. Ahearn raised his eyebrows and said: "I wondered what Phil was doing! I didn't even see Paul!"

Balance does it. If Hebron isn't able to work the ball in, Ken Spooner, a set shot artist, makes 'em from beyond the key-hole. He made two long ones when Crystal Lake's defense was momentarily diverted to Schulz and the Judsons. Don Wilbrandt is the playmaker, and not to be taken lightly if he is left alone in a corner for a second. Wilbrandt loves to drive around an opponent and lay one up. Bill Thayer is the No. 1 reserve of a not-so-weak bench. There is no letdown when Thayer goes in, either. He's got one of those devastating drives like Phil Judson's.

One thing, if you're interested in attending the tournament. Don't go. It's murder. The writer spent the major share of the first game with his back against a wall, while standing in the aisle of the bleachers. Only the kindness of Ahearn, who made a space on his bench for us during the second game, enabled us to report this to you.

Lowry B. Crane, Hebron coach from 1928 to 1939, as a student at the University of Chicago.

After the sectional championship of 1940, former coach Lowry Crane and coach Ed Willett hoist the trophy. [*Elgin Courier-News*]

Sparks

Fans light a bonfire in the streets of downtown Hebron to mark the school's first appearance in the state finals. [*Elgin Courier-News*]

The 1939-40 team that paved the way for Hebron's success in 1952. First row: John Ryan, Les Bigelow, Ervin Norgard, Howie Judson, Harry Behrens. Back row: Gordon Burgett, Kenneth Rehorst, Russell Voltz, John Kjellstrom, Keith Johnson, Coach Ed Willett. [*Elgin Courier-News*]

The 1942-43 Green Giants, the fifth consecutive Hebron team to win at least 23 games, met their Waterloo at Elgin. Front row, from left: Gustav Seavall, Wally Tibbits, Ford Burgett, Howie Judson, George Simes, Elwyn Behrens, Harold Drake. Back row: Coach Les Harman, Bill Judson, Cyran Zank, William Henrichs, Robert Sommer, Tony Slavin.

Bittersweet

Howie Judson, Hebron's first All-State athlete and future major league pitcher.

The result of the infamous "staple game." [Elgin H.S. yearbook]

The five-year-old Judson twins tussle for a rebound off an old hoop attached to their house by their father. Neighbor children David Weter and John Prehn look on. [*Chicago Daily News*]

Town Kids

The Judson family, about 1940. Front row, Phil, Ruth Ann, and Paul; back row, father Clarence, Howie, and mother Jessie.

Jim and Don Wilbrandt, about 1939.

Ken and Wayne Spooner with their father, Harold, about 1939.

Far left: Russ Ahearn as a freshman pitcher at Illinois State Normal University in 1931. [ISNU yearbook]

Near left: Advertisement for the Streator All-Star game of 1934.

Russ and Marie Ahearn out on the farm about the time they were married in 1941.

Russ Ahearn and John Krafft look over a spiral notebook in 1944. [Elgin H.S. yearbook]

Duke

The Ahearn family just before moving form Elgin to Hebron in 1948. From left: Russ's mother Mary, Judy, Marie, Billy, and Russ.

Russ Ahearn's 1948-49 varsity squad, his first at Hebron. Front row, from left; Phil Judson, Don Wilbrandt, Paul Judson, Bob Schoenbeck, Jim Judson. Back row: Coach Russ Ahearn, Ray Halstead, Cliff Wiersma, Earl Seavall, Ron Elliott, Dave Nichols, Bob Nichols.

Building a Winner

The 1949-50 Hebron varsity and JV squads. Front row, from left: Bill Thayer, Ken Spooner, Jim Wilbrandt, Lynn Judson, Wayne Spooner, Hank Oleson, Ed Okeson. Second row: Jim Judson, Paul Judson, Bob Nichols, Dave Nichols, Ray Halstead, Ron Elliott, Cliff Wiersma. Back row: Coach Floyd Sorenson, Wendell Calhoon, Don Wilbrandt, Bill Schulz, Tom Kuecker, Phil Judson, Coach Russ Ahearn.

The 1950-51 team that finished with a 28-2 won-lost record. Front row, from left: Duane Feuerhammer, Jim Wilbrandt, Clayton Ihrke, Bill Thayer, Ken Spooner. Back row: Coach Floyd Sorenson, Phil Judson, Ron Elliott, Coach Russ Ahearn, Bill Schulz, Paul Judson, Jim Judson, Superintendent Paul Tigard.

Howie Judson poses with brothers Phil and Paul at Great Lakes Naval Training Center, during his brief time in the service.

Wearing street clothes, Howie pitches to the twins in the driveway next to the Judson home. The driveway also served as a basketball court.

Big Brother

Howie towers over the twins just prior to their freshman season. [*Elgin Courier-News*]

Three years later, Paul and Phil have turned the tables. The twins are wearing the same uniforms they wore as freshmen.

Bill Schulz, the lanky farm boy, was a favorite of the news photographers assigned to the Hebron story.

Bill in the Model A Ford he drove to school. Russ Ahearn once lured a photographer to Hebron by telling him that Schulz had to cut a hole in the roof of his car in order to see the road.

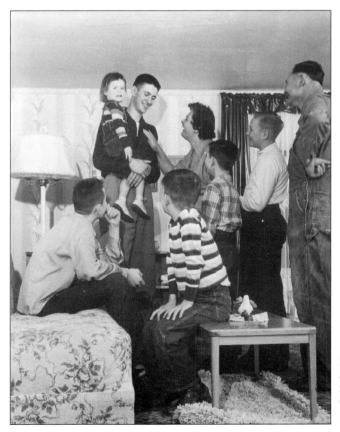

Farm Boy

Bill Schulz holds his sister Marybeth as the rest of the family gathers round. From left: John, Russ, mother Helen, Jim, Ken, and father Fred. [Larry Burrows]

A famous shot of the 1951-52 starters from the top of the backboard. When posing, the five always lined up in the same order: Ken Spooner, Paul Judson, Bill Schulz, Phil Judson, and Don Wilbrandt. [Don Peasley]

Starting Lineup

The starters and Coach Russ Ahearn in another pre-season shot. Little number 0 is the coach's son, Billy. [Elgin Courier-News]

The balcony and main floor of the Hebron gym are packed long before the contest begins. [Alden-Hebron H.S. yearbook]

Paul Judson reaches to block a shot during the 1951-52 season. [Alden-Hebron H.S. yearbook]

On
Stage

Timeout in the Hebron gym. The players cluster near the benches along the wall, while the cheerleaders successfully avoid the four-foot drop at the edge of the court. [Alden-Hebron H.S. yearbook]

Don Wilbrandt shoots over a defender in the regional championship game at Elgin while Bill Schulz waits for the rebound. [Don Peasley]

Tournament Trail

Captain Don Wilbrandt accepts the sectional championship trophy at Waukegan, sending Hebron to the state finals for the first time since 1940. Just behind Coach Russ Ahearn, reporters Frank Reichstein and George Sullivan applaud. [Don Peasley]

The entire student body of Alden-Hebron High School gives the team a rousing send-off prior to the long trip to Champaign. [*Rockford Morning Star*]

Fans

Russ Ahearn's mother and a collection of nieces and nephews pose with a television set in Streator. The semifinals and the championship game were the first tournament contests ever televised. Front row, from left: Sharon Gotch, Linda Gotch, Sheila Higgins, Mary Whitmer, Mary Ahearn. Back row: Marilyn Gotch, Marcia Gotch, Cathy Higgins, Tommy Higgins.

Hebron fans seeking tickets for the next state tournament session besiege Superintendent Paul Tigard at a booth inside the University of Illinois Armory. [Don Peasley]

Paul Judson shoots a free throw against Champaign in the opening game at Huff Gym. Sunlight coming through the windows creates a glow in the gym. [Don Peasley]

Huff Gym

The cover of the 1952 state final souvenir program.

A close-up of the scoreboard shows the map of Illinois, 12 feet high, with a shining light representing every team still in the running. [Don Peasley]

Phil Judson charges toward the basket, while Champaign's Larry Hopkins tries to catch up. [AP]

Champaign

Bill Schulz moves a Champaign defender out of the way as Ken Spooner looks on. [AP]

Cheerleaders

The Hebron cheerleaders pose in front of the faithful in Huff Gym. From left are Shirley Schroeder, Joan DeYoung, Judy VanderKarr, and Helen Borgeson. [*Champaign News-Gazette*]

Helen Evers, Hebron's entry in the Miss Sweet Sixteen competition, joins the cheerleaders. The girls didn't like their new uniforms, which they said made them look like penguins. [Don Peasley]

Paul Judson drives to the hoop as Lawrenceville's Kay Gosnell makes a futile attempt to block. [*Champaign News-Gazette*]

Lawrenceville

Phil Judson rises above the Lawrenceville defense for a reverse layup in the state quarterfinal game. [*Champaign News-Gazette*]

Phil Hadley and Russ Ahearn clutch their notebooks while contemplating the next game at Huff Gym. [*Champaign News-Gazette*]

On the Bench

Russ Ahearn, at far left, shouts while Phil Hadley, with head down, scribbles during the quarterfinal game in Huff Gym. To Hadley's right are George Sullivan of the *Woodstock Sentinel*, Dr. Louis Tobison, and Charles and Bob Hall. In front of the players are Tom Kuecker, student sportswriter and Wally Adams, team manager. Players on the bench are Bill Thayer (clapping), Clayton Ihrke (head to left of Kuecker), Jim Bergin (clapping in second row), Joe Schmidt (with glasses), and Jim Wilbrandt (partially visible at far right). [Don Peasley]

chapter 10

Onward to State

Four years of preparation had gone into this moment. Russ Ahearn's goal, ever since he took the head coaching job at Hebron, was to beat his mentor, John Krafft, on the basketball floor. And now, even though Krafft was no longer the head coach, Ahearn desperately wanted to beat Elgin. With a win in the regional championship, Ahearn would prove to Krafft, and just as importantly, to himself, that he was worthy of being a coach.

This obsession with Krafft meant nothing to his players. John Krafft did this or John Krafft did that — well, they didn't know Krafft from Adam. But they did know Elgin. To motivate his players, all Ahearn had to do was bring up last year's loss, and remind them how after all the toil and tears, Hebron had still finished on the short end of a 54-51 result.

Tonight was the night when the Hebron Green Giants would go after their revenge. And when he got done with his X's and O's in the locker room, Ahearn talked straight to the players.

"Do you fellows *really* want to go to Champaign?" he asked. "The team that wins tonight will be the favorite to go to the state tournament. And so I'm calling on you players to give a superhuman effort tonight. You have to give a lot of extra effort, every man on the team. *"Tonight we have to win."*

Ahearn had prepared for this game since the day after the previous year's loss. He'd covered every conceivable angle, down to the tiniest detail, even which end of the court to shoot at. The embarrassing memory of the 1943 "staple game" might have been long forgotten in Elgin, but it was legendary in Hebron. Before the game, the Green Giants chose to come out in the first half and shoot at the end of the court with the balcony, so that in the second half they would not need to worry about any unidentified flying objects.

Most teams were leery of matching up with Hebron man-to-man, but Elgin's defense was particularly tough. In the opening minutes, the Maroons put the clamps on the Judsons and also managed to penetrate the Green Giants' coverage. Midway through the second period, Elgin led, 23-16. Not even Crystal Lake had had such success in shutting down Hebron. The only thing Elgin could not stop was Hebron's 6-10½ center. Bill Schulz was the sole bright spot for the Green Giants, with six baskets in the first half.

Just before the horn sounded, Paul Judson finally hit his first field goal of the game, a long jumper, to bring Hebron to within three at 27-24. The Hebron players went to the locker room feeling a little exasperated. It was the first time all season they had trailed at halftime.

The numbers told the story. Schulz had kept Hebron in the game with his 12 points. But Paul Judson had only four points, and brother Phil had managed just a single free throw.

Elgin kept up its pressure as the game resumed, and still the Judsons couldn't find their shots. Ken Spooner put in four points to help out Schulz, and Hebron finally pulled even at 36-36 in the first minute of the final period.

Then Schulz really went to work. He scored three quick baskets on a tip-in, a lay-up, and another tip-in, and Hebron led for the first time since the early going, 42-40.

That was just enough to keep Elgin at bay for the last four minutes. Phil and Paul did the rest of the scoring for Hebron, seven points in all. Elgin scored a couple of baskets in the closing seconds, but it was not enough. The final score read Hebron 49, Elgin 47.

It was unthinkable, but true. Elgin had held the Judson twins to a total of only three baskets — and lost. Schulz, with 23 points, was the only Hebron player in double figures.

Captain Don Wilbrandt accepted the plaque from Elgin High School principal Roscoe Cartwright, who then asked Ahearn to say a few words to the crowd. The local fans listened intently as the former Maroon coach stepped to the microphone.

Elgin used to be his first love, Ahearn declared, but now it was all Hebron. There were very few sore losers in the Elgin gym that night. On the principle that if you can't beat them you might as well join them, many Elgin rooters had already ceded their loyalty to Hebron. Some of them had tears in their eyes as the Maroon cheerleaders sent the Hebron team off with a rousing cheer.

In the locker room, Ahearn was ecstatic. He clutched the regional tournament plaque tightly as one Elgin school official joked within earshot of a reporter.

"Remind us, Russ," he said, "that if we ever let another coach go, to send him to Kansas or some place far away."

Two thousand miles west, Howie Judson sat in his room at Pasadena's Hotel Green, waiting on pins and needles for a knock on the door. He'd sent T-bone steaks to Edna Thompson, an aunt who lived in Elgin, with instructions to feed them to the twins after the game if Hebron won.

He didn't have long to wait to find out whether Aunt Edna would be firing up the broiler. Back at the high school, Louie Wilbrandt was already on the phone, dictating a telegram announcing that, at long last, the Elgin Maroons had been conquered.

Upsets All Over

By the end of the week's play, only 60 regional champions and four Chicago Public League teams were still alive in the state tournament. Those Green Giant fans who'd spent the time to plot out the bracket took notice of some very good fortune. Unranked, unheralded, and virtually unknown teams had cleared out the tournament field, upsetting some of Hebron's most dangerous potential opponents.

It started on the very first night of regional play. Waukegan had ended up with a sub-par season, including a loss to Hebron. Nevertheless, the Bulldogs still had the potential to win their regional, as the competition was quite weak. Fans sensed a possible rematch between Hebron and Waukegan on the Bulldogs' home court in the final game before the state tournament. Playing a sectional game in the opponent's gym was always a tough proposition, and going in, it looked like a real possibility. But Waukegan bombed on opening night against Niles Township, a team that had won only three games all season. Seven Waukegan players fouled out, and the Bulldogs frittered away the win, finishing the game with just three players on the floor.

Then, on the Friday night of the regional finals, as Hebron was beating Elgin, the state shook with the sound of some of the tallest trees in the basketball forest being felled. Two of those upsets had an immediate impact on Hebron's path to the state championship game.

The biggest loser was Danville, ranked No. 4 in the state, and Hebron's potential first-round opponent in the state finals. Danville fell by one point to unheralded Homer, a small school near Champaign. In another huge reversal, No. 7-ranked Collinsville, which might have played Hebron in the quarterfinals, lost to a "district school," Madison.

The complexion of the bracket changed substantially. If it kept winning, Hebron would now play four consecutive games, all the way into the state semifinals, without having to meet another "ranked" opponent. All of this was great grist for the hot-stovers, but it meant little to the players, if indeed they noticed at all.

Of the 60 teams that won regional titles and qualified for sectional play in 1952, Hebron was not the littlest of the Little Davids. That honor fell to Perry, a school from far western Illinois, with only 64 pupils. Unlike Hebron, Perry did not have to play in the district tournament stage just to qualify for the regional meet.

Armstrong, Augusta, Forrest, and Varna, all with enrollments under 150 but none of them district schools, rounded out the list of the smallest schools still alive. Three other district schools besides Hebron qualified for the sectionals: Madison, Waterloo, and Attucks, a segregated school from Carbondale. All of these schools had enrollments larger than 150.

Sportswriters were astonished and excited by the small schools' success. In a state with so many high schools and such a wide span of enrollments, the question of whether to divide the field had been debated on many occasions since the first tournament in 1908. Seizing on Hebron's success, a columnist for the *Elgin Courier-News* wrote:

> For years many high school basketball coaches in Illinois have been advocating the division of the state title eliminations. They have proposed that the smaller schools compete in Class C tournaments, the medium-sized schools compete in Class B meets, and the larger schools play for the Class A crown. The little northern McHenry County school would have little trouble taking the Class C title this year. But what would such a crown mean? Just that the Green Giants were the "biggest fish in the little puddle." Now they have the opportunity, as has each of the state's 752 other teams, to become the "big fish in the BIG pond."

Whatever the class, none of the sportswriters needed to be convinced of Hebron's supremacy in its upcoming sectional tournament. The Associated Press traditionally polled its writers across the state to select the sectional winners. In the Waukegan tournament, Hebron was the unanimous selection of all 21 writers.

Their logic was indisputable. Hebron's first game was with Barrington, a 22-3 team that the Green Giants had already buried by 44 points. The other two teams in the tournament were DeKalb, 14-11 and a 30-point loser to Hebron, and Niles, which had managed to stumble through the weak regional at Waukegan and now had a grand total of six wins to its credit.

Warming Up

Ahearn tried to keep his team up for the Wednesday night game with Barrington, even though a letdown after the Elgin win seemed inevitable.

"We are not counting too much on that victory we scored over Barrington two weeks ago," said Ahearn, "because we know

Wednesday night's game will be a tough one and we are taking each game as it comes."

But Barrington was a broken team. Hebron held the Broncos scoreless for almost the entire first quarter. Barrington made a brief run at the Green Giants in the second period, but Phil Judson doused any comeback hopes with a 40-foot basket as the horn sounded. Hebron led by 17 points at halftime.

As if to put the final nail in Barrington's coffin, Don Wilbrandt hit a 40-footer of his own to end the third quarter.

While his team nursed a 20-point lead in the final period, Ahearn sat on the bench, looking for all the world like a coach whose team was on the verge of collapse. He slid his spiral notebook in and out of his pocket, squirmed in his seat at every turnover and missed shot, and called out notes constantly to assistant coach Phil Hadley. Only when the clock ticked under a minute did he finally pat Hadley on the back and admit that the game was won.

Sportswriters covering the game that night agreed that Hebron's 64-42 victory was "not as close as the score indicated." A first-time fan in the stands turned to a reporter and commented, "I guess this team can do anything it wants to. It can't do anything wrong."

The Green Giants were one win away from their next goal: a berth in the state tournament and a trip to Champaign. A win would put the 1952 team on equal footing with the 1940 team in the annals of Hebron basketball. It would take a win over DeKalb to do it.

As the teams warmed up on the Waukegan floor, a familiar face appeared out of the crowd and greeted Ahearn near the bench. Lowry Crane had traveled up from Chicago to witness the event, and he'd brought along his eight-year-old son, Carter. The boy was fascinated with the Green Giants, the amazing team from the school where his father had coached so long ago. Ahearn offered Crane a place on the Hebron bench, but Crane politely declined and took a seat in the bleachers with his son.

The bench was getting pretty crowded as it was. Besides Phil Hadley and the players, there was Tom Kuecker, the student reporter, and Wally Adams and Ed Okeson, the team managers. For this game, Billy Ahearn, the coach's son, sat next to his dad, eager to be a part of the historic evening. And George Sullivan of the Woodstock paper claimed his usual spot between the players and the coach.

Frank Reichstein, the bespectacled, bow-tied reporter from Beloit, was also in the gym, covering his second Hebron game of the week and third in eight nights. His hometown readers must have been wondering if he was ever going to cover another game in Wisconsin. Ahearn slid his team down and gave Reichstein a seat as well.

Even with the new addition, Hebron's bench was no more crowded than the rest of the stands. The Waukegan gymnasium was packed with over 3,500 shouting, stomping fans. Almost all of them were Hebron partisans, if not actual Hebron citizens, who'd come from near and far, ready to see a Green Giant victory and send the team off to Champaign. That left DeKalb out in the cold as far as fan support was concerned.

But George Dertinger, the DeKalb coach, knew Hebron well. Twelve years before, at Huff Gym in Champaign, his Lewistown team had stunned a tall "Little David" team from the north. Now he had another chance to put a stop to Hebron's state tournament hopes. It would take a terrific upset, but anything was possible.

Except this was not 1940 and DeKalb was not Lewistown. Dertinger's team lasted just four minutes before that became apparent.

Ken Spooner was the star on this particular evening. He hit five straight baskets from long range, putting the game out of reach by halftime. Hebron expanded its lead to 34 points by the start of the fourth quarter, when Ahearn ordered his team to stall. Then, and only then, did DeKalb finally discover a chink in the Green Giant armor. Hebron threw the ball away several times, and DeKalb managed to grope back to an almost respectable 68-46 final score. But the game had been over for a long time. The horn sounded with Billy Ahearn sleeping peacefully at his father's side.

The fans whooped it up as Captain Don Wilbrandt accepted the sectional trophy, but there was no great outburst of enthusiasm from the players. Their win was expected and they took it remarkably straight-faced, perhaps a little embarrassed they had let DeKalb back within 25 points. In their minds it had been just another ballgame, maybe even a subpar effort, except for Spooner. That did not stop dozens of autograph seekers from surrounding the players after the trophy presentation, delaying their showers.

As Hebron fans finally settled down and filed out of the gym, word spread that Centralia, the state's No. 2-ranked team, had lost to Pinckneyville. The forest was being cleared, one redwood at a time. Hebron's first opponent in the state tournament at Champaign had also been determined. The Green Giants would face off against the hometown team, Champaign High School, which had beaten Bloomington for the sectional championship.

Memories of 1940 abounded as the caravan of fans made its way back from Waukegan to Hebron. The players had heard about the celebration that followed Hebron's first sectional championship and practically demanded an equivalent bonfire. By the time the team reached home, the flames leapt high over Prairie Avenue again, signaling Hebron's long-awaited return to the Sweet Sixteen.

Counting the Days

When the sun rose the next morning, the business of basketball overtook Hebron. Game time at Champaign was Thursday, March 20, at 2:30 p.m., the fifth of eight first-round games. But for Russ Ahearn, there were far too many things to do before then and precious little time to do them.

Reporters and photographers roamed all over town, looking for a new angle or a unique picture. Every time one showed up, Ahearn had to call the boys out of class to answer questions and set them up in a variety of poses. Dribble! Shoot! Block! There was no end to the combinations. The coach couldn't turn down an invitation to have his team appear on a television show, so he spent Monday evening ferrying the starters to Chicago and back.

The telephone in Ahearn's office rang off the hook with fans looking for tickets and old friends wishing him well — and looking for tickets. The games at Huff Gym were always sold out, but this year they promised to be more popular than ever. As a participating school, Hebron was allotted exactly 300 seats at each session it played. That wasn't enough for any school, but Hebron's following was bigger than the big schools' and there was no way to satisfy all the requests. Saying no fell to Ahearn and to Superintendent Paul Tigard, who did their best to keep the situation under control.

Wednesday could not come soon enough. Russ and Marie decided to leave Billy and Judy at home with friends. If everything went as planned, they could watch the Saturday games on TV.

Meanwhile, the official Hebron entourage kept growing and growing. There was Superintendent Tigard, Coaches Ahearn and Hadley, the ten-man tournament squad, school sportswriter Tom Kuecker, managers Wally Adams and Ed Okeson, Dr. Alex Leschuck, and Dr. Louis Tobison, a chiropractor from Harvard whom Ahearn had enlisted to give the team rubdowns.

In addition, the high school would send its four cheerleaders, Shirley Schroeder, Joan DeYoung, Judy VanderKarr, and Helen Borgeson, sporting brand-new green-and-white uniforms for the tournament. As its candidate in the annual Miss Sweet Sixteen competition, Hebron offered Helen Evers, a tall, blonde cousin of Bill Schulz.

Following right behind were the players' parents and families, and dozens upon dozens of diehards who had traveled with the team all year. They were all headed for Champaign, whether or not they had tickets. If they couldn't get them in Hebron, they'd bargain for them outside Huff Gym, because this was a once-in-a-lifetime, not-to-be-missed experience.

When Wednesday morning finally arrived, the team took one victory lap around town, horns blaring, and then headed down the long road to Champaign. An old-timer in the crowd shouted words of advice as the team trailed out of town.

"This time," he joked, "let's get to the gym a couple of hours early."

Setting Up Camp

Russ Ahearn and the Hebron administration were not about to repeat the mistake of the 1940 team. Hebron's first state tournament team had stayed in Paxton, 28 miles away. This crew set up camp in the Alexander Hamilton Hotel, right in downtown Champaign.

Even so, the hotel was not the center of tournament action. Most of the other teams chose to stay in the Inman Hotel, a couple of blocks away, which was the unofficial headquarters of teams, reporters, and fans alike. By choosing the Hamilton, Ahearn could shield his team from some, if not all, of the hubbub.

Ahearn and Hadley checked out the rooms at the Hamilton and assigned them to the team members. Most of the players had to share a bed with a teammate or a manager; only Bill Schulz and the twins got to sleep alone.

Ahearn strictly controlled their activities. He ordered the players to stay together if they went out. There were movie houses just down the street, and he allowed them to watch the cartoons if they wanted. He told the players to disconnect the phones and keep fans and reporters away. They could nap, but not close to game time. And they could listen to the radio in their rooms, but not to any of the tournament games.

The players knew this would be the first state basketball tournament ever televised, but they had no hope of seeing any of the games. For one thing, the hotel rooms didn't have TV sets — Champaign-Urbana didn't even have a television station. And of course, Mr. Ahearn would never have allowed it in the first place. But more importantly, since only the Saturday games would be broadcast, the players planned to be in Huff Gym preparing for the second semifinal game by the time the first semifinal hit the air.

The coach had a million and one things to do when the team got to town on Wednesday afternoon. As principal, he had to submit his list of eligible players to Al Willis, the executive secretary of the IHSA, to certify their participation in the tournament. He had to arrange tickets for a few of his entourage. He had to track down some new balls for practice and some medical supplies from the staff over at the university.

But mostly, Ahearn had to keep his team and himself focused on the task at hand. It wasn't easy. He was still besieged by well-wishers and ticket-seekers.

Back in his hotel room, Ahearn leafed through a stack of telegrams. Many came from Hebron, of course. But there were also some from fans in Harvard, Crystal Lake, McHenry, and Woodstock, rivals defeated on the court but now standing behind his team.

One was from Harold Beth of the First National Bank of Woodstock. "STEAK DINNERS RESERVED AT HEIMANNS 6:30 SUNDAY EVENING WIN OR LOSE," it said. Well, at least his players wouldn't go hungry when they got back.

The coach opened another envelope, looked at the sender, and laughed out loud. "BEST WISHES FOR SUCCESS FROM ONE GREEN GIANT TO ANOTHER," the telegram read. Who knew that the Green Giant Company of LeSueur, Minnesota, had been keeping tabs on them?

At four o'clock, Ahearn gathered his players for practice at the Champaign Junior High School gym. They were met by local photographers, who had not yet had their shot at documenting the curious team from the north. The Taylorville squad was in the gym at the same time, and one of the photographers posed a shot of the Tornadoes' 5-foot-7 All-State guard Bill Ridley, perched on top of a staircase, looking decidedly uncomfortable shaking hands with Bill Schulz.

After the practice, Paul Judson and Schulz both complained of sore arms, so Doc Tobison took them aside and worked them over while Doc Leschuck rubbed down the rest of the team. It was eight o'clock before the coaches and players sat down for their usual steak dinner.

At the same time, Ahearn and Phil Hadley caught up with their scouts at the hotel. Like a snowball rolling downhill, Hebron had picked up the accumulated braintrust of teams it defeated along the way. Max Brady, head coach of Crystal Lake, was scouting for the Green Giants now, as was Ahearn's good friend, Bert Nafziger of Richmond. Most important of all, John Krafft of Elgin had joined the ranks of Hebron scouts. Once his Maroons had fallen, Krafft switched his allegiance to help Ahearn on his title drive. The five men met in the hotel room and talked about strategy.

The two Wednesday quarterfinal games had just concluded, and the conclave of coaches was already dissecting the results. Mt. Vernon, a potential title-game opponent, had been pushed to overtime, barely beating Kankakee, a team Hebron had handled easily at Christmas. That was good news, but it couldn't be taken too seriously. They might have survived a squeaker, but Mt. Vernon had won the state tournament two of the last three years and would not be the least bit in awe of Hebron or anyone else.

Pinckneyville, another southern Illinois school with a long-standing tournament tradition, had won the other game, knocking off the Chicago Public League's entry, Roosevelt High School.

Ahearn checked the *Champaign News-Gazette*, where sports editor Jack Prowell provided a full scouting report on first-round action. Champaign was abuzz. Not only was the city lucky enough to host Hebron, the biggest phenomenon ever to hit the tournament, but the hometown school was scheduled to play the Green Giants in the first round. Prowell's column, a must-read for anyone interested in high school basketball, gave tournament-goers an idea of what to expect.

Prowell started by detailing the strengths of each of the Hebron starters, but he seemed most impressed with the general demeanor of the ballclub.

"The Judsons never crack a smile," he wrote. "They are all business, and during a timeout it is not unusual to see one twin raising hob with the other. Phil didn't smile until 30 minutes after the game."

Hebron entered the state finals with the best record of any team, 31-1, riding a 16-game winning streak. Although the question of whether Hebron was the best team in the tournament had yet to be settled, there was no question that a school with an enrollment of 98 students would be the sentimental favorite.

Still, there were indications that Hebron's support was soft. Despite the unsavory overtones, the *Urbana Courier* ran a handicap sheet — "Condition of track: dry, fast" — and installed Hebron and Quincy as co-favorites, at odds of 4-1. Taylorville, Thornton, and Rock Island were next at 5-1.

Hebron Can Be Beaten

By Jack Prowell

Champaign News-Gazette

How good is Hebron? What are Champaign's chances against the fabled Green Giants in the opening round of the state tournament?

Hebron is good, but not unbeatable by any means.

Hebron is good because (1) it is a gang of amazing shooters, (2) it has some amazing passwork, (3) it is strong on the boards, and (4) it is strong fundamentally.

Its weaknesses are: (1) a porous defense, (2) lack of reserve strength, (3) possibly a slight case of nervousness when an opponent goes into a pressing defense.

Champaign will have to be at its best to beat Hebron. The Green Giants have size. With that height, Hebron will give most teams trouble on the boards. Phil Judson is one of the best defensive rebounders who'll be on view in the state tournament.

But Hebron has not won 31 of 32 games by rebounding. It has won by shooting. The Green Giants averaged .460 from the field all season.

One of Hebron's favorite plays is the simplest one in the books. Paul Judson screens for Ken Spooner outside the free throw circle, and Spooner unleashes a one-hand push shot. More often than not, Spooner connects.

Bob Menke, former Illinois cager from Elgin who is now coaching at Woodstock, is high on Spooner. "I'd like to pit him in a '21' game with anybody. He rarely misses."

Another favorite play starts with Paul Judson controlling the ball out in front. He passes to twin brother Phil on the right side, then breaks toward the basket. Taking the return pass from Phil, Paul jumps as if to shoot. This forces the defensive man guarding 6-10 Schulz to come out after Paul, who thereupon dumps an easy pass to Schulz, who has an easy two or three-foot jump shot.

Phil Judson is a hard driving forward. Don Wilbrandt will also drive, but he's toughest on a one-hander from the side.

The Judsons are excellent feeders. All the Hebron players like to slide under the basket, and once there they may expect a baseball peg from one of the Judsons. They are exceptionally good at spotting a man in the clear and at getting the ball to him.

Schulz is not the best center in the world, but he is a long way from the poorest. He can move, has a fairly good left hand, and offers quite a problem because of his height.

The Judsons are about as good as you will ever see at blocking shots. They have amazingly fast hands.

In the Barrington game, a Barrington boy was bringing the ball down the floor. Paul, instead of slapping at the ball, trapped it against the floor at the bottom of the dribble. Then he flipped the ball to one side, picked it up, and went the length of the floor to score.

The Sweet Sixteen
at Huff Gym

Mt. Vernon (29-3)

Kankakee (15-13)

Roosevelt (Chicago) (23-3)

Pinckneyville (26-3)

Taylorville (27-1)

Manual (Peoria) (20-8)

Quincy (25-4)

Freeport (23-3)

Champaign (23-6)

HEBRON (31-1)

Lawrenceville (19-8)

Madison (28-4)

Ottawa (25-3)

Jacksonville (21-7)

Thornton (Harvey) (25-3)

Rock Island (23-4)

1952
STATE
CHAMPION

chapter 11

March Madness

For fans of the schools talented and lucky enough to qualify for the "Sweet Sixteen," a trip to Champaign-Urbana meant being part of a unique experience.

The state basketball tournament had been the premier high school athletic event in Illinois almost from the moment of its inception in 1908. But it wasn't until after 1934, when the tournament expanded from eight teams to a "Sweet Sixteen" format, that the event really took on a personality all its own.

They called it "March Madness." For four days every spring, this incomparable "short-pants pageant" played out on the dimly lit basketball court of Huff Gym. Superstars like Lou Boudreau, Andy Phillip, Dike Eddleman, and Max Hooper thrilled the crowds here. Unstoppable fives from Thornton Township, Taylorville, and Mt. Vernon certified their legends here.

But March Madness wasn't confined to Huff Gym. It consumed the entire landscape of the twin cities of Champaign and Urbana and the campus of the University of Illinois. As the tournament approached, no corner of the community was unaffected. Every hotel, every restaurant, and every store girded itself for the onslaught of out-of-towners.

For tournament management, housing was the primary concern. There were only a handful of hotels in the two towns, and they were allocated almost exclusively to the teams and others directly involved in the competition. The rest of the fans had to make do, either by securing accommodations in private homes or fraternities or by sleeping on cots in designated university buildings.

"Do not plan to stay overnight in Champaign-Urbana unless it is absolutely necessary," the University advised. "Men and boys should bring their own bedding."

The state tournament had become so popular by 1952 that Hebron fans who'd made the trip twelve years earlier marveled at the changes.

In 1940, anyone could walk right up to the window at Huff Gym and get a ticket to most of the sessions. That was a pipe dream by 1952. Every seat for every session was spoken for long before the opening tip-off.

The University had also instituted a huge event called the Sweet Sixteen Circus, now in its fourth year. Located in the University Armory just across the street from Huff Gym, the Circus provided wholesome entertainment for thousands of visiting students. In the past, many tournament-goers simply wandered around campus to kill time between sessions, leading to frequent reports of vandalism. The Circus was the perfect antidote for that problem.

A huge cutout of a clown surrounded the entrance to the Armory and called attention to the event. Inside, various forms of entertainment beckoned the flock, including acrobats, music, and dancing. The culmination of the festivities was the crowning of the annual Miss Sweet Sixteen.

All of this fun, however, was off-limits to the Hebron players. While the students played at the Circus, the Green Giants plotted their strategy for Thursday's game with Champaign.

One Down: Champaign

After breakfast at the Hamilton Hotel, Russ Ahearn called the team together for his final chalk talk prior to taking the floor in Huff Gym.

Champaign was a traditional state tournament entrant but somewhat of a surprise in 1952, simply because Danville was expected to emerge from that area. But after Danville had suffered its ignominious loss to Homer, Champaign stepped up and grabbed a berth in the state finals. The Maroons had won 23 of 29 games, playing in the tough Big Twelve Conference.

The Maroons' best player was Bert Leach, a 6-foot-1 forward who could drive or shoot from the outside. Ahearn assigned Phil Judson to guard him. Then the coach laid out some specifics for his team to consider.

"You have to expect anything in state tournament play," he said, "such as a press, a stall, tricky defenses, or cockeyed zones. You'll probably see a lot of driving, especially in the first quarter to foul you out of the game. *Holler at them!* And talk to each other to prevent getting caught in a block."

Although he never raised his voice in anger, the coach now warmed to the topic.

"We have come here to play basketball," he began. "Everything else is of minor importance to our big goal — winning the state championship. Fifteen other clubs have the same goal in mind. To accomplish our goal we can't look ahead to the final game. We must beat each team that we play."

There were rumors that national publications had taken an interest in Hebron's story, and Ahearn now used them as a motivational tool.

"We coaches challenge you to be alert every second and play your best defensive ball of the year, every game. We challenge you Giants to put a glorious finish to a glorious year of basketball. If you fellows win this tournament, *LIFE* and *TIME* magazines and the *Saturday Evening Post* are going to film our team and furnish us a police escort back to Hebron. But all of these fine things will happen only to the winner."

Ahearn then emphasized the philosophy that had brought his team this far.

"This is just another tournament to us," he said. "Huff Gymnasium will be packed with howling students from Champaign High, but no more than at Oak Park, Waukegan, Danville, or the regional or the sectional. Just go out and play *basketball*. Remember that everybody will be trying so hard to beat Hebron that they will be worried, excited, and trying *too* hard. But we will be calm, cool, poised, and yet desperate every second."

He finished with a flourish.

"Are you ready for a battle? Then go get 'em, Giants!" Ahearn shouted.

By now, the Hebron contingent was already tumbling into Huff Gym. They'd seen games in big gyms before, and yet they were still awed by the sheer size of the arena. They were a long way from Hebron's little stage gym.

Jessie Judson, mother of the twins, was one of the first in the doors. She spotted George Sullivan, the newspaperman from Woodstock, and smiled.

"I know we are in the right place when you are here," she told him.

It was the right place. They hoped it would be a friendly place as well.

Once the game started, both teams showed jitters. It took a while for the players to get accustomed to the big gym floor and the sea of fans around them. Ken Spooner broke the ice for Hebron with a short push shot in the first minute, and Hebron edged out to a 14-8 lead.

Only Clarence Burks, the Maroons' 6-5 center, kept Champaign in contention. He seemed to be able to maneuver against big Bill Schulz and had six of his team's points. Near the end of the quarter, Phil Judson picked up his third foul and Champaign pulled close at 16-14.

Even with Phil in foul trouble, Hebron's defense responded in the second quarter, shutting down Leach and Burks and effectively ending the game. Wilbrandt and Schulz broke into the scoring column, and by halftime Hebron's lead had grown to 36-21. Down so far so fast, the hometown crowd sat on its hands the rest of the game. Champaign never pulled closer than nine points in the second half, as Hebron won a decisive, if not overwhelming, 55-46 decision.

Even though his team was out of the game after the first quarter, Champaign coach Harold Jester was unimpressed with Hebron's showing. "I wish we could play them five straight games," Jester told reporters. "Look at the scorebook. Outside the second quarter we outscored them 39-35.

"They're a good team," Jester continued, "but neither the best in the state nor this tournament. I don't think they're going to go all the way. We've played better teams, and those Judson boys are good, but not the best we've seen."

In the Hebron locker room, Ken Spooner tried to explain his team's lackluster performance. "We really were hitting in that second quarter, but otherwise, we weren't up to our regular pace."

"I suppose it was the halftime rest that got us nervous again," added Phil Judson. "Those fouls kept me from driving in, and I'd have liked to press a little more. But this game gave us the feel. We were so excited that we didn't play as well as usual."

Paul chimed in. "When you get this far, every move is important. I caught myself tensing up just when I'd shoot. This quit bothering me when I forgot about myself and began to worry about Phil's fouls." The reporters chuckled.

Russ Ahearn took the commentary in stride. He was not upset by his team's showing.

"The boys are like a bunch of racehorses," he assured the reporters. "They're high-strung, and they were over-jittery today. I'm afraid I was a little bit jittery myself. You know this is the first time I've ever brought a team to the state finals. I was with Elgin here three times, but it's not the same pressure when you're an assistant coach."

One writer expressed doubts Bill Schulz could make it through a three-day, four-game grind.

"For a kid built like he is, he's got amazing stamina," said the coach. "In fact, I wouldn't be a bit surprised if he plays his best ball the last two games."

After the writers got their fill, Ahearn hustled his team back to the hotel. Paul Judson had a couple of blisters on his feet and everyone needed to be rubbed down. While Doc Leschuck and Doc Tobison worked on the muscles of some of the players, Ray Long, editor of the *Elgin Courier-News*, came by and offered to buy dinner for the team — steak, of course.

That evening, Ahearn talked over the day's results with his scouts.

With Mt. Vernon and Pinckneyville already in, Taylorville and Quincy had taken the remaining slots in the top bracket. Of those four, Quincy seemed like the probable survivor. The Blue Devils had beaten the Freeport Pretzels, the defending state champs, and looked strong in doing so.

Joining Hebron in the bottom bracket were Lawrenceville and Jacksonville. And in a big surprise, Rock Island had demolished Thornton, 56-35. Thornton had been ranked No. 6 at the end of the regular season but could do nothing right against the up-and-coming Rocks.

For the quarterfinal, Hebron was looking at Lawrenceville, and practically everyone predicted that the game would be a walkover. Coach Joe Fearheiley's team had eight losses on the year and did not play in a particularly strong conference or region. But it did have one outstanding performer, a player who could make a difference if he had the game of his life.

Tom Kelly had broken his neck playing football in 1950, and in a subsequent accident, lost the middle finger of his left hand. Bloodied but unbowed, the 6-foot senior forward was now playing in the Sweet Sixteen. And he wasn't just playing — he was thriving. He'd scored 33 points in an upset of Mattoon in the sectional final and had to be considered a serious threat.

The Hebron players went to their rooms that night in high spirits and ready for the next day's contest. Their coach rested as well, with confidence in his team and his game plan. They had one win under their belts. It wasn't a pretty win, but it was a win nonetheless.

Two Down: Lawrenceville

The team had some time to kill on Friday, since their quarterfinal game wasn't scheduled until 7:30 that night, a full 29 hours after the start of the first-round game.

Nevertheless, most of the Hebron contingent was up early, talking and reading the newspapers. Only Phil Hadley dozed on.

"I wish I would sleep like that guy," wrote Doc Tobison, who was keeping a tournament diary for the *Harvard Herald*.

The morning columnists were unimpressed by Hebron's showing against Champaign. Despite registering an easy win over a Big Twelve team with only six losses, Hebron somehow left the writers expecting more. Bert Bertine of the *Urbana Courier* was particularly perplexed.

"Are the Green Giants good?" he wrote. "They were at times against Champaign, other times looking ordinary. They will have to play better to beat the likes of Rock Island. Quincy is clearly the popular choice to win the tournament."

After lunch, some of the adults gave the team an auto tour of the Twin Cities. Their drive took them through the downtown areas and around the elm-lined streets of the university campus. There were high schoolers everywhere, easily visible in their brightly colored letter sweaters. The university looked as if it had been taken over by teens.

The players were restless. They hadn't come to Champaign to sightsee and were anxious to make amends for the drab showing the night before. They made their way back to the hotel and counted the hours until game time.

That evening at Huff Gym, from the moment the Green Giants took the opening tip, it was obvious that the nerves that had plagued them on the first day were gone. This time Hebron got it right from the get-go.

With typically balanced scoring, the Green Giants jumped to a 20-12 lead after one quarter and expanded it to 38-21 by halftime. As they left the court at intermission, the Green Giants were shooting 52 percent from the field. Despite a strong effort from Tom Kelly, Lawrenceville had just about run out of options.

Although the downstate school closed to within nine points early in the fourth quarter, nine straight Hebron points put the game away. With Hebron leading 65-47, Ahearn cleared the bench, and all the reserves got to play. For everyone except Bill Thayer, who had played briefly the day before, it was the first taste of action on the Huff Gym floor. The final score was 65-55.

The victory over Lawrenceville assured the Hebron team of three important things. First, it meant that Hebron would be the first team from McHenry County ever to win a state tournament trophy.

Second, the team would play on television. When the semifinal game started, everyone left behind in Hebron would be watching.

And no matter what, Hebron would be one of only four teams still playing on Saturday. It promised to be a real endurance test, with each team required to play two games in the span of several hours.

One of the reporters asked Ahearn what instructions he'd give his players.

"Go get a steak and get right to bed," he told them, "then get up about 9:30 and have another steak."

Paul Judson offered that he didn't think he'd be hungry enough for another steak in the morning. "We'd rather have the extra sleep, with two games tomorrow," he commented.

One of the photographers, thinking ahead to his early deadlines the next evening, asked the team to group together and let out a yell, pretending they had won the championship.

The players balked at the request. "Wait till tomorrow for that," muttered one.

The boys made their way to the showers but the reporters still surged forward, pressing Ahearn for details of the Lawrenceville victory.

"All season the boys have played just hard enough to win," he noted. And that was his strategy in Champaign as well. "In a tournament like this you've got to pace yourself or you'll burn out."

For Ahearn it was all part of a larger equation. "We're shooting for the big one, you know," he said with a smile.

The last question came from a reporter who wanted to know why Hebron was such an overwhelming favorite of the crowds.

"I guess it's because we're just small-town boys," the coach answered, and then he was off.

By the time the team got back to the hotel, the semifinalists had been determined. The end result of Friday's action was that all four schools with names ending in "-ville" had lost. That meant Quincy, which beat Taylorville, and Mt. Vernon, which beat Pinckneyville, would play in Saturday's first game.

In the second semifinal, Hebron's opponent would be Rock Island, a 61-49 winner over Jacksonville.

Three Down: Rock Island

Illinois Route 47 runs from Mahomet, a small town just west of Champaign, due north through Hebron to the Wisconsin border. Late Friday and early Saturday it was jammed with cars and trucks making the four-hour trip from Champaign to Hebron and then back again.

Many of Hebron's faithful fans were dairy farmers. And for these fans, the only thing more important than the state tournament was the cows. The cows didn't ask to be milked; they demanded it. And so the caravan started, shortly after the Friday night game concluded at nine o'clock, and continued on through the night, as Hebronites made the long trek back home. These farmers and farmer's wives and farmer's children caught a few hours' sleep, rose at dawn to milk their stock, and set out back down the road to Champaign in time to make the second semifinal game at 2:30.

Meanwhile, Ahearn and his advisers concentrated on the upcoming contest. Rock Island had lost just four games and seemed to be on a late-season surge. The coaches knew little about the Rocks other than what they had gleaned in the past two days. But Coach Wilbur Allen, who was in his first season at the school, was well known to the group, having coached at Waukegan for several years prior to taking the Rock Island job.

Hebron's match-up with Rock Island presented some different obstacles. The Rocks' offense was based around a center named Jerry Hansen, who averaged almost 20 points per game. The Rocks were big and athletic, and had gained many backers with their easy wins over Jacksonville and highly regarded Thornton. But they were also slow, and Ahearn reminded his team that the key to the game was keeping the pace where Hebron wanted it — fast.

"Run 'em ragged," he told his team. "If we can be quicker, we have a chance."

But finding ways to wear out the opposition would soon be the least of Ahearn's concerns.

The Quincy team was still downstairs celebrating its semifinal win over Mt. Vernon and the Hebron players had barely broken a sweat when disaster struck.

It was the kind of disaster that the Green Giants had been able to avoid so neatly all year, but Hebron's luck had finally run out. In the fourth minute of the game, in the span of just 55 seconds, Paul Judson was whistled for three consecutive fouls.

Russ Ahearn was concerned, but his expression never wavered. Paul had run into foul trouble before, and he had always played through it. The coach knew that Paul had a level head and could rein it in when he had to. Now Ahearn gambled that this was one of those times.

He left his star player in the game.

Hebron pressed on, unfazed by Rock Island's rough-and-tumble, crash-the-boards game. Wilbrandt and Schulz each had a hot hand, and Hebron had built a 15-12 lead by the end of the first quarter. But barely thirty seconds into the second quarter, Paul was whistled again, this time for running into Stuart Thoms. It was Hebron's fourth foul of the game — and all of them were on Paul Judson.

There was no room left for mistakes. Still Ahearn left Judson on the floor. The coach instructed him to take it easy on defense. But Ahearn knew he couldn't stop Judson from playing aggressively on offense, and that was nearly the end of him.

Twice in the next minute, Paul Judson and Stuart Thoms mixed it up and the whistle blew, stopping the hearts of thousands of spectators. Paul held his breath, too. But both of these calls went against Thoms, and now *Thoms* had three fouls. Hebron's lead grew to seven points, 21-14.

Ahearn had seen enough for one half. He calmly pointed down the bench to Bill Thayer, who removed his warm-up jacket and ran onto the court. Thayer had filled the sixth-man role for half the season, but rarely played when anything was at stake. Now, on the floor of Huff Gym, the fiery redhead finally had a chance to contribute when it really mattered.

Thayer proved to be a capable backup for Judson, running the offense and surprising many fans who'd assumed Hebron's bench would be easy pickings for a good team like Rock Island. Instead, Hebron maintained its margin and led 32-26 as the teams made their way to the locker room.

By now, the big panel on the scoreboard that indicated personal fouls was filled with rows of red lights. A string of four glowed next to the names of both Paul Judson and Stuart Thoms. Schulz, with three lights by his name, was in foul trouble, too. Did officials really call it tighter at the state tournament? The proof was on the foul board.

Judson returned to start the second half. With his help, Hebron's offense kept battering the Rocks, sustaining the lead throughout the third quarter. Schulz managed to foul Thoms out of the game midway though the period, and with Rock Island down by seven points and playing shorthanded, the Green Giants appeared to have the game well in hand.

But Rock Island had plenty of fight left. Merrell Clark, the Rocks' 6-foot-5 center, hit three straight baskets, followed by a long jumper from Jerry Hansen. Suddenly Rock Island led by one, 46-45, as the quarter came to a close.

Milt Scheuerman made a jumper of his own to start the fourth quarter, and Rock Island was up by three. The Rocks were on the verge of breaking the game open. But after Wilbrandt and Bill Geisler traded baskets, the Hebron players decided it was time to put an end to the nonsense.

With all the starters except Spooner getting into the act, Hebron made the next 14 points, holding Rock Island scoreless for almost six minutes. When the run ended, Hebron led, 61-50, with only a minute and a half left on the clock. The final score was 64-56.

They'd made it to the championship game. Everything they'd worked so hard for was now within reach.

The Green Giants didn't waste time celebrating. There was still a job to be done and little time to prepare, especially when the postgame interviews took longer than expected. As usual, the twins held court with the reporters. They were describing Phil's technique of counting out loud on out-of-bounds plays when the coach decided enough was enough. It was well after four o'clock. They'd have to be on the floor for the championship game in a little more than four hours.

Ahearn hustled his team out of the gym and back to the hotel for a few minutes of rest. He had scheduled another steak dinner at about six o'clock, and then one last team meeting before returning to Huff Gym for the Saturday night finale.

Hebron's starters were in pretty good shape physically. Other than a few blisters, the only problem was Schulz's back. He'd suffered spasms throughout the second half of the season, and sometimes he had to wear a corset to control the pain. The injury had flared up again this weekend, especially after he took a nasty fall during the semifinal. Ahearn sent Doc Leschuck down to Schulz's room to take a look.

Meanwhile, he and Phil Hadley attempted to plot out strategy with the braintrust of Brady, Nafziger, and Krafft. John Krafft was feeling ill. He thought he might have gotten food poisoning somewhere along the line. Too many restaurants and not enough home cooking, he said. But time was of the essence, and he damped down his queasy stomach as the five kept working.

Not only would this be Hebron's biggest game of the season, but it was clear that Quincy would be its toughest opponent. The Blue Devils came into the final game with four losses, but all of them were against top-notch competition: Centralia, East St. Louis, Taylorville, and Thornton. What could little Hebron do against a team like Quincy?

Everyone knew about the Blue Devils' 6-foot-5 center, Bruce Brothers, who averaged over 20 points per game. He'd started for Quincy the last three years and each time finished the season in the state finals, right here on the floor of Huff Gym. In 1951, when Quincy finished third, he'd been an All-Tournament selection, and this year he was a virtual lock for All-State honors.

Bill Schulz had never matched up against a player of Brothers' talent. The championship game would be a true test of how far the Hebron center had come in four years of intense instruction.

Quincy was not a one-man team. At forward were 6-4 Charlie Fast and 6-2 Jack Gower, good shooters and rebounders who would have a slight height advantage over their Hebron counterparts. Phil Harvey and Dick Thompson, the guards, gave away a few inches to the Hebron backcourt, but both were quick, with good ballhandling ability.

146

Ahearn was concerned about the zone press Quincy had used in its quarterfinal game against Taylorville. His advisers felt certain that George Latham, the Quincy coach, would call for it again in the championship. Hebron had rarely seen a zone press, certainly not one as well executed as Quincy's, and Ahearn wanted to be sure his men would be ready for it. As the clock ticked down to the biggest game of his life, Coach Ahearn scribbled some final notes into his spiral notebook.

One To Go

Bundled up against a bone-chilling north wind, the crowd gathered early for the championship session. The anticipation of the match-up was enough to make even the most jaded sportswriters giddy. Only once before had a school climbed all the way up from the district level to reach the championship game. Braidwood had accomplished an amazing feat in 1938, but at the time the district tournament setup was brand-new, and no one had recognized how special that accomplishment really was.

It was different now. Out on Fourth Street, hundreds of hopeful fans searched in vain for scalpers with an extra ticket, but there were few to be found. Almost everyone who had a ticket planned on using it. The few lucky buyers who found a seller paid as much as $20 over the $1.25 face value.

The crowd packed into the smoke-filled corridors that ringed the main court. Huff Gym was a palace built in a cornfield when it opened in 1926, but now, just a quarter century later, it was past its prime. It was far too small to hold the people who wanted to see the University of Illinois team, and it was equally unsuitable for the crowds now desperate to get into the high school tournament.

The bleacher seats on the main floor provided a great view, if you were lucky enough to get one. Fans in the first row were right in the action. If they weren't careful to keep their legs tucked in, their feet would stick over the sideline and right onto the court.

The balcony was far less inviting. The rows were too short and the slatted theater-style seats too narrow for a normal adult male. Making things worse, the view from a fair number of the seats was obstructed by the pillars that supported the roof.

Still, Huff Gym was one of the biggest arenas in Illinois, and it had the advantage of being centrally located, a critical factor where the state tournament was concerned. A *News-Gazette* editorial warned readers that there was agitation to move the tournament to Chicago Stadium or to Bradley University in Peoria, and advised the University to expedite its plans for a new arena. The official attendance for all state tournament sessions at Huff Gym was 6,905, but twice as many tickets could have been sold on this night.

Still, the ticket situation might have been worse. By coincidence, many Champaign-Urbana fans who might otherwise have joined the rabble clamoring for tickets outside Huff Gym were at Chicago Stadium instead. There the Fighting Illini were preparing to play Duquesne University in the finals of the NCAA regional tournament, scheduled to start about half an hour after the state title game. The basketball fever that enveloped the Twin Cities on this evening was an exciting interplay between the high school game at Huff Gym and the college game at Chicago Stadium, where the team from the state's flagship university was trying for its second consecutive appearance in the Final Four.

The Hebron team arrived at Huff Gym about eight o'clock, with the consolation game already in progress. In what had become something of a state tournament tradition, the third-place contest was a freewheeling, high-scoring affair. Mt. Vernon and Rock Island put on a show that went down to the wire before Mt. Vernon finally earned a 71-70 decision.

Now the stage was set for the game everyone had come to see, or at least, for the *team* everyone had come to see. As talented as the Quincy team was, they had few rooters in the stands, outside close friends and family.

Down in the locker room, Russ Ahearn brought his players together to discuss strategy prior to the final struggle. He pulled the notebook out of his pocket and read from his observations, one point at a time.

"I want you to work the pivot a lot."

"Watch out for the blocks."

"Work running screens all over."

"Stop the pass from going in to Brothers as much as possible."

"Paul and Phil—watch your contact and don't be overanxious."

"Use a shifting man-to-man defense all over."

"Drive, drive, drive."

He flipped the page and continued.

"Against the zone — do not dribble."

"Work to the forwards."

"Do not attempt to dribble without a screen."

"You can fast-break them on their press."

"Get their defense spread. You can drive them."

"Be great rebounders again."

Finally, the coach stopped talking strategy and addressed the team.

"Boys," he said, "Hebron loves to play when the chips are down. Quincy is nearly out of gas, so let's run the daylights out of them. We won't settle for anything less than the state championship."

He took a deep breath. And then Coach Ahearn gave his final advice before the big game. "It's time to play. Go get 'em, Giants!"

Upstairs, the cameras were about to roll on the first television broadcast of an Illinois state championship game. Some observers had predicted that televising the games on the final day might cut into attendance at the tournament, but they needn't have worried. The fans in the wooden bleachers were packed in like sardines.

Illinois Bell Telephone Company was in charge of the telecast and pulled out all the stops. For this inaugural state championship broadcast, viewers would be treated to a first-class production. Not one, but two cameras were prepared to document all the action. The on-air crew was also first-rate. Jack Drees, the play-by-play man, was a former basketball player at the University of Iowa and now a popular Chicago broadcaster. Chick Hearn, who would handle the interviews at halftime and after the game, was the radio voice of Bradley University athletics. As the clock ticked down, the two men went over their notes one last time at courtside.

The radio booth at the top of the balcony vibrated with the chatter of announcers from several stations, beaming a stream of commentary back to those parts of Illinois still beyond the reach of television.

Veteran sportscasters Fritz Sorenson of WKRS in Waukegan and Bob Philbin of WJOL in Joliet got ready for their network broadcast, to be carried on twelve radio stations in northern Illinois. Meanwhile, Fred Corray and Harold Hill of WILL, the station operated by the University of Illinois, prepared for a dual role. They'd be calling the Hebron-Quincy game for folks in central Illinois while at the same time relaying updates on the Illinois-Duquesne game for those fans who wanted to keep tabs on the Fighting Illini.

Down on the floor, Don Peasley, the reporter from Woodstock who'd covered Hebron all season, chatted with a young Englishman named Larry Burrows. Burrows had just arrived in America from London and was making his first trip across the country, taking pictures as he went. He'd never seen a basketball game in his life, but had picked up on the story of the small-town team from the Chicago papers. Now he was documenting the team's progress for a magazine feature called "*Life* Goes to a Party." If Hebron won, Burrows hoped to follow the team back home the next day and get shots of their homecoming for next week's edition. As they chatted, Burrows took shots of the crowd.

The Hebron cheerleaders worked the sidelines, doing their best to urge the crowd into a cheer. The girls didn't like their new green-and-white uniforms — made them look like penguins, one grumbled — but they had plenty of spirit, especially considering there were only four of them. Their cheers couldn't possibly carry throughout a gym this large. So they concentrated on the small group of fans from Hebron, located right behind the team bench for the first time in four state tournament games.

Ahearn and Latham shook hands as the players finished their warm-ups. As usual, Ahearn showed his loyalty by wearing a green tie and green socks with his favorite light-blue, double-breasted suit. The men joked that while the outcome of the game was in doubt, at least one thing was certain: the winning coach would be a graduate of Illinois State Normal University. Latham had played on the ISNU football team right after Ahearn finished his four years on the baseball team. Wasn't it ironic, Ahearn remarked, that they should meet here and now on a *basketball* court?

The gym grew quiet as the starters were introduced. The public address announcer boasted that the spectators were about to enjoy "the best high school basketball in the United States." Twenty-six previous state championships had been decided on the floor of George Huff Gymnasium, but never had more eyes been focused on this place at one time. In parlors and living rooms across Illinois, families sat together to watch or listen to the game that would decide whether Hebron or Quincy would reign as the basketball champion of Illinois.

The crowd sang the national anthem.

The lights over the balcony dimmed.

And on the big map of Illinois, high above the floor, two red lights blinked into the darkness.

Bill Schulz provides a big obstacle as Rock Island's Merrell Clark attempts a shot. [AP]

Rock Island

Ken Spooner tries to steal the ball from Charles Thomas in the semifinal game against Rock Island. [AP]

As the teams warm up for the championship game, Russ Ahearn gives Bill Schulz some last-minute instructions. [Larry Burrows]

"Nothing less than the state championship," wrote Russ Ahearn in his notes for the final contest against Quincy.

Pre-Game

Russ Ahearn and Quincy Coach George Latham shake hands prior to the title game. [*Champaign News-Gazette*]

Phil Judson drives out of trouble
in the championship game as
Quincy's Bruce Brothers and Jack
Gower defend. [AP]

Quincy

Hebron's 6-foot-10½ Bill Schulz soars
to the basket as Quincy's Phil
Harvey, a 5-foot-8 guard, is powerless
to stop him. [AP]

With a five-point lead and five seconds to play, Paul Judson can barely contain himself at the free throw line. These were the blurry images that first-time television viewers saw.

Victory!

The Hebron players celebrate as the final gun sounds. Visible in the dark uniforms are Bill Schulz (partially obscured), Don Wilbrandt (8), and Phil Judson (in mid-air). [Don Peasley]

Chick Hearn conducts a television interview after the state championship trophy presentation. To the right of Russ Ahearn are Superintendent Paul Tigard and IHSA Executive Secretary Albert Willis. [Don Peasley]

Victory!

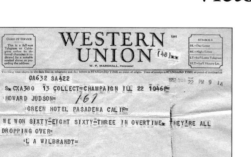

Louie Wilbrandt sent this telegram to Howie Judson after Hebron won the state championship. In his excitement, he got the score wrong.

Hebron's win was bigger news in Champaign than the Fighting Illini, who made it to the Final Four the same evening. [*Champaign News-Gazette*]

Coach

This picture was taken 2 minutes after the end of the tournament.
It clearly shows the affect of the terrific strain experienced in winning a state tournament.
The kids fought too.

Russ Ahearn

P.S. Dr. Leschuck worked on me for ½ hour in the hotel after the game. Determination is the word.

Russ Ahearn's inscription speaks for itself. [Larry Burrows]

Jubilation

Russ Ahearn is greeted by Jeff Balke, his wife's brother-in-law, at the Hamilton Hotel in downtown Champaign. In the background, Marie Ahearn's brothers, Johnny and Jerry Gotch, are all smiles. [Larry Burrows]

George Sullivan, sports editor of the *Woodstock Sentinel*, gives the No. 1 sign as the Hebron contingent goes wild. Visible to Sullivan's right are Barbara DeHaan, Helen Borgeson, Vera Lemmerhirt, and Jim Judson. In the far background are Paul Judson, former players Wally and Gordie Tibbits, and Clayton Ihrke. [Larry Burrows]

Louie Wilbrandt's Cadillac leads the caravan over the Illinois River bridge and into Morris. The players greeted the crowd from a flatbed truck in the background. [Larry Burrows]

Morris

Jim Bergin signs an autograph as teammates Clayton Ihrke, Jim Wilbrandt, Don Wilbrandt, and Bill Schulz look on. [Larry Burrows]

Fire engine sirens blare as the caravan enters the brick streets of Woodstock's Town Square. [Larry Burrows]

Woodstock

Bundled up against the cold, the players emerge into the waiting crowd. Behind the car are Phil Judson, Jim Bergin, Ken Spooner, Bill Thayer, Bill Schulz, Clayton Ihrke, Jim Wilbrandt, and Don Wilbrandt. [AP]

In the middle of Main Street, homebound Hebronites await the return of the triumphant team.

Hebron

The long line of cars pulls into Hebron for its final stop as the high school band plays in the foreground.
[Larry Burrows]

Fans surround the lead cars on Hebron's Main Street and raise the players to their shoulders one by one. Bill Schulz is in the air and Ken Spooner is about to get a lift. [Larry Burrows]

Hometown Heroes

Team members raise Russ Ahearn and Phil Hadley to their shoulders. The players are Bill Thayer, Ken Spooner, Paul Judson, Clayton Ihrke, Don Wilbrandt (wearing fireman's hat), and Jim Bergin. Bill Schulz peeks in from behind Hadley. [Don Peasley]

Back home at Ernie Heimann's Hebron Café, Russ Ahearn answers questions from radio reporter Fritz Sorenson. Billy Ahearn, on dad's shoulder, got to say a few words, too. [*Rockford Register-Republic*]

Feast

While Ernie Heimann chats with Phil Hadley, Russ Ahearn and Bill Thayer admire the championship trophy. In the background, two reporters phone in their stories. Visible at the table to the right of the trophy are Phil Judson, Bill Schulz, Louie Wilbrandt, Superintendent Paul Tigard, and Ken Spooner. [Larry Burrows]

The town honors the team at a banquet on the stage gym floor. [Don Peasley]

Tribute

Chicago reporters Tommy Kouzmanoff and John Carmichael stop for a pose with the Judson twins, Paul and Phil. [Don Peasley]

Phil Judson receives his letter from Russ Ahearn. [Don Peasley]

Hebron's tournament team poses with the trophies it won during the 1951-52 season. In front of Russ Ahearn is the regional tournament plaque that marked his most cherished victory. The mysterious seventh trophy, added for symmetry, is the team free-throw shooting award. Front row: Coach Russ Ahearn, Ken Spooner, Paul Judson, Bill Schulz, Phil Judson, Don Wilbrandt. Back row: Jim Bergin, Jim Wilbrandt, Joe Schmidt, Bill Thayer, Clayton Ihrke. [Don Peasley]

Hardware

Coach Russ Ahearn's daughter Judy and son Billy flank the six-man varsity squad and its trophies. The players are Ken Spooner, Bill Thayer (standing), Paul Judson, Bill Schulz, Phil Judson, and Don Wilbrandt. [Don Peasley]

The 25th anniversary reunion, held at the state tournament in Champaign-Urbana, came shortly after Russ Ahearn passed away. Front row, from left: Paul Judson, Bill Schulz, Phil Judson. Back row: Ken Spooner, Phil Hadley, Marie Ahearn, Don Wilbrandt. [Don Peasley]

Reunited

Coach Ray Meyer of DePaul University was a special guest at the dedication of the Hebron water tower in 1986. From left: Paul Judson, Ken Spooner, Phil Judson, Bill Schulz, Ray Meyer, Don Wilbrandt. [Don Peasley]

Cheerleaders joined team members at the 40th anniversary reunion in Hebron. Front row, from left: Photographer Don Peasley, Joan DeYoung Peterson, Helen Borgeson O'Dierno, Shirley Schroeder Ihrke, Judy VanderKarr Siwkowski. Back row: Clayton Ihrke, Ken Spooner, Paul Judson, Bill Schulz, Phil Judson, Don Wilbrandt. [Don Peasley]

Legacy

Hebron's starting five pose in the shadow of the water tower that commemorates their achievement. They lined up in the same order as always: Ken Spooner, Paul Judson, Bill Schulz, Phil Judson, and Don Wilbrandt. [Don Peasley]

chapter 12

Game of Games

Clyde McQueen and Russell Shields, dressed in gray pants and striped shirts, sprinted to their positions at the center of the floor. Both were experienced basketball officials. It was the first championship-game assignment for either man, although both had officiated at the state finals the year before. In their full-time professions, McQueen was dean of boys at Feitshans High School in Springfield and Shields worked as an undertaker in Greenfield.

The starters for both teams ambled to the center circle. For Hebron, of course, it was Bill Schulz, the Judsons, Don Wilbrandt, and Ken Spooner. There were no surprises in the Quincy lineup, either. George Latham sent out Bruce Brothers, Jack Gower, Charlie Fast, Dick Thompson, and Phil Harvey to meet the Hebron squad. The players shook hands all around before they took their places for the opening jump ball.

SORENSON: "We have one more game to go, and this is really the big one. At the end of this 32 minutes of basketball play, a new champion will be crowned."

Schulz won the tip, and true to form, Hebron immediately raced downcourt, where Wilbrandt took a long shot from the left side. He was fouled by Gower and made good on the free throw. Just ten seconds into the game, Hebron led, 1-0.

Quincy took the ball the other way, worked it around the perimeter, and found Bruce Brothers underneath, where he was fouled by Phil Judson. The score was tied 1-1.

Thus the pattern was established early. Hebron liked to race down the court and take the first available shot, attempting to catch Quincy before its defense was set up. Running up and down, they also hoped to tire the Blue Devils quickly. On its end of the court, Quincy tried to slow the game down, patiently working the ball around for a good shot, preferably a short one by Brothers.

Hebron had to be careful, of course, to keep its players out of foul trouble. Another episode like the one in the semifinal would almost certainly be fatal in the championship contest. Bill Thayer was available for relief, but he'd taken only one shot in three games. None of the other reserves had played at all except for a minute or so at the end of the Lawrenceville game.

All of this was standard procedure for Hebron, but barely a minute into the game, it happened again. Phil Judson leaned into Gower on a hook shot and was whistled for his second foul. He'd have to play cautiously now, and that was definitely not his style.

Baskets by Paul Judson and Spooner had pushed Hebron out to a 5-3 advantage when the big scoreboard on the wall malfunctioned. As Quincy's score inexplicably showed zero, the crowd hooted and cheered. The basketball gods seemed to be rooting against Quincy, too. After all, they were the Blue Devils.

But then the Quincy players, showing the savvy that had gotten them all the way to the championship game, slowly began to assert themselves. Fast scored twice, on a push shot and a rebounded miss, and Brothers, who shot his free throws underhanded, made a pair. Suddenly it was 10-6, Quincy.

Ahearn knew what the problems were — Hebron was making too many turnovers and Paul couldn't quite find his shot. But how to fix it?

Near the end of the quarter, the boys finally got loose on a fast break and then Wilbrandt scored on a rebound that wowed the crowd.

Paul followed seconds later with his second basket, a jumper from the right side. The quarter ended with Quincy in front by only two, 16-14.

PHILBIN: "Here's a telegram from Frank Rogers, who went to Hebron High School and graduated in 1908. What do you know about that? Frank Rogers, pulling for Hebron, went to Hebron in 1908 — well, Frank, we sincerely trust they come through."

As the second quarter opened, it began to look like Quincy might run away with it. Quincy's Dick Thompson made a pair of jump shots to get things started. Moments later, Phil Judson, playing aggressively as usual, was called for another charge. With three fouls, he was now in real trouble. But with Hebron six points behind, Ahearn left him in the ballgame anyway.

Schulz responded with a pivot shot, his second basket of the game. Then Gower tried a shot that Phil Judson knocked out of bounds. The official at first signaled for the ball to go to Hebron, but suddenly reversed his decision and gave the ball to Quincy instead. Hebron, already setting up an out-of-bounds play, was caught off guard, allowing Brothers to score an easy basket that put his team up by seven points, 23-16.

Things were threatening to get out of hand when suddenly Schulz caught fire for Hebron. He banked in an angle shot for one basket and rebounded a Wilbrandt miss for another. Bruce Brothers, All-Stater or not, still gave up five or six inches in height and was having trouble containing Schulz and his tricky left-handed pivot shot.

The rest of the Quincy team, however, picked up the pace. Gower hit a couple of jump shots and Phil Harvey sank a set shot from long distance. Just as quickly as Quincy had lost its seven-point lead, the Blue Devils regained it at 33-26.

SORENSON: "Quincy is just hitting those shots right and left. They're hitting jump shots from the corners very well. When you're hot you really begin to roar, and Quincy's Blue Devils look like champions."

Ahearn called a timeout. There were less than three minutes left in the half — enough time to make up the deficit before the break, or enough time to fall so far behind that a comeback would be difficult. He told his boys they had to slow down the Quincy shooters. In addition, Hebron needed to squeeze some more offense out of someone besides Schulz, who already had 10 points. No one else had more than five.

Bill Schulz's dominating play was something of a surprise. Schulz was carrying his team, when most fans had assumed he would be easy pickings for the highly touted Brothers. The Quincy center was having a good game on the offensive end of the floor and led all scorers with 13 points, but he could not seem to keep the ball out of Schulz's hands. Brothers fronted the big center whenever he could, but the Hebron players simply lobbed it over Brothers' outstretched hands. Worse still, Brothers had fouled twice while trying to stop drives by Spooner and Phil Judson.

The teams broke from their huddles. Schulz scored again a short time later, on another looping pass from Phil Judson. After Brothers made a basket from the free throw line, Phil scored from the side. Then Paul faked his man into the air and hit a jumper before time ran out. The first half ended with Quincy ahead by one, 35-34.

Both teams had enjoyed a hot-shooting first half, but Brothers was hottest of all with 15 points. Quincy had made 14 of 29 field goals, while Hebron had shot 14 of 30.

So far, it was the closely-contested, back-and-forth game that everyone anticipated. And more.

Tuning In

Back home, Hebron was practically a ghost town. Just about everyone who wasn't required for some essential service had traveled to Champaign.

Those who remained — the policeman, the volunteer firemen, the hostess at the tavern — stayed glued to a fuzzy television screen or tuned in a radio broadcast, or both. Only a few Hebron workers, such as the town's telephone operator, were shut out altogether.

Two television stations, one in Chicago and one in Rock Island, carried the broadcast, which was visible throughout the northern third of the state. Even as far south as Champaign-Urbana, it was possible, on a good night when atmospheric conditions were right, to adjust a set's rabbit ears to tune in the ghostly image of WENR from Chicago.

But it was not a good night in Champaign-Urbana, and those fans who huddled around the few television sets in town saw a whole lot of snow.

In Hebron, reception was much better, for which everyone was thankful. A number of northern Illinois basketball fans, their interest piqued by the Hebron story, had flocked to stores to buy their first TV sets. Few of them had witnessed a state tournament, and now they could watch the whole thing, from tip-off to the final gun, right in their living rooms.

A Superhuman Game

Ahearn brought his team back to the floor and into the huddle for the second half. He made a last pass over the notes he'd dictated to Hadley in the first half, and then reminded the team of the things he'd been telling them since the beginning: Keep calm, cool and poised. Run them ragged. And play a superhuman game.

The lights dimmed once more, and the game was in motion.

> DREES: *"Sixteen minutes to go, sixteen minutes to determine which of these splendid teams will know the joy of championship and which will know the heartbreak of defeat. And, brother, that heartbreak is very real here for the team that can't go home with the bacon."*

Charlie Fast and Don Wilbrandt traded baskets to start the third quarter. A minute later, Brothers lost the ball to Wilbrandt and then fouled him trying to get it back. Now both teams had a star with three fouls — Brothers and Phil Judson — and things were getting tense. Schulz scored after rebounding a miss by Wilbrandt, and Hebron led for the first time since the early going, 38-37.

Schulz made another bucket, but baskets by Gower and Brothers put Quincy back ahead. No one but Schulz seemed to be connecting for Hebron in the second half. Thank goodness he was open and hitting his shots.

Paul Judson brought the ball down and set up the play for Hebron in the forecourt. Brothers was fronting Schulz again, and the big man stepped toward the basket just as Judson looped a rainbow his way. Schulz made the easy lay-up and the Green Giants were on top by a point once more.

HEARN: "Beautiful pass, Jack."

DREES: "Yes, sir, that was right on the mark, just out of the reach of Bruce Brothers, who is a pretty tall man himself. That makes the score 42-41, in favor of HEB-ron."

But the lead did not last long, mostly because Quincy was racking up points at the free throw line. Even after Spooner dropped in one of his patented rainbow shots from the left side and Schulz scored on another tip-in, Quincy still held a two-point lead with half a minute to go in the third quarter.

The Judson twins got to work. Rebounding a Quincy miss, Judson steamed down the length of the court and tried to force a pass inside to brother Phil. Thompson deflected it into the air and Phil grabbed the ball, immediately twisting to put up a shot. Brothers went up to block and caught the ball squarely, but he came down with a foul — his fourth. The Quincy crowd stood and booed. Paul realized the implication immediately and whispered to his teammates that Brothers was sitting on four fouls. For the first time, Tom Payne, a lithe sophomore, entered the game for Quincy, replacing Brothers. After Phil made the free throws, the quarter ended, all tied up at 48.

Early Exit

One quarter was all that remained to decide the championship of the state of Illinois, and it was still a stalemate.

As Quincy continued searching for a way to stop Bill Schulz, Hebron had figured out that the way to neutralize Bruce Brothers was to put him on the bench. Ahearn knew that it would be rough sailing for Quincy without Brothers on the floor. He told his team to attack on the inside against the inexperienced Payne, and against Brothers when he returned, in hopes of fouling him out of the game.

Smelling blood, Hebron went to work. Wilbrandt quickly scored on a rebound after a Schulz miss to make it 50-48. At the offensive end Quincy missed Brothers badly, misfiring on three shots in a row. The All-Stater had 18 points in the game but was burning time on the pine as Hebron started to pull away.

Judson's basket forced George Latham's hand. With a little more than six minutes to go in the championship game, the last game of Bruce Brothers' high school career, the All-State center was not doing his team any good on the bench. It was do or die. Latham put his star back in the lineup and hoped for the best.

Latham sent in a play as well. When the game resumed, Phil Harvey dribbled across the timeline, and at the moment when Brothers moved up from the low post to the middle of the free throw lane, Harvey lobbed him a pass. Brothers took the pass and faked Schulz into the air, letting go with a turnaround jump shot that swished. Schulz shook his head, disgusted with himself. Only two points separated the teams once again. Clearly Brothers hadn't grown cold during his forced rest.

After Phil Judson and Brothers traded misses from long range, Hebron had the ball again. Phil tried to drive on the left side against Payne, then stopped and threw back to Paul, who set up past the free throw line with his back to the basket. Harvey and Thompson, in a zone defense, both jumped forward to meet Paul and then simultaneously backed off. Paul sensed an opening. He wheeled around and threw in a push shot that swished. Just like that, Hebron was up by four again.

Quincy's players looked to Brothers to get them out of their predicament. Running the offense, Harvey tried the same play that had worked a few moments earlier, but this time his pass to Brothers was a little high. Schulz reached over his head and tapped it away.

On the next play, Paul Judson made one of two free throws, and with the score now 55-50, Hebron was on the verge of breaking the game open. Latham called another timeout.

> PHILBIN: "Well, it's a championship play if there ever was one. Quincy, of course, a little bit the favorites, maybe, down around this neck of the woods, but up north they're pulling for those Green Giants from Hebron. They'll be the only team, only Little David ever to win this coveted Sweet Sixteen crown. Brother, if they do, they'll blow the lid off the northern part of Illinois tomorrow."

Quincy ran its play, but Fast missed the short shot. The Blue Devils couldn't afford too many more misses. The game was slipping away.

Paul Judson brought the ball across the timeline and flipped it to brother Phil near midcourt. As Phil surveyed the court, Wilbrandt cut across the lane and ended up in the right corner, undefended, behind a screen set by Schulz. Phil made a quick chest pass to Wilbrandt, who drove the base line and went up for a lay-up. Brothers slid over from the lane to help out, leapt high, and stopped the ball at the top of Wilbrandt's shot. Both Wilbrandt and the ball crashed to the floor.

Russell Shields blew hard on his whistle and pointed at Brothers.

The crowd fell silent for an instant. Then, as people began to realize what had just happened, there was a scatter of nervous cheers. Brothers stared straight forward in disbelief. He looked as if he might say a few words to Shields. But the Hebron players were already coming over to shake hands with him, starting with Phil and Paul Judson. Quincy's star center had no choice but to back away gracefully, aware only now that he would watch the rest of the game as a spectator.

A few Hebron players celebrated, raising their fists in the air. With Brothers out, it seemed next to impossible for Quincy to make up the five-point deficit. Wilbrandt missed the first free throw but made the second. Hebron led 56-50 with four and a half minutes to play.

But Hebron's celebration was premature. Even with Brothers gone, Quincy refused to give up. First Dick Thompson scored for the Blue Devils on a pair of free throws. Then Hebron turned the ball over, missed a short shot, and turned the ball over again, this time on a full-court pass that sent Spooner hurtling over the line of photographers at the end of the floor. They were getting careless. Ahearn called a time-out and calmly reminded the players to settle down and stick with their game plan.

After Quincy brought the ball down, Charlie Fast missed a short shot from the left side, and Wilbrandt was immediately whistled for reaching in. Surprised at the call, he lobbed the ball underhanded into the air, aimed at no one in particular. But Fast had already stepped to the free throw line and the ball came down squarely on the top of his head. He glowered at Wilbrandt for a moment, regaining his composure quickly enough to make the second of his two free throws.

Quincy had pulled back to within three.

Three minutes to play, and Ahearn had his team take some time off the clock by running a weave play. But after a few passes, Thompson knocked the ball away from Wilbrandt, and Payne got into the scorebook at the other end with a crucial turnaround jump shot. Quincy had scored five points in a row. Hebron's lead had shrunk to 56-55.

The Green Giants stayed with their weave, patiently trying to run some time off the clock and at the same time poke holes in the Quincy zone. Phil Judson got the ball on the left side of the lane and drove to the right corner, taking Fast with him. He passed back out to Paul, who found Schulz all alone for an easy basket.

Payne missed a long jumper. Paul Judson traveled on a drive. Fast missed a side shot, then Harvey, then Fast. The teams were trading sloppy punches like two heavy-armed boxers in the fifteenth round.

With little more than a minute to go, Harvey found Gower open for an untouched drive to the left side of the hoop. Quincy was back to within one.

Hebron fought the ball over the timeline against Quincy's tenacious press. Wilbrandt took a pass in the forecourt and pivoted, backing into Jack Gower as he did. The whistle blew — an offensive foul on Wilbrandt. When Gower went to the line, he had a chance to tie the game at 58-all. The big forward stepped to the free throw line, dribbled the ball a couple of times, eyed the basket intently, and swished the shot. In a span of four minutes, Quincy had made it back from a six-point deficit, without its All-State center.

The face of the scoreboard clock glowed red, indicating there was less than a minute to play. The momentum was completely in Quincy's favor.

> DREES: *"From this point on I don't know how well you'll hear me, but we'll do the best we can."*

Fans stood, screaming and shouting, as Paul Judson brought the ball up the right side of the court, deep into Quincy territory. He crossed over on his dribble, and in an instant Harvey tapped the ball loose, sending Paul and Dick Thompson scrambling to the floor. A whistle blew, and the officials signaled a jump ball. Thompson won the jump, and suddenly, despite its handicap, Quincy had a chance to win the game.

The Blue Devils brought the ball into the front court and waited, looking for options. Harvey made a tentative drive, then pulled back out, giving the ball to Payne, who flipped it to Thompson. The junior guard drove right again, rose and launched a running 20-foot jumper that clanked off the iron and lurched toward the baseline. Gower flew out of bounds trying to save the ball, falling in a heap on the floor underneath the basket.

Jack Gower didn't get up. The crowd stood on its toes and strained for a view of the injured man. The other players paced nervously, waiting for the circle of officials to break up around Gower. He lay on the ground for almost two minutes while the team trainer gave him smelling salts and mopped up some blood with a towel. Finally, after some prodding, Gower rose slowly, motioned that he was all right, and walked toward the bench.

Sixteen seconds still showed on the clock. George Latham called his last timeout.

CORRAY: "If I recall the play clearly, it's going to be Quincy's ball out of bounds. Let's wait and see. I've forgotten now."

SORENSON: "I think it's going to be Gower at the line, although I'm not sure. It may be an out-of-bounds play. If it's a foul, there may very well be your ball game. No, it's an out-of-bounds play, and Quincy has the ball."

The teams broke from their huddles. Latham had sent in a special play, hoping to break the 58-58 tie. An out-of-bounds play at the offensive basket was an opportunity not to be missed, especially when there were only a few seconds left in the game. The *championship* game.

Dick Thompson took the ball for the throw-in underneath the basket. The Quincy players set up in a straight line across the free throw lane, then broke from their positions, pulling their defenders with them. Thompson looked for his options. There was no one open under the basket.

The official ticked off the seconds left on the throw-in. Payne had floated all the way over to the sideline and finally Thompson spotted him. As the count reached three, Thompson shot a pass over Wilbrandt's outstretched arms in Payne's direction. The sophomore got a hand on it, but he was off-balance, and the ball bounced on the sideline near the Hebron bench. The whistle blew — Hebron's ball!

Now all the Hebron fans jumped to their feet. Ten seconds to go. Wilbrandt drove deep down the right side, looking for an opening, but Harvey cut him off. He passed back out to Paul Judson at the right side of the key, catching Thompson out of position. While the defender scrambled, Paul had an open shot. He considered taking it, but hesitated an instant too long. Instead he tried to lob to Schulz, but Fast reached in and knocked the ball away. Payne grabbed it in the lane and rifled a pass ahead to Gower, already sprinting downcourt with a full head of steam. Schulz and Paul Judson raced furiously to block his path. Gower was headed straight for the hoop.

Three! Two! One! Gower never looked up as he tore down the floor, dribbling as he ran. He passed the top of the key, overtook the free throw line, and then... *Rrrrrrn*...the horn sounded just as Gower dribbled the ball off Schulz's foot, ten feet from the basket.

They were out of time, and the score was tied 58-58.

Overtime!

The fans gasped for breath. Overtime? After the roller coaster ride they'd just endured, they didn't know whether to be thrilled their teams were still alive, frantic at the prospect of facing more of this, or just plain exhausted. No wonder they called it "March Madness."

Unfortunately, the break in the action came too late for two Hebron spectators. During the intense fourth quarter, Ruby Boelter, a Hebron High School student, had fallen down a flight of stairs and injured her elbow. She had to be taken to the hospital.

John Lopeman, son of superfan Ken Lopeman, also succumbed to the excitement. Like many Hebron fans, John had driven back and forth to Champaign each day and was tired from the exhausting grind. He'd eaten a big steak, too, just before coming to the game. The narrow seats at Huff Gym proved to be the last straw. Packed in shoulder to shoulder in a sea of humanity, he was finally overcome by the heat. Medical personnel dragged John, so stiff he could barely bend his legs, out of the stands and down into the musty basement of Huff Gym, where a doctor kept an eye on him. The end of regulation time found John and his father, Hebron's biggest fans, out of the action for the first time all season, listening to the roar of the crowd above and wondering what it might mean.

Al Willis, executive secretary of the IHSA, found himself in a similar predicament. With about a minute to play, he had taken the huge first-place trophy down to the locker room for the presentation. Now he waited, alone, surprised that neither team had shown up. Afraid to leave the trophy unattended and not wanting to lug it any further, Willis decided to remain in the locker room for the duration. It would be a long wait.

Back upstairs, the fans fidgeted in their seats, tried to remember to breathe, and prepared for the exciting conclusion.

It was overtime — the first ever in an Illinois high school state championship game.

Overtime

It was the first overtime Ahearn had ever coached in a varsity game and the first for the players, too. The coach reminded them that the game was still basketball, and it was played exactly the same way they'd been playing it all season. Despite Quincy's comeback, Ahearn knew Hebron still held a huge advantage with Brothers out of the game. He told his team to be patient, look inside, and attack the boards. The overtime was three minutes long. There was no need to rush things.

Schulz again controlled the tip, giving Hebron the chance to work the ball down into the corner and then back out. Standing near the top of the key, Wilbrandt paused for a second, noting that Schulz had gained position on Fast, who was making a futile attempt to front him. He lofted a strike to the big man. Schulz gathered the ball in, took a short left-handed jumper, and then watched as it rolled around the hoop and in.

Hebron 60, Quincy 58. The Green Giants were back on top.

After Thompson missed a long shot for Quincy, back came Hebron, taking its time, passing back and forth at the top of the key, looking for an opening. Wilbrandt drove down low and found a crack in the Quincy zone. He tossed the ball out to Paul Judson, who snapped a return pass to Phil, standing alone under the basket. Hebron was up by four, with 1:45 to play.

On the Quincy side, desperation began to set in. Thompson dribbled downcourt and launched a wild pass over Fast's head that sailed past the endline.

Hebron was in control now. Paul Judson raced toward the basket and passed back into the lane to Wilbrandt, who was immediately fouled by Gower. Before moving to the line, Wilbrandt pulled Paul aside and asked if he should try to bounce the ball off the rim to Schulz, who was stationed in the first position at the right side of the lane. Judson shook his head. There was no need for a trick play when Hebron was four points ahead. He told Wilbrandt to make the free throw, and when it swished, Hebron led by five, 63-58. A minute and a half remained.

Quincy missed a couple of shots, but gained some hope when Phil Harvey was fouled by Paul Judson. Harvey made the free throw. The clock was under a minute now, but Quincy had pulled back within four.

The Blue Devils had to foul to get the ball back, and they picked on Schulz in the backcourt. The big man missed his free throw, and Quincy stormed down the court. Thompson was forced to shoot first and worry about high percentage shots later. He put up a long miss from the left side and Bill Schulz corralled the rebound. Schulz got the ball away to Phil Judson, who was fouled in the backcourt with thirty seconds left.

Phil made his free throw. Hebron led, 64-59, and the Hebron crowd was on its feet once more, sensing that victory was only a heartbeat away. When Quincy missed two more shots, Hebron came away with the ball. Paul Judson dribbled back into the corner, and with time running out, Harvey had no choice but to foul him. Just five seconds remained on the clock. Paul moved toward the free throw line, and for the first time in the tournament, he cracked a smile on the court.

The roar from the Hebron crowd reached a crescendo as Paul raised his hands into the air and shook a fist back at the Hebron bench.

CORRAY: "Paul Judson, shaking his hands high over his head to the crowd — 'We're in! We're in!' He's so excited now he can hardly contain himself, as he stands at the free throw line, and I don't blame the boy."

As he danced nervously at the line, Paul Judson couldn't have made the free throw if he'd been shooting a marble into a swimming pool. The ball clanked off the rim and bounced back to the floor, where Paul recovered the rebound, missing a driving lay-up just as the timekeeper fired his gun.

This was it! *This* was what everyone had come to see.

The scoreboard said it all: Hebron 64, Quincy 59. The Green Giants had won the state championship!

As the roar of the crowd engulfed them, the Hebron players leapt in the air — the Judson twins, Wilbrandt, Schulz, and Spooner — followed across the court by Don Peasley and his camera, as a cascade of Hebron fans tumbled out of the stands. Diminutive Russ Ahearn was swallowed up by the crowd and disappeared from sight. Louie Wilbrandt fought his way out of the bleachers and pushed past a burly usher, bouncing up and down, looking for Don and Jim. Helen Schulz rested her head on her husband's shoulder and cried tears of joy. Then she and Fred and the rest of the parents carefully made their way to the floor, beaming with pride, eager to embrace their sons.

There were hugs and backslaps all around. The cheerleaders raced into the melee and kissed the players one by one, as the announcers scrambled to find someone, anyone, to interview.

HILL: All right, down here in the middle of the floor, everything is pandemonium as Hebron wins the state championship.

PHIL JUDSON: That's right!

HILL: Where'd the coach go? Anybody find the coach? Where's the coach? ... Coach Ahearn, how's it feel to have your team be state champions?

AHEARN: Aw, it's wonderful. Quincy has a great ballclub. We just got the breaks tonight and it's our night, I guess, to win.

Someone in the crowd shouted Bill Schulz's name, and a cluster of Hebron fans rushed to surround him. Slowly and somewhat awkwardly, they hoisted the tallest Green Giant onto their shoulders. His 24 points in the championship game — 11 more than Paul Judson, Hebron's next highest scorer — had saved the day for his team. Not a bad game against the state's premier center. Not bad for a boy who'd never seen a basketball game until four years before, who'd started for the varsity for just four short months.

The fans released Schulz as they latched onto a more convenient victim. This time, they took the little Irishman, Russ Ahearn, and tossed him lightly up above the crowd. He locked his hands above his head in a victory embrace and then blew a kiss to his wife. His never-failing belief that Hebron could win, even against the longest of odds, had ended in triumph and vindication.

One by one the other players were lofted into the air. The fans would not let them out of their grasp, not even to attend the trophy presentation.

Some of the team members surged toward the end of the court shouting, "We want the net!" Policemen held them back until someone finally produced a ladder and cut the nets down.

After the commotion on the floor had finally subsided and the players retreated to the locker room, Louie Wilbrandt ran out into the concourse and found an open pay phone. When he reached Western Union, Wilbrandt dictated his final telegram to Howie Judson: "WE WON, SIXTY-EIGHT SIXTY-THREE IN OVERTIME. THEY'RE ALL DROPPING OVER."

It didn't matter that he'd misremembered the final score. By the time the telegram was delivered to the Green Hotel in Pasadena, Howie had already received a long-distance call from Martha Strebe, his girlfriend back home in Chicago, who'd been watching the game on television. All through the night, the news-starved major leaguer celebrated, sharing the victory with anyone who cared to hear about it.

Impromptu

Meanwhile, there was plenty of celebration back in Hebron.

The lone telephone operator, Myra Vanderpal, had been tied to her switchboard all night, but she ended up getting a second-hand account of the final minutes, anyway. A reporter at the *Champaign News-Gazette* called her with a minute remaining in regulation time to get the reaction back on the home front, but ended up feeding her a play-by-play account of the final moments.

When Paul Judson got the final rebound and the gun sounded to end the game, Myra whooped out loud. "You ought to see my switchboard now!" she cried. "It's lit up like a Christmas tree. We won! Gotta go now!"

Before she picked up the calls, she blew the fire whistle — against the advice of Hebron's fire chief, William Perry — and the engine, manned by a couple of volunteers, rumbled out of the station, driving slowly around the six or seven streets of Hebron at the head of an impromptu parade. It was going on eleven o'clock, but no one in town was sleeping. Residents who had been unable to make the trip fell into line behind the blaring engine, soon to be joined by cars from the neighboring towns of Alden, Harvard, Richmond, and Woodstock, as well as Lake Geneva, Wisconsin, who came to share in Hebron's biggest moment.

Afterglow

When midnight fell in Champaign, there was no sleeping in the tournament district. The Inman Hotel was the center of the action, but basketball fans filled the lobbies and restaurants and taverns all around town with tournament talk. They recounted again and again the story of the heroic struggle of the "Little David" team that had fought against incredible odds and won. They were all hoping for a barnburner, an epic game, and that was what they got, overtime and all.

Out in the crowd somewhere, the Hebron players made their way from station to station, receiving congratulations from old friends and strangers in equal measure.

Russ Ahearn relaxed in his room at the Hamilton Hotel, where he gave a reporter from his hometown newspaper, the *Streator Times-Press*, the inside scoop on the biggest sports story of the year.

"Give my boys the credit," the coach began. "They were absolutely great. These kids came down here with only one purpose in mind

— to win this title — and they achieved their goal, one we had our minds on since the season started."

He ran a hand over his forehead, still not quite believing it was over. "I knew we had the ability to win here. I predicted it after the 1950-51 season and I never once changed my mind. These boys united into a team that wouldn't be beaten. They obeyed instructions to the letter and pulled together all the way. This surely paid off today when we beat two great teams within a period of six or seven hours."

The reporter asked him if he'd changed his team's style of play for the Quincy game.

"Not too much," he mused, "although I did instruct our guards, Paul Judson and Ken Spooner, to feed it in to the Tower more than in previous games. I had a feeling Schulz would be on, and he had to be for us to win. He never let us down, did he?"

A cheer rose up from the crowd in the streets below, where a snake dance had broken out.

"I'll bet Schulz is the cheerleader down there," he said with a laugh. "I'm going to let them have fun tonight. They earned it after all the pressure that's been on them since the tournaments started. They have to relax now. Tomorrow, we head home for the big celebration."

As Coach Ahearn continued his interviews, the players made the rounds of the hotels and restaurants. At one establishment they ran into Bill Veeck, the owner of the St. Louis Browns, who'd been in the stands for the championship contest. The players were surprised to find a celebrity in town, but Veeck impressed them with his down-home manner.

"This proves there's still hope for the Browns," he joked.

Veeck told the Judson twins he'd give their regards to Howie the next time they met in St. Louis. And then the players moved on to the next stop.

Bill Schulz, used to keeping dairyman's hours, soon grew tired and headed for bed, but the party continued on through the night without him.

Back at the hotel, the tournament itself had already provided enough excitement for another member of Hebron's winning team.

"It's all over but the shouting and there's plenty of that going on," wrote Doc Tobison, making the final entry in his tournament diary. "It looks like everyone is celebrating except me. I guess the game was too much for me. I dare say those that attended that last game will never forget it."

Then he wrote his final thought on the Green Giants' trip to the top. "This has been the most interesting and exciting week in my life."

Green Giants Become Team of Destiny

by Don Peasley

Community News

Hebron's Green Giants kept their rendezvous with destiny last week and are kings of all they survey.

Move over, Andy Phillip, in the IHSA tourney hall of fame. Paul Judson, Hebron's quarterback and guiding force, is stepping in beside you. So also is twin brother Phil, the rebounding demon and scoring ace whose play causes fans to debate which Judson is better. (We can answer that one — they are both equally great and have indelibly carved their names in the high school Hall of Fame.)

And you, too, Max Hooper and Dike Eddleman — step aside to make room for Bill Schulz, the 6-11 Green Giant whose exploits when scoring punch was most needed are now inscribed in what is called "the greatest state cage tourney final of all time."

Move over far enough, you all-time heroes, for you must also make a place for Don Wilbrandt and Ken Spooner — the duo whose sniping from far out and close in repeatedly kept the Giants in important battles (Elgin, Champaign, Rock Island, and the big one — Quincy), when the remaining trio of this team of destiny was stymied.

And don't forget Coach Russ Ahearn. Whenever stories of state tournament play are written, henceforth they will always include "Duke." Ahearn's insistence on meticulous coaching detail pays off. His famous notebook, which Asst. Coach Phil Hadley kept during those tourney games, no longer is a joke with those who used to needle Ahearn with cracks about it. The Green Giants reflect Ahearn. You see in them the will to win, the result of his perfectionist technique, the cool confidence that, well, after all, "You are *the Green Giants*. Remember that."

"Who's going to keep those Green Giants down?" the cheerleaders asked, and the crowd roared back, "Nobody! Nobody! Nobody!"

Hebron reigns supreme!

chapter 13

Celebration

It was five o'clock in the morning before the revelry ceased and the players finally rested.

By then, the ink was already dry on Sunday morning editions across the state. Hebron's triumph was front-page news just about everywhere. The *Champaign News-Gazette* trumpeted the Hebron story with a banner headline at the top of page one that read: "HEBRON GIANTS REIGN SUPREME." And what of the University of Illinois' bid for a berth in the Final Four? Fans looking for that result had to search for a small teaser, buried halfway down the Hebron article, that read, "ILLINI WIN! (DETAILS IN SPORTS SECTION.)" Their six-point victory seemed almost an afterthought.

Page after page across the state sang the praises of Hebron's Green Giants. The doubters and the naysayers had been silenced once and for all. There was no more disputing whether Russ Ahearn's team had the talent or tenacity to win the state title. Now the Green Giants' achievement was a matter of record.

Almost every sportswriter hammered out a lead that touched on the historic nature of Hebron's championship. Bob Novak of the

Urbana Courier was perhaps the most succinct when he wrote, "For the first time, a Lil' David is king of Illinois high school basketball."

Jerome Holtzman of the *Chicago Sun-Times*, who had followed the team for the better part of two seasons, reflected on the trials and tribulations along the road to basketball immortality. "Hebron's fabulous Green Giants," he wrote, "dreaming a wonderful dream for four long years, can't be blamed if they pinch themselves in disbelief. The dream has come true."

But it was Jack Prowell, the basketball maven of the *News-Gazette*, who summed up the events of the weekend, and perhaps of the whole basketball season, most poignantly:

> *The 1952 state high school basketball championship belongs to Hebron as it never belonged to another team in history. When memories of other state championships have long been forgotten, the fans will remember Hebron, for Hebron and its David and Goliath story belong to every basketball fan everywhere.*
>
> *If ever a blow were struck to keep the present tournament structure and keep it from being changed to a division of classes for small and large schools, Hebron did it Saturday night.*
>
> *Hebron is the champion of the small towns. It has set an example for the Homers, St. Joes, Fishers, Carrier Mills, and other small towns around the state. There is hope now. Hebron proved it.*

Waxing Philosophic

As the team roused itself for the long trip home, Russ Ahearn still couldn't pull himself away from the reporters. He spent some time in the hotel lobby recounting the events of the weekend with T.O. White of the *Champaign News-Gazette*, who asked him how he felt, ten hours later, about winning the state title.

"It was a matter of a team setting a goal and achieving it," Ahearn said. "And since we had the best team there is nothing remarkable in our victory. I am most proud of our team for its ability to withstand pressure.

"Some people made a point of the Judson twins not smiling — in fact, you did," he told the reporter. "They are happy kids but down here they had a job to do and were serious about it. Maybe you expected them to whistle while they worked."

Cracking a smile, he added, "Seriously, I find a lot of personal satisfaction out of coaching a championship team. I'm repaying some debts, to John Krafft of Elgin, for example, who taught me a lot about coaching when I was his assistant.

"Then I was able to provide tournament seats for our games for Chuck and Bob Hall of Normal. Before I started to Normal, my father and sister died and I was almost without friends or money. The Halls took me in, I worked at their candy store, and they put me through school. I was so glad to have the opportunity to make them proud of what I've accomplished."

When White asked about the inevitable rumors that he might leave Hebron, the coach answered, "My whole life, right now, is at Hebron. I like it there and I don't want anyone to think you have to win a state title to be a successful coach."

Now Russ Ahearn waxed philosophic. "In fact, you can be a good coach and not get to the finals, ever. I like to believe our boys will be better men because they have played high school basketball. Outstanding success such as we have had is fine, but it isn't a necessary adjunct to the aims of coaching.

"It is all right for losing coaches to talk about 'building character' and no doubt they do it. But it would certainly be a shame if the winning coaches didn't also build character. I think we have at Hebron and my experience is most coaches are doing the same. If they aren't, they'd better get out of the business."

White asked the Hebron coach if he'd prefer some relaxation instead of the celebration that loomed ahead.

"Assuredly not," Ahearn replied. "The post-tournament celebration is as much a part of success as the games we played and the preparation we made for them. I assure you we would all be disappointed without the hustle and bustle and the honors which people will bestow on the boys."

The Caravan

There seemed to be little that could outdo the events of Saturday night, but Russ Ahearn had big plans. A 180-mile return trip remained, and he was determined to make it as memorable as possible. Radio announcers had been getting the word out since the middle of the championship game that the Green Giant caravan would travel north from Champaign on Route 47, headed straight for town. At the Kane County line, a full sixty miles from Hebron, police would meet the group to escort them the rest of the way. The police would also communicate the progress of the procession so that it could be announced to the public on the radio.

The caravan, some thirty cars in all, got a late start — no doubt due to the late bedtimes of some of the players — and pulled out of downtown Champaign at about eleven o'clock. Louie Wilbrandt led the way in his Cadillac. Russ Ahearn drove the car right behind, accompanied by his wife, Marie, Fritz Sorenson, the radio man, and Larry Burrows, the *LIFE* photographer, who'd gotten the story he came for. The trailing cars included those members of the Hebron crowd who had not already left to make the morning milking, and a bevy of journalists, from local newspapers to big-city dailies.

From Champaign to Mahomet and on to the north, the cars flew past the unplowed fields of central Illinois, honking their horns at each farm family that waved from the porch. The caravan snarled traffic coming out of church in Gibson City and Forrest. The first large group of well-wishers met the team at Dwight. At Mazon, townsmen from Kinsman, Ahearn's birthplace, cheered from both sides of the road, shouting, "Duke, Duke!" at their old friend as the caravan passed.

The next stop was Morris, where Ahearn had once starred on the local semipro baseball team. Three fire trucks greeted the team, offering the players a ride down the main street on one of them. Friends and well-wishers flocked to the curbs to catch a glimpse of the team and shout their congratulations to Ahearn, the returning hero. The coach beamed as he signed autographs for children from a flatbed truck parked at the side of the road.

By Yorkville, the caravan had lengthened to about a hundred cars and traffic trying to cross Route 47 found it nearly impossible to make any progress. The state police met the procession north of town. Near Burlington, the entire group turned east toward Elgin.

Ahearn had planned a homecoming here, taking the parade right past his old house in the shadow of St. Edward's High School. From there, they proceeded across the Fox River and through downtown to Elgin High School, where hundreds of fans turned out to cheer the team. If the Elgin faithful harbored any hard feelings over losing to Hebron in the hard-fought regional final, they were nowhere to be seen. The Green Giants were the "People's Choice," and the citizens of the big city were eager to show their admiration for the new champions. A cluster of fans held up a huge painted sign that said, "ELGIN IS PROUD OF HEBRON."

The line picked up more cars and veered north again, entering Dundee, home of Hebron's other archrival. The caravan grew longer still as it snaked through the neighboring communities of Carpentersville and Algonquin, where a fire truck led the parade and Bill Schulz acquired the chief's hat, which he wore for the rest of the trip. Louie Wilbrandt, who'd grown up in Algonquin, stopped his car and handed out green and white ribbons to anyone who wanted to join the parade.

Onward the lengthening line crawled towards Crystal Lake, yet another of Hebron's vanquished foes. There, in the same place where the Green Giants had lost their only game of the season, a huge crowd greeted the team in the center of town. The caravan was only slightly delayed when Paul Judson, who was driving his brother Howie's car, turned his attention to the crowd for a moment and ran into the car in front of him, knocking off part of the grille.

The line of cars finally opened up a bit as it surged toward Woodstock, where 3,000 more fans awaited the procession in the brick-paved town square. The lead vehicles inched their way completely around the square, parting the sea of people with their bumpers, and then perhaps unwisely decided to make a second circuit. As the head of the caravan merged with cars from the middle of the pack, the whole line knotted into a mess that took over an hour to untie. In the general bedlam, the order of the lead cars became hopelessly confused. When the group finally untangled itself and set out down the eleven-mile homestretch to Hebron, Ahearn's car ended up well back in the pack.

As the head of the parade neared its destination, it slowed to a crawl. Automobiles of every make and model lined both sides of the road almost a mile from town. As the crowd milled slowly in the center of the street, the waters parted slightly, and the lead cars, honking wildly, rumbled to a halt right in the middle of the street under a banner that read "HAIL THE STATE CHAMPS." There the procession was immediately engulfed.

Flurries were falling and the wind was howling, but no one seemed to care. The Hebron High School brass band, decked out in their green caps and capes, struck up the school song. The assembled townspeople, reporters, well-wishers, and onlookers pressed forward as the coaches and players slowly emerged from the cars, a little dazed at what they saw.

"Lift them up! Let's see them!" shouted a dozen or so photographers from their vantage point atop Okeson's Hardware Store. One by one each player was raised to the shoulders of the crowd as flash bulbs popped. From behind the storefronts, a local man named William Cox set off blasts of gunpowder from a miniature cannon, shaking the entire town.

The crowd shouted for Ahearn to speak, and he moved to the microphone to address the crowd. But the public address system gave out, and the little coach mounted a car and shouted out his words instead.

"This is the realization of a dream that started four years ago," Ahearn told the Hebron faithful. "I can't believe it yet. It's simply a great thing to have all these people here to greet us. We are very proud."

When someone asked Mayor Mark Spooner, grandfather of Ken, if the team would get the key to the city, he replied there was no key to the city, but added, "The place is yours to do what you want with."

Then Ahearn gave the message that many students had been hoping to hear.

"As principal of Hebron High School," he said, "I hereby declare that there will be no classes on Monday."

As the crowd roared, a newspaper reporter caught up with Marie Ahearn. Through the years Marie had been a solid rock of support while Russ pursued his dream of coaching a championship team. With that goal reached, she had now a chance to reflect on the practical aspects of ending the season with a victory.

"Of course I am thrilled and happy that we won," she said, "but I am also happy to have my husband back. He's been missing, it seems, since the basketball season started."

The crowd swarmed around and around, overwhelming the normally sleepy streets of Hebron. On one bustling street corner, Paul Judson got caught in a wave and bumped into a reporter he recognized, Tommy Kouzmanoff of the *Chicago Herald-American*.

"You know, Mr. Kouzmanoff," said Judson, "there are a lot of people here today I never saw before."

Kouzmanoff thought for a moment and replied, "Paul, there are a lot of people here today you'll never see again."

Dinner at Ernie's

Finally the dignitaries ushered the team out of the milling crowd and into Ernie Heimann's Hebron Café, right on Main Street. The First National Bank of Woodstock had promised a steak dinner for the team, win or lose, and now Ahearn and his crew were ready to take the bank up on its offer. The whole Hebron entourage gathered in the single room. In the dim light they looked a little haggard from the events of the past few days. A few hangers-on stood in the background, watching the proceedings. Dolph Stanley, the Beloit College coach, was propped up against the wall, still hoping to snag the Judsons, or at least one of them, for his team.

As the team slowly gathered, Fritz Sorenson, the announcer from WKRS, moved forward to interview the team for his live radio audience. He pulled the coach aside and asked him about the police escort that had led the team on the second half of the journey home.

Russ Ahearn, a notoriously bad driver, couldn't help but smile. "It was about the first time I was ever glad to see a policeman," he said, bringing down the house.

Sorenson called the twins to the microphone and asked Paul Judson what was going through his head as he pumped his fist prior to the last free throw in the championship game.

"Well, I was looking at a pretty girl in the second row over there," he answered. The crowd laughed again.

On down the line Sorenson went, bringing the voices of the players into the homes of northern Illinois for the first time. He asked Don Wilbrandt how the team had developed its winning work ethic.

"We play during the summer," Wilbrandt said, "and we start practice early in the year. I think that's what helped us. We all get along, and with our fine team spirit and heart, and our desire to win, we will come through."

Ken Spooner showed the resolve of a true athlete, even when asked about breaking training after the championship game.

It wasn't a big deal, he said. "I enjoy the training and playing ball, so I'll train and play." And being only a junior, what were his plans for next season? "Train and play ball again."

As the players finished off their steaks and the reporters called in their copy, Larry Burrows, who'd pursued his story all the way into the restaurant, took one last photograph of the Hebron team.

Russ Ahearn was exhausted. He stared blankly into space while the rest of the party chatted on into the night. It was time to rest.

But there was very little rest to be had.

Hebron

By Dr. Martin T. Bergsjo
(writing as "The Heckler" in the *Harvard Herald*)

Let Milton sing of giants of old
That were ancient Hebron's right,
But give me those much younger giants
That beat Quincy Saturday night.

Green Giants they are, in modern garb,
The finest team in years.
If Dumas were alive today
He'd write, "Five Basketeers."

These Giants would not be appeased;
Their goal, if you would ask it,
Was victory in the "Sweet Sixteen."
Thru basket after basket.

Each opponent met in combat
Would give no quick retreat,
But when four quarters ended
It ended in their defeat.

And when the Game of Games was on,
On that fateful Saturday night,
It seemed the Hebron fans
Must surely die of fright.

But when the final gun went off
Their opponents all but cried.
Poor Quincy had a big sore throat
From swallowing their pride.

So hail the conquering heroes,
Those angels of the court,
The finest five alive today
In the Basket-balling sport.

With basket hoops for haloes,
The world is now their all.
No wonder that the world is shaped
Just like a basket ball.

chapter 14

Road Show

The 180-mile-long caravan home had not satisfied Hebron's legions of well-wishers. Towns not lucky enough to have been on the parade route clamored for a chance to congratulate the conquering heroes. The folks in Huntley, in particular, were disappointed that the caravan had detoured over to the Fox River towns and bypassed them completely.

And so on Monday, with school officially canceled by the principal, the entire student body of Alden-Hebron High School set off on a victory lap, the likes of which had never been seen in Illinois.

Crammed into seventeen cars, the students made a great loop around McHenry County, cruising past the high school campuses at Harvard, Marengo, Huntley, Woodstock, Crystal Lake, McHenry, and Richmond. They even crossed the state line to mingle with fans at Genoa City, Walworth, and Lake Geneva. At each high school building, students came outside to shout their pride in Hebron, the little school that represented the hopes and dreams of so many others. At McHenry, the entire group of travelers was pulled into an all-school assembly where the local students applauded their rivals for fifteen minutes.

That evening, Russ Ahearn took his team to a testimonial dinner in DeKalb, where basketball players from around that county turned out to show their appreciation for the new champions. Ahearn had barely slept since winning the title 48 hours earlier. But this was just the start of an extended road trip that would take him to all parts of Illinois and beyond.

By virtue of Hebron's sensational victory, the coach had risen to the top of the high school "knife-and-fork" circuit overnight. To handle all the requests for speaking engagements coming in, Ahearn could have used a booking agent, a chaffeur, and a valet. Some of the groups requested the whole team, while others wanted the coach by himself or with a player or two. All of them wanted a piece of Hebron. All of them got a piece of Russ Ahearn.

Within a week of winning the championship, the coach had already spoken in LaSalle, Savanna, Freeport, and Streator and was booked on practically every evening for the next month as well.

At every Lions and Elks Club hall, at every church banquet or supper club, Ahearn's future was the favorite topic of conversation. Rumors had him taking head coaching positions at any number of prestigious Illinois high schools, from his hometown of Streator to Batavia to East Aurora. There were even job offers from as far away as Colorado and Tennessee. The coach always said that his home and future were in Hebron, but he never officially said he was staying.

There was no end to the requests, and no saying no to them, either.

The four Hebron seniors — Paul Judson, Phil Judson, Don Wilbrandt, and Bill Thayer — even appeared as guests at the Champaign High School basketball banquet. It was Harold Jester's way of admitting he'd been wrong when he said Hebron wasn't the best in the state.

Twice the Hebron players were feted in the city of Chicago, first at the Bismarck Hotel and then at the Drake. At the latter occasion, kicking off Air Force Recruiting Week, the team got to meet Mayor Martin H. Kennelly himself. Bill Schulz, seated next to the mayor, managed to get into a predicament when he was confronted with an unfamiliar hard "bullet" roll. Trying to figure out how to open it up with his knife, he accidentally shot the unyielding bread directly into Kennelly's lap.

Kudos

Elsewhere in Hebron, life carried on. To no one's surprise, Paul and Phil Judson were selected as first-team All-State players by the *Champaign News-Gazette*, making the family the first in Illinois history with three brothers who'd received that honor. Bruce Brothers of Quincy made the team as well.

The only disappointment came at the newsstand. The townspeople eagerly awaited each new issue of *LIFE* magazine, but Larry Burrows' photo essay was never published. Burrows had become friends with Russ Ahearn, however, and sent copies of the best shots to the coach, who proudly displayed them in his office.

In the wake of the championship, the second busiest man in Hebron was the postmaster. Mail poured in from across the state and also from more remote outposts, from folks who'd watched the historic game on television or read about the remarkable champions in newspapers across the country.

The players received many letters, most of them from admiring high school girls who'd seen them on TV. The Judsons heard from several sets of twins. One girl even offered to drive to Hebron in her boyfriend's car to take her favorite player out on a date.

The starting five also sparked interest from many college coaches. Any coach worth his salt had heard about the Hebron team by now. Quite a few were eager to take a chance on the most famous high school players in the state, especially since the seniors, Paul, Phil, and Don, had not made any decision yet on where to enroll.

The mail brought Russ Ahearn hundreds of letters of congratulations from friends, relatives, former teachers and teammates, college roommates, and a slew of other admirers. He saved them all in a folder. But on the top of the stack, he kept the two letters that meant the most.

One was written on the stationery of the Santa Rita Hotel in Tucson, Arizona.

March 26, 1952

Dear Russ,

Just finished talking with Ken at home and it sure sounds like everyone is having a good time. I am sure happy for everyone and especially for you, Russ. There is no one who put in so much time and hard work on a club as you did on this one. You deserved all you are getting and a little more.

At times I second-guessed you, but believe me, it is much easier to sit out in the crowd and think what should be done than it is to sit on the bench and have to make the decisions right then. Anyway I want to tell you you did a great job and congratulations.

Your friend, Howie

The other letter, sitting on top, came from the athletic department of Elgin High School.

March 26, 1952

Dear Russ,

Congratulations again, and power to you. I waited to write since I know you were awfully busy at first. I dug out Saturday night at the end, in a hurry to get home. I was so weak from the poisoning I stayed in bed all day Sunday. Didn't know you were coming through Elgin or would have gotten up a couple hours for it.

The boys came through great and deserved everything. They were a nice bunch. You got one notch on me now, you know. That's swell, I am mighty glad for you. You worked hard for it.

Sincerely, John

He'd guided a team of teenagers to an accomplishment that many had deemed impossible. He'd earned fame within his chosen profession. He'd put his name in the record books for all time. But in the end, the blessing of his old friend and mentor, John A. Krafft, meant more than anything to Russ Ahearn.

The Missing Half

Two weeks after the unforgettable victory, the town of Hebron lauded its heroes with a banquet on the floor of the stage gym that had been the site of many of the team's exploits. Four hundred students, parents, and fans turned out, eager to show their appreciation and hear what sportswriters Jack Ryan, Bud Nangle, and John Carmichael of the *Chicago Daily News* and Tommy Kouzmanoff of the *Chicago Herald-American* had to say about Little Old Hebron and its famous team.

After their remarks, Wilbur Peak, a representative from Illinois Bell Telephone Company, took the podium to introduce a film of the championship game. The historic broadcast had been a great success, Peak related, based on the responses the TV crew received. About half the telegrams accused the announcers of favoring Quincy and about half thought they favored Hebron, so they must have been doing a good job. A small portion of the telegrams voiced displeasure that the announcing team never seemed to pronounce "Hebron" the same way twice, for which Peak apologized.

The biggest apology was still to come. Peak explained that the film was made using the kinescope technique, which involved pointing a movie camera at the live TV picture. As he now sheepishly revealed, something had gone wrong in the control room that night, and the first half was over before the technicians finally figured out what the problem was. Only the second half and the overtime were preserved on film. Peak thanked Don Wilbrandt for making the foul that allowed Quincy to tie the game and force the overtime period, giving him a little more to show.

The audience enjoyed the show, brief as it was, but the most important moment of the evening as far as they were concerned came when Coach Russ Ahearn took the podium. He was lavish in his praise, thanking the players, the parents, his coaches, the community, the managers, the cheerleaders, the sportswriters, and on down the line, elaborating on each group as he came to it.

Ahearn talked about the next year's schedule and team for a bit, and then, finally, he answered the question that had been on so many lips for the previous two weeks.

"Don't be surprised," he said, "if Russ Ahearn coaches the Green Giants next year."

The Price of Success

Ahearn had other irons in the fire as well.

He never slowed down anyway, but now was certainly not the time to start. There were many people knocking at his door, and the offer that seemed to suit him best was as an agent with the Franklin Life Insurance Company. Ahearn had always had to work a summer job to make ends meet. Now he'd never have to work at Auto-Lite again. He could use his contacts, his personality, and his newfound fame to move ahead in the business world.

Franklin Life recruited many coaches to become agents. Coaches networked for a living, with teachers, parents, players, and the community at large. Ahearn was as good at the game as anyone.

But fame, fortune, and success came at a cost. He was recognized everywhere he went, and everyone wanted to talk about Hebron's championship season. "Aren't you Russ Ahearn?" a stranger might inquire, and the conversation was off and running. The gregarious Irishman was always happy to relive the memories of 1952 in glorious detail.

For his family, the routine could sometimes grow old, especially when the questions interrupted a quiet dinner when there were family matters to discuss. It was unfortunate, but it seemed there was nothing else to do. The after-dinner speech he'd long since memorized, the evenings and weekends away from his family, the long hours behind the wheel — those were the price for getting ahead in the world.

The coach understood that the secret of Hebron's popularity wasn't just that the Green Giants were a great team; it was that they were a great team that thousands of fans had adopted as their own. Ahearn wasn't about to turn his back on a person or group of people who merely wanted to share a few thoughts about the fairy tale season and what it meant to them.

And it was never a one-way conversation. Ahearn had plenty to talk about, too, and it didn't end with winning the 1952 championship. He had plans, big plans for the future.

chapter 15

Back to Earth

Russ Ahearn had set a very high goal for himself and for his team. Against all odds, they'd achieved that goal. They'd won the state championship. But what could Coach Ahearn possibly do for an encore?

He thought he might have the answer. He'd become the first coach to lead a small school to two consecutive championships.

And who could blame him for his high hopes? With Bill Schulz and Ken Spooner back and a crop of capable reserves ready to move up into starting roles, anything seemed possible. Jim Wilbrandt and Clayton Ihrke, just juniors, were ready for starting roles, and Jim Bergin and Lynn Judson would compete for the fifth position. Of course, winning another championship was a long shot, but then so was all of 1952.

There was no letdown in the competition, as Ahearn strengthened Hebron's schedule yet again. Hebron was now a household name, and fans across the state and beyond were eager for a chance to see the unusual champions. The 1952-53 team played only four home games and didn't make its debut on the stage gym floor until January 10. The Green Giants took their show on the road to Joliet, West Aurora, and the Kankakee Tournament. They also visited nearby Beloit, Wisconsin, and made longer trips to Hammond, Indiana, and Davenport, Iowa, to play championship clubs from those states.

But Hebron stumbled out of the gate. Schulz was by now such a potent scoring threat that team balance suffered. He did all he could, averaging 21 points per game, but Hebron lost five in a row at mid-season and dropped to 9-8. Then Schulz really cut loose, scoring 310 points in the last ten games of the season. Hebron lost only to St. Edward's during this span, but the second time came in the finals of the district tournament.

It was a bitter disappointment for a team that had started with such great expectations. The defending state champion had not even qualified for the regional tournament.

That loss seemed to signal the end of the high times for both Ahearn and Hebron.

It was apparent, for example, that Ahearn had scaled back his sights for the 1953-54 Hebron squad. The team played a normal schedule of nine home games, including only a couple of large schools, and was not even entered in a Christmas tournament. The surnames recalled the triumph of two years earlier — (John) Schulz, (Lynn) Judson, (Jim) Wilbrandt, (Wayne) Spooner — but Ahearn now seemed to concede that the results could never be the same. John Schulz suffered a broken ankle in practice before the season began and missed ten games. The team limped to a 13-8 record and once again lost the district title to St. Edward's.

A month later, Ahearn announced he would resign in June to become athletic director and head basketball coach at a new high school, Woodland, near his old stomping grounds of Streator.

"I don't like to leave Hebron," he told a reporter from the *Elgin Courier-News*, "but it seems to me when you've won a state title, the peak has been reached. The job is done, there's no more to do, and both the coach and the boys lose incentive."

Florence Wilbrandt took issue with the comment. She pasted the article into her son Jim's scrapbook, took out a pen, and scratched through the last sentence. "The boys?" she wrote. "No!"

Ahearn's departure for Woodland tore the heart out of the Hebron athletic program. Not only did the school lose its famous basketball coach, but it also lost its football coach, Phil Hadley, when Ahearn persuaded his assistant to follow him to his new outpost in central Illinois. Hebron fans were sorry to see Ahearn go, but few were really surprised. A proven winner seldom sticks around in a small town. And for Ahearn, the lure of going home to share his success with family and old friends was far too strong to resist.

At Woodland, a school of about 300 students, Ahearn saw steady improvement in his teams over the next three years. His first squad won only four games. But the next year the team won twelve, and in the 1956-57 season Woodland won 21 games and a regional title before losing to Ottawa in the sectional. He had the small-school magic working all over again.

Under other circumstances, Ahearn might have developed an enduring program at Woodland. But he had one final goal, and that was to coach at his alma mater, to inherit the proud legacy of Lowell "Pug" Dale, now affectionately known as "Pops," who had coached at Streator Township from 1918 to 1946. When the head coaching position came open in the spring of 1957, Ahearn made the leap without hesitation, even though he would no longer hold the position of athletic director. Woodland had been a stepping-stone. At Streator, Ahearn was finally home.

Ahearn's first Bulldog team finished one game over .500 and the signs were bright for the next season. But in his second year at Streator, he ran into trouble. A dispute within the athletic department turned personal and dragged on throughout the basketball season. Despite the friction, Ahearn's team went into the regional with an excellent 17-6 record and high hopes for success in state tournament play. But the season ended two games later in a stunning 70-69, double-overtime loss to Marseilles in the regional semifinals.

Nine weeks later, he was removed as head basketball coach. Officially, the school board shifted him to a new position as supervisor of the basketball program and executive assistant to the athletic director. But there was no power behind the title. Ahearn was not allowed any say in choosing a successor to lead the program.

Wounded and confused, Russ Ahearn was faced with one of the most important decisions of his life. He and Marie had just had a new baby, Mary Jane, born in January. Their older daughter, Judy, was a junior at Streator Township and deeply involved in drama, student council, and synchronized swimming. Billy was an athletic eighth grader, well on his way to being a star in three sports. The insurance business Russ had built from the bottom up was a great success. It was no time to look for a job at another school in another town.

A day later, Ahearn issued a written statement announcing his resignation from the coaching profession. He was 46 years old and had been a head coach for only eleven years.

He wrote, "May my successor as varsity basketball coach perpetuate the historical tradition of winning with honor, which has been so indelibly inculcated into Bulldog teams of the past. It is with profound regret that I hang up my whistle, which has been such an amicable companion."

chapter 16

The Legacy

Since those amazing days in March of '52, scrapbooks have crumbled and memories have faded. Yet this one small team, this small name — Hebron — still occupies a special place in the hearts of basketball fans who call Illinois home.

Nowhere do the flames of memory burn brighter than in Hebron itself.

On the surface, little has changed in Hebron. The town is still virtually indistinguishable from thousands of other small towns across the American Midwest. The high school, the houses, and the buildings downtown all still look pretty much as they did during that magical moment in 1952.

There is one very big difference, however, and for that Hebron's citizens can thank Lynn Ellison.

In 1985, Ellison was mayor of Hebron and searching for a solution to a perennial problem: water pressure. For years the town's water system had depended on a rickety wooden "tower" only 25 feet tall. The pressure it supplied was barely enough to supply a couple of good, hot showers, let alone fight a major fire. The village leaders were aware of the danger. But their requests for aid were turned down regularly, and without financial assistance the town simply couldn't afford to build a real tower.

That's when Ellison came up with a novel idea.

Speaking before a meeting of the Community Development Assistance Program in Woodstock, he detailed his vision: a tower topped by a spherical reservoir, painted like a basketball, with a message commemorating the 1952 state championship. In a county where stories of the Hebron team passed from generation to generation, Ellison's brainstorm received an enthusiastic response. The town got its money, $400,000 in all, the only full grant given by the state that year.

When the project was completed a year later, the town threw an all-out celebration to dedicate the tower, with Ray Meyer, head basketball coach of DePaul University, as the guest of honor. Visitors toured a room at the base of the tower that contained Hebron basketball memorabilia and a big screen showing the videotape of the second half of the championship game. And, of course, the 1952 starters were invited back to greet spectators and play short games against alumni teams. Besides the trophy case in the high school, the water tower was Hebron's first permanent commemoration of the historic event.

Even today, the unique landmark draws visitors who simply want to see the water tower and perhaps bring back memories of another era.

Rising 155 feet above the center of town, the tower can be seen from almost any vantage point in Hebron, especially in winter when the leaves are off the trees. But the most nostalgic view of the tower requires approaching the town from the south, just as the team caravan did in 1952.

A mile out of town, not far from the farm that the Wilbrandts still own, Route 47 straightens out of an S curve. Suddenly the tower appears, bearing the proud message: "HEBRON, HOME OF 1952 STATE CHAMPIONS." The bright orange ball looms larger along the final mile of highway, where cars once parked bumper-to-bumper in anticipation of the Green Giants' triumphal return home.

There are thousands of water towers across America, but none of the others, so far as anyone knows, looks like a basketball. When the

Basketball Hall of Fame in Springfield, Massachusetts, found out about Hebron's tower, the museum developed an exhibit around the team that had inspired it. Now travelers who go to Springfield to learn about the legends of basketball learn a little about the Hebron legend as well.

It had a practical purpose, but Lynn Ellison's tower provided a lot more than good water pressure. As long as the tower stands, it will serve as a symbol of just how much the town cherishes its memories of the 1952 team.

Being From Hebron

If the town seems to be clinging to its fame, perhaps it's because fame has resolutely refused to let go of Hebron. Even fifty years later, "Hebron" still means something to an amazing number of people.

Almost everyone from the town has an anecdote about being on vacation in some distant place and being asked where they were from.

"Oh, it's a little town in Illinois," the Hebronite will say. "It's a ways outside of Chicago — you've probably never heard of it — a place called Hebron."

And then, as the stories go, a glimmer of recognition will cross the stranger's face, and then a smile.

"Oh, yeah, that's the little town with the basketball team."

It happens again and again. At a gas station in New Mexico. In a beachfront store in Monterey. On the streets of Toronto.

And it's not just people from Illinois who remember that something good happened in Hebron, although the out-of-staters sometimes get the story confused.

Folks from Hebron, Indiana, the largest Hebron in the U.S. with about 3,600 residents, often run into the same response when they give the name of their hometown.

"Hebron, isn't that the town that won the state championship?" comes the question. Much to their dismay, the Hoosiers are forced to answer, "No, that was Hebron, *Illinois*."

Even in 1991, when the Indiana town's high school (enrollment 240) made its own bid for a basketball state championship, they found they had to share space in news stories with the famous team from

Illinois. There is no escaping Hebron's legacy, even in the state that claims to be the basketball capital of the U.S.

Not *Hoosiers*

But give credit where credit is due. On the subject of basketball, Indiana still has one up on Illinois, at least as far as Hollywood is concerned. That is a source of humor and irritation to the 1952 Hebron players. They're not *Hoosiers*, they say, although maybe *Hoosiers* should have been written about them.

Released in 1986, the fictional classic depicts the struggle of tiny Hickory High School in the 1952 Indiana state basketball championship. *Hoosiers* was based, apparently, on the high school team from Milan, Indiana, that won the state championship in 1954. The screenwriters had no Illinois ties. But curiously, Gene Hackman, the film's star, grew up in Danville and was a student at the University of Illinois in 1952, the year Hebron won its title.

So why 1952? Why pick the year Hebron won in Illinois? Some people think it's because *Hoosiers* looked to Hebron for inspiration.

In the film, Hackman plays Norman Dale, a hard-nosed basketball coach who's running from a blow-up that ruined his college career. He's given one last chance by a friend at a backwater Indiana high school. Coach Dale takes over a ragged team, angers the diehard fans who want him to play a shoot-'em-up game, survives a vote of no-confidence, finds romance with a pretty teacher half his age, rehabilitates the town drunk *and* coaxes his superstar son back to the team, all in 115 minutes of running time. Good story, but pure Hollywood.

"We didn't have a town drunk," said Phil Judson, "and there was nobody in the gym telling Mr. Ahearn how to coach."

But perhaps the most important difference, according to the players, was that Hebron had an enormous following right from the start. Folks came from miles around and waited for hours on end to watch them play. The players basked in the attention and adulation, hardly coming out of nowhere just in time to take the championship.

"The fans didn't follow the bus to the game like in the movie," Phil said. "If you weren't at the game by the time our bus got there, you didn't get a seat. Sometimes *we* didn't get a seat. We'd have to stand in the corner to watch the first game."

Comparisons between Hebron and Milan are inevitable, but so far as a scorecard can be kept in these matters, Hebron wins on most counts. Milan High School was substantially bigger, with an enrollment of 162 to Hebron's 98. Milan had to win nine games in a row to capture the state title; because of Illinois' unique district setup, Hebron had to win eleven. Milan lost only two games that winter but was a decided underdog against Muncie Central in the title game; Hebron was ranked No. 1 in the state most of the season (9 out of the 13 weeks). Milan liked to play a cat-and-mouse, stall offense, as it did during the championship game (and as Hickory did in the movie); Hebron played racehorse basketball and could outrun and outgun any team in the state.

Comparisons can also be drawn with another tiny school, not so well known, but one that claimed its state championship on the very same evening Hebron did. The Cubs of Cuba, Kentucky — not far from Cairo, Illinois — came from a school with an enrollment of just 139 students. In 1952, Cuba won 37 games and lost five, beating a large school, DuPont Manual of Louisville, for the state championship.

But things have always been a little different in Kentucky. There were fewer schools to begin with, and in the Bluegrass State there was a long history of very small schools challenging for the state title. Cuba itself had qualified for the state tournament the year before (as had Milan). Just fifteen miles from Cuba an even smaller school, Brewers, had won an undefeated state championship in 1948. After its victory in 1952, Cuba joined the growing list of tiny rural teams that had won Kentucky's fabled one-class basketball title.

But on Illinois' list there is only one.

Not that others didn't come close. Cobden, a school of only 147 students from deep southern Illinois, made it to the championship game in 1964. In many ways the Cobden story paralleled that of Hebron. The team was filled with brothers and cousins. The starting lineup was exceptionally tall. And the school had a colorful nickname: the Appleknockers.

Cobden fought its way through district, regional, sectional, and supersectional play to reach the state championship game against a team from Pekin. During the game the Judson twins were interviewed on television and asked whether they were rooting for the Appleknockers. "No," came the reply in unison. Nothing against Cobden, the Judsons said, but they wanted Hebron's accomplishment to remain unique.

And so it has.

A House Divided

Cobden lost that game to Pekin and finished in second place.

Seven years later, the one-class tournament was abolished, ensuring that Hebron's one-of-a-kind achievement would always hold a place in the record books.

That, too, is Hebron's legacy.

The argument against the one-class tournament was that small schools no longer had a fighting chance against the large urban and suburban schools that came to dominate the field in the 1960s. From 1965 to 1969, no school with fewer than 500 students, and only three with fewer than 1,000 students, qualified for the Elite Eight tournament. The rumblings to split the field grew louder, led by Toluca High School coach Chuck Rolinski, whose own Little David teams had suffered repeatedly at the hands of the local Goliaths.

But ironically, in 1970, just as the state's high school principals were about to vote on whether to split the tournament, small schools made a resurgence. Okawville, with an enrollment of 250, and St. Anthony of Effingham, with 280, both qualified for the Elite Eight. To the shock of just about everyone, St. Anthony came within a point of upsetting the state's No. 1-ranked team, undefeated Lyons Township of LaGrange, in the quarterfinals. But it was too little, too late for the traditionalists. After the tournament, the principals of the IHSA's 791 member schools voted to divide the field into two classes — small (Class A) and large (Class AA) — starting in 1972.

Classification was the most divisive issue the Illinois High School Association had ever tackled. Coaches at large schools were generally against the two-class system. Ron Nikcevich, coach of Lyons Township's state champions, reflected that sentiment.

"Illinois has been robbed of its one true sports classic," he said. "We will no longer have a true state champion."

Small school coaches were generally in favor of the move, although Coach John Keller of St. Anthony, whose team had sparked reminiscences of the great Little David teams, took no solace in the vote. For him it had come a year too late. He opined that the talk about the "color" that small schools added to the tournament was "garbage."

"We had our finest team in 15 or 20 years," he told a reporter for United Press International, "and we came away empty-handed. We didn't get a trophy — we just lost."

Though he recognized it as the end of an era, the man behind Hebron's championship found it hard to defend continuing the one-class tradition.

Interviewed in 1972, Russ Ahearn thought splitting the tournament sounded like a good idea, as long as a playoff was held between the winner of the two classes to determine a single state champion.

"It is a highly justified move," he said. "We have a fighter fight in his own weight class, and a wrestler in his own, don't we?"

But the ultimate championship game that Ahearn envisioned — a showdown between the Class A and Class AA champions — never materialized. Thirty years later, the tournament remains exactly as it was in 1972: two classes, with two separate champions, season over.

Looking back on two-class tournaments that have now spanned a generation, the Hebron players have softened somewhat on the subject.

"I can see the two-class system," said Ken Spooner. "I can understand why they went about it, because it's very difficult for small schools to get anywhere in the tournament. This way it gives a lot of kids that opportunity to play, win, and be champions. It probably is better for the kids' sake, with more kids involved in the tournaments."

"I have mixed emotions," said Bill Schulz. "One class was nice when we were in school, but today one class would not be too good. The kids from small schools could not compete with the larger schools. In its time the one-class tournament was fine, but today two classes is better. It gives more players the opportunity to succeed."

But the Judsons remain unconvinced that the two-class system doesn't water down the final product.

"It would be a shame if there had been a two-class system in 1952," said Phil. "We'd have been beating Class A teams by 20 points, and what would that have meant? We wouldn't have been competing against the best, so how could we have been state champs?"

"I certainly favor a one-class system," added Paul, who coached at a small school, Hampshire, for many years. "However, I do understand the good things that can come out of a two-class system. At Hampshire they were really proud of what they did in Class A, and that's good, and you can't take a thing away from that. But it seems to me it's worth it to have that small team come along every ten or twelve years and put some excitement into the [one-class] tournament."

The players' sentiments are shaded, of course, by the fact that, against all the odds, they won the state championship. Would things have been different if they'd lost that championship game to Quincy?

"I'd rather have finished second in a one-class tournament," said Paul. "At least then you would know there was only one team ahead of you. If you win Class A, you've still got all of AA ahead of you, and you're not sure where you stand."

The argument over classification still smolders now and again, but nothing like it did in the years right after the system was implemented. Popular opinion now favors two classes. Until and unless that sentiment reverses itself, Hebron's accomplishment will remain singular.

A Cinderella Story?

Over the years, Hebron's story has taken on mythic proportions. To hear some tell the tale, the idea of the Green Giants winning the state championship was a stunner, a shocker, and practically supernatural.

But let's set the record straight. Hebron's win over Quincy was not a miracle, not even an upset.

The Green Giants were good. Very good. And they earned every victory.

A majority of the sportswriters had ranked Hebron No. 1 during the regular season, even though they ran like rats from a sinking ship after the lackluster showing against Champaign and the near-disaster against Rock Island. At that point, the writers gave Quincy the advantage. Many reiterated their oft-stated belief that "a team of five players cannot win the state title," arguing that Hebron would run out of gas before the three-day grind was over.

Contrary to the writers' expectations, the Green Giants never hit the wall in the championship game. The starters were so well conditioned that they played all 35 minutes, four quarters and an overtime, without requiring a substitution.

Yes, Hebron won. But for a school that small to prevail, it must have been an upset, right?

Absolutely not. Unlikely, to be sure. "David vs. Goliath," you bet. A Cinderella story? Maybe. But an upset? Not on your life.

Hebron won because it was the best team.

One of the few writers to raise any doubt on that point in the post-tournament commentary was Merle Jones, sports editor of the *Southern Illinoisan*. Lewis "Pick" Dehner, the head coach from East St. Louis, had made some derogatory comments about how poor the tournament field was — the teams were so evenly matched that no one dominated, he felt — and Jones agreed, pointing out that of the last eight games of the tournament, none was decided by more than 12 points.

Never mind the fact that that sounds a whole lot like a good tournament, not a bad one.

When it came right down to it, even Jones didn't question Hebron's supremacy. "I didn't realize till I got to Champaign," he wrote, "that [in the regular season] Hebron had defeated St. Edward's twice, Marmion twice, Joliet, Oak Park, Danville, Kankakee, Belvidere, DeKalb, and Riverside. These schools have more students than Hebron has people. So the Green Giants are no fluke champions. They deserve the championship more than anybody else in the state."

"We Didn't Know What We Had Done"

After all the exuberant celebrations, weeks of testimonials, months of after-dinner speeches, and years of interviews, surely everyone knew that this Hebron team was something special. And yet, the players will tell you that they had absolutely no idea what they had done.

They knew they had won the state championship, of course. But they had no real idea of its significance or of the role it would play in their lives and in the lives of others.

The final scene on the floor of Huff Gym still has Phil Judson scratching his head.

"When the horn went off," he said, "I can see myself jumping. My heels are way up in the air, knees bent, and for the life of me I don't know what I'm jumping about. None of us ever stopped to say, 'This is for all the marbles.' None of that went through our minds. I'm not sure why. Part of it was that it never entered our minds that we were going to be beaten. And part of the reason was we never listened to the tournament on radio or saw it on TV. We didn't know how big it was. It never sank in, even after we got honored in Chicago and Harvard and Woodstock, none of it. Not until Paul and I went to Illinois and watched several Sweet Sixteen tournaments did we know what we had done."

"It seemed like we always took one game at time," said Ken Spooner. "It was just another game. Yes, we knew we'd won the whole thing in the state of Illinois, but it was really many years after, maybe even ten years later, before we really realized what an impact it had on so many people. Over the years people would talk about it. After ten years or so it finally soaked in that, hey, this was really something — this was quite an accomplishment. It's strange that it would take that long but that's the way it was with me."

Man on the Street

Whether or not the players had any concept of what they had done, it didn't take long for them to notice the impact it was having on their own lives. They were genuine celebrities, whether on the dinner circuit with Russ Ahearn or just walking down the street miles from home.

For the starters especially, being recognized very quickly became a part of life. Whenever they were out in the public, they might be subject to a furtive glance, then a longer stare, until finally the stranger worked up the courage to approach and ask the question. What the players never suspected was that they would still be recognized and remembered decades later.

"We were in Spain one time and the shops closed at one o'clock for the siesta," Bill Schulz said. "We were standing outside a store, looking at china, when a guy came up and introduced himself. He said, 'You're Bill Schulz, aren't you?' He worked for Caterpillar in Peoria, and recognized me from basketball thirty years ago.

"Another time a fellow came up and asked, 'Didn't you use to be Bill Schulz?' and I just had to say, 'I still am Bill Schulz.'"

Schulz added, "Ninety-nine percent of the people that you meet are interesting people, not trying to hit you for something, just interested in what you're doing or what you did."

Fifty years later, Schulz still stands out in a crowd, and many people naturally think of basketball when they see such a tall man. But Schulz isn't the only recognizable character, as the other starters can attest.

Don Wilbrandt had a different trait that helped people identify him.

"Two strangers stopped me in a tavern a while ago," he told a reporter in 1972. "I run into that all the time. They look at my ear and find out my name and say, 'I know who you are.'

"It was never publicized, but everybody could see it. Everybody knew it. My dad used to want me to have a skin graft, but I wanted everyone to know me like I am."

Ken Spooner was giving an interview on camera in 1992 and was stopped in mid-sentence by someone who walked by and recognized him.

"It's kind of fun," he said, "because people are so surprised to meet somebody from the team, and they remember so much about it."

It wasn't just the starters who were recognized. While stationed in London with the Marines, Bill Thayer and his wife traveled to Norway, where they met some travelers from Barrington. When

Thayer revealed that he was from Hebron, a woman in the party stared hard at him for a few seconds and then asked, "You're the little red-head from the '52 Green Giants, aren't you?"

The Judson twins played basketball on a high-profile team at the University of Illinois and were connected to the high school basketball scene until they retired, so it's not surprising they've run into any number of strangers over the years who recognize them and want to talk about their Hebron days. They were frequently interviewed on state tournament television broadcasts, and those who remember seeing them after they went bald — by their early thirties — have no trouble recognizing them even fifty years after the championship.

Phil Judson was standing in line at Wrigley Field one morning before dawn, waiting for tickets, when a television reporter came over and started interviewing him and some of the other folks who'd camped out. She taped her piece and went back to the truck. A few minutes later she returned to the line with a big smile on her face. "Ladies and gentlemen," she said, "we've got a celebrity here!" Her tape editor had recognized Phil in the background of one of the interviews.

And even when they aren't recognized, the Judsons, ever playful, find a way to bring up the topic, especially if they spot a U of I cap or other mark identifying a sports fan from the Land of Lincoln.

"I see you're from Illinois," the conversation might start. "Ever heard of Hebron?"

"Oh, sure, that's the town with the basketball team," is the usual reply.

"Do you remember any of the players on that team?"

"Well, let's see, they had those twins..." And then a spark of recognition usually stops the little game.

Opening Doors

Most important of all, the Hebron legacy meant a different way of life for the five players who spent most of the time on the floor during the 1952 season. It's hard to imagine in today's world, but Hebron's entire starting lineup, five boys out of 42 in the school, earned scholarships to major universities.

The Hebron players are clear about the impact winning the championship made on their lives.

"By winning that state title, I got to go to the University of Illinois and get a good education and a chance to play Big Ten basketball," said Paul Judson. "If we'd gotten beat by Quincy, or by Elgin, I'm not sure that would have happened. It's not like today, with colleges recruiting you in your junior year. We didn't have that many offers."

"Winning the championship meant a college education," brother Phil said. "At the University of Illinois I got to play basketball in the Big Ten, see some of the country, and I also met my wife, Lesley. When I graduated, I got a teaching and coaching job which I really enjoyed."

And, Phil added with a twinkle in his eye, "I get to talk to lots of people about Hebron and Illinois basketball."

Before 1952, Ken Spooner envisioned a life in Hebron, much like his father and grandfather before him.

"My life changed tremendously from what it would have been," said Spooner. "I probably wouldn't have gone to college. I probably would have stayed in Hebron, doing something with my dad, maybe. Winning the championship opened up a lot of opportunities for me. It totally changed my life from what I thought it would be."

Undoubtedly, the changes that came with the hard work and the success that followed meant the most to Bill Schulz.

"It certainly affected my life," said Schulz. "I was a farm boy, and there was no way in the devil I would ever have gotten to go to college. Instead, I graduated with a great education from Northwestern University, where I met my wife, Karin. It has to be the big point in my life — that and my marriage. It really opened up the world to me."

The End of an Era

In 1952, as the residents of Hebron found themselves caught up in basketball fever, the world was becoming a different place.

Senator Joseph McCarthy was at the peak of his power, the House Un-American Activities Committee was gearing up to grill members of Hollywood's elite about possible Communist ties, and peace eluded U.S. and U.N. officials in Korea. Later in the year, Vice Presidential candidate Richard Nixon would deliver his famous "Checkers" speech, and Harry Truman would make way for Dwight Eisenhower in the White House.

Supermarkets, superhighways, TV dinners, rock 'n roll, Ozzie and Harriet, *Brown v. Board of Education*, Sputnik, and the chilliest days of the Cold War loomed just over the horizon.

America was changing.

Perhaps that's why the Hebron Green Giants caught the fancy of the public in their own time, and why so many people remember them so fondly, even now, fifty years later. They represent something sweet and innocent, a sense of small-town America at its industrious, modest, uncomplicated best.

The only district school in Illinois ever to win the state championship, the only Little David to prevail against the Big Boys, Hebron represents the end of an era.

For some of the players, the state championship unveiled a whole new range of possibilities. College, careers, and big-city life suddenly became viable choices. They saw themselves as different people now, and they believed in the power of their own abilities and accomplishments enough to take on risks and challenges they'd never dreamed of.

For others among the team and entourage, the big win set a very high standard. As they faced the rest of their lives, it seemed that nothing else could quite measure up. It was as if they were stuck in the golden memories, frozen in time, never quite able to find their way to a thaw.

And for a third group, winning it all was simply one more link in a chain of grand adventures. They bundled up all the innocence and excitement of their championship season, and they carried those gifts along with them on every step of their life journeys. What feats and follies awaited them around the next corner? Who could say? And wasn't that the best kind of storybook ending?

They were a team in 1952, and yet individuals, too, so it was fitting that their biggest accomplishment should have affected them differently.

And in the end, they did their legacy proud. The Green Giants of Alden-Hebron Community Consolidated High School stood tall.

What Ever Happened To?

The Starting Five

The **JUDSON TWINS** attended the University of Illinois together on athletic scholarships. For all his efforts, Dolph Stanley could not persuade them to attend Beloit College. The boys briefly considered playing at the University of Wisconsin, where their brother Howie said they needed players and the twins could play right away. But eventually, loyalty to their home state overcame all the other arguments, and the twins enrolled at the Champaign-Urbana campus.

Paul was a star on the varsity basketball team for three years (freshmen could not play varsity ball in those days), and was named captain and Most Valuable Player in his junior year, All-Big Ten in both his junior and senior years, and All-America his senior year. Phil played on the varsity three years as well and was also a standout catcher on the baseball team. After graduation they were drafted and served together at Ft. Leonard Wood, Mo., playing on many service basketball teams. Later they barnstormed with the Illinois All-Stars, a team of UI alumni, against the Marques Haynes All-Stars, the Goose Tatum Magicians, and the Harlem Globetrotters. Among other highlights, they took on Wilt Chamberlain in his first professional game (with the Globetrotters) before a sellout crowd of 21,000 people at Chicago Stadium. Marriage eventually separated the twins, as they pursued their own lives and careers.

PAUL JUDSON was drafted by the Syracuse Nationals of the NBA but had not yet signed when he received another draft notice — this time into the United States Army. Although Syracuse was still interested when he left the service, Paul decided he'd played enough basketball. Instead he embarked on a coaching career that took him first to Mattoon High School and later to Hebron's archrival, Dundee. He was already head baseball coach there when he took over a girls' basketball program in its infancy. In 1978, his second year at the helm, he led the team downstate to Champaign. The next year Paul became head coach of the boys' team. When Dundee High School combined with Crown in 1983, he moved within the school district to Hampshire High School. At Hampshire, he coached the boys' team for three more years and also served as athletic director until his retirement in 1993.

Paul was inducted into the Illinois Basketball Coaches Association Hall of Fame in 1973. The entire 1952 Hebron team was inducted in the same ceremony.

Paul and his wife, Jackie, live in Florida. They have three children: Jennifer (married to Roy Schumacher, with children Jillian and Justin); Jeff (married to Carol, with children Jessica, Jason, and Brock); and Jerry.

PHIL JUDSON began his coaching career in 1959 at North Chicago High School. One day at North Chicago, his basket-shooting prowess earned him an enduring, and endearing, nickname. Today almost everyone, including his wife and kids (but not Paul or Howie), calls him "Swish." In 1969, he moved to a varsity coaching position at Adrian High School in Michigan, where he stayed for five years before trying one year as freshman coach at Adrian College. In 1975, he returned home to Illinois to coach at Zion-Benton High School. At Zion-Benton, his son, Rob, became the fourth member of the Judson family to be named a first-team All-State basketball player; he's now the head coach at Northern Illinois University. Swish retired in 1995, but still works as a substitute driver's education teacher and basketball official.

Phil was inducted into the Illinois Basketball Coaches Association Hall of Fame in 1979.

Phil and his wife, Lesley, live in northern Illinois. They have two children: Rob (married to Kimberly, with children Karin, Matt, and Kristin) and Gary (married to Susan, with daughters Rachael, Emily, and Alissa — the last two are twins).

BILL SCHULZ attended Northwestern University on a basketball scholarship and played on the varsity team for three years. He was captain of the squad in his senior year and completed his undergraduate degree in education during the middle of the season, taking graduate courses the rest of the spring.

After college, Bill embarked on a successful business career, working his way up the ladder at Motorola. When the Consumer Products Division of Motorola was purchased by Matsushita, he became national distribution manager of its Quasar Division, in charge of all of its warehousing, importing, traffic, car fleets, and scheduling. In 1986, the company downsized and let many of its executives go, which led Bill to a new career as a hardware store owner and operator in Chicago. In 1998, he bought a different hardware store in Waukegan, which he still owns and operates from seven in the morning until seven at night. Bill still eats an apple every day and in his wallet he still carries the original, handwritten copy of Russ Ahearn's "Recommendations for Bill Schulz."

Bill and his wife, Karin, live in northern Illinois. They have three children: Julie, Pamela, and Bill. They also have two surrogate grandchildren, Haley and Collin.

KENLEY SPOONER attended Northwestern University on a basketball scholarship, but stayed only one year. He then transferred to Northern Illinois State Teachers' College (now Northern Illinois University) to pursue a teaching degree. After graduation, Ken taught for several years at Richmond-Burton High School and his alma mater, Alden-Hebron, before entering the real estate business. A few years later, while waiting for his real estate license to be transferred, he took an interim job in retail clothing that ended up lasting until his recent retirement.

Ken and his wife, Katy, still live in northern Illinois. Ken has three children: Leslie; Todd (married to Sofia, with daughters Maresa and Laura); and Kristin (married to John Smrt, with children Katie, Joe, Jake, and James).

DON WILBRANDT attended Valparaiso University in Indiana on a basketball scholarship, where he played all four years. After leaving college, he returned to the family business and bought calves for a few years. Later he became a truck driver for E.M. Melahn Construction Company, hauling heavy construction equipment, a job he held for over thirty years. Throughout his adult life, Don played on many amateur basketball teams and officiated in several different sports. He was proudest of the fact that he was captain of the 1952 state champions, and even late in life he signed his name "Capt. Don Wilbrandt."

Don died in 1998 at the age of 64. He left three children: Clara Koenig (with children Matthew, Nathan, and Jennifer); Mary; and Jason.

The Reserves

JIM BERGIN attended Marquette University in Milwaukee and DePaul University before getting his master's degree in school administration at Illinois State University. After graduation, he pursued a variety of occupations: teacher, accountant, educational salesman, computer programmer, and director of maintenance for a fast food franchise.

Jim and his wife, Angie, live in central Illinois. They have nine children: Tim (married to Kate, with son Connor); Dave (married to Anne, with son Christian); Mary (married to Mike McCracken, with sons Paddy and Brendan); Patrick; Anne (married to Steve Grosklaus); Kate; Molly (married to Peter Carl, expecting in January 2002); Michael; and Meg (married to Brian Rincker).

CLAYTON IHRKE took a job at Northern Illinois Gas Company and worked his way up the ladder for many years before retiring and moving to South Carolina in 1993.

Clayton died in 1997 at the age of 61. He was survived by his wife, Shirley Schroeder, one of the 1952 cheerleaders, and three children: Valerie (married to Lee Maule, with sons Matthew and Michael Henline); Bruce (with children Steven, Jennifer, and Randy); and Malinda (married to John Gibson, with sons Daniel, Trevor, Kirk and Colin — the last two are twins).

JOE SCHMIDT was drafted into the Army after graduation, serving a tour in Korea. When he returned home in 1957, he farmed with his father on a farm outside of Hebron. In 1961 he enrolled in electronics school in Chicago and for a short while took over Harold Spooner's TV shop in Hebron. Joe worked for Admiral Corporation in Harvard for a few years before becoming service manager at a television repair shop in Rockford. He moved to Florida in 1978, where he's still working in television repair.

Joe and his wife, Janet, were married in 1961.

BILL THAYER went to college at LeTourneau Tech in Longview, Texas, where he played two years of junior college basketball. He joined the Marines in 1956 and served all around the world, with tours in Vietnam and London, before retiring in 1986 with the rank of Master Gunnery Sergeant.

He and his wife, Marybeth, live in California.

JIM WILBRANDT attended Valparaiso University on a basketball scholarship, but ended up playing football and baseball instead. After graduation, he served in the Army in Italy before returning home to teach in the Dundee school district. He was head football coach and athletic director at Crown High School from 1970 to 1974. After four years as dean of students at Dundee High School, he returned to Crown as assistant principal. He served there and at the combined Dundee-Crown High School as principal from 1987 until his retirement in 1994.

Jim and his wife, Sue, still live in northern Illinois. They have four children: Cindy (married to Louis Saia, with sons Michael, Joseph, and John Paul); Cathy (married to Greg Miller, with sons Chris, Brad, and Steve); Jim, Jr.; and Cheryl (married to Jeff Leitner, with children Daniel and Roslyn).

The Coaches

 **RUSS AHEARN** continued with his successful insurance business and taught civics at Streator Township High School until his retirement in 1974. He never lost the passion to coach. He gave instruction at summer camps and clinics, and even late in his teaching career Ahearn was heard to comment that he'd like to take over Streator's current team and turn it into a winner. Not long after his retirement, he was inducted into the Illinois Basketball Coaches Association Hall of Fame, in the same class as the late Lowell Dale of Streator.

"Duke" was also inducted into the Illinois State University Athletic Hall of Fame as a baseball player. In his letter of thanks, the old southpaw wrote, "I loved baseball as much as life itself — especially on a Redbird mound."

Not long afterward, Russ Ahearn was hospitalized with cancer. He died just a few months later, in November 1976, just before the 25th anniversary of Hebron's championship. He was 64 years old.

Those close to him say that although Ahearn lived with lingering regret over the way his coaching career ended, he never lost his charm, his sense of humor, or his faith.

Russ Ahearn was laid to rest in St. Mary's Cemetery in Streator, with Howie Judson and Phil Hadley among the pallbearers. Serving as honorary pallbearers were the starting five of the 1952 championship team.

Marie Ahearn, Russ's rock of strength, passed away in 1994.

Judy Ahearn married Peter Benda and has three children: Scott (married to Patty), with daughters Gabrielle and Gentry; Jill (married to Matt Countie), with children William and Grace; and Brian (married to Marci).

Bill Ahearn is married to Marlain and has three children: Amy (married to Neil Eidel), with daughter Isabelle; Ryan; and Nathan.

Mary Jane Ahearn married Brad Lovins and has two daughters: Lindsey and Brittany.

PHIL HADLEY remained loyal to Russ Ahearn to the end. He became athletic director at Woodland High School after Ahearn's departure, but in 1963 followed his mentor to Streator Township. There he worked as a science teacher and football coach until his retirement in 1990.

Phil Hadley died in 1999 at the age of 74. He was survived by his widow, Marilyn, and a son, Craig (married to Jennifer).

The Opponents

GEORGE LATHAM took his Quincy Blue Devils to the state finals at Huff Gym three more times before leaving Quincy in 1956. Pursuing a career in administration, he moved to Waukegan and served first as a division chairman and later as high school principal and assistant superintendent. He also served one year as interim superintendent of the Waukegan School District.

Latham was inducted into the Illinois Basketball Coaches Association Hall of Fame in 1973. Now retired, he and his wife, Josephine, still live in northern Illinois.

BRUCE BROTHERS, Quincy's All-State center, played basketball at the University of Illinois with the Judson twins, often rooming with one or the other on road trips. He later rejoined George Latham at Waukegan, where he taught and coached, before moving to Maine East High School in Park Ridge. In 1976, the Illinois Basketball Coaches Association honored Brothers for his outstanding basketball career by inducting him into its Hall of Fame.

He remained good friends with the Judsons, often riding with them to Champaign to attend Fighting Illini basketball games.

In 1985, Brothers collapsed in his classroom, suffering from a brain tumor, and died less than a year later at the age of 52. During all the time he and the Judsons spent together, they never once discussed the 1952 championship game.

The Sideline Characters

LOWRY B. CRANE finished his teaching career at Senn High School. He never coached varsity sports after leaving Hebron, preferring to stay out of the limelight. Instead, he coached freshman and sophomore basketball for many years. Some of his players went on to win the Chicago Public League championship for Senn in 1945, playing in the state tournament at Huff Gym. Crane gave up coaching when he became assistant principal in 1955. The coach who turned Hebron into a basketball town retired from teaching in 1969 and died just two weeks later.

Lowry Crane and his wife, Lucia, are buried in Linn-Hebron Cemetery, on a hill outside of town.

HOWIE JUDSON was traded by the Chicago White Sox to the Cincinnati Reds in 1953. When his arm gave out in 1954, Howie left major league baseball and returned home to Hebron, where he worked until his retirement in 1985. Howie was inducted into the Illinois Basketball Coaches Association Hall of Fame in 1986.

In 1987, Howie and his wife, Martha, moved to Florida, where they still reside.

JOHN A. KRAFFT left Elgin High School in 1956 and moved to Pasadena, California, where he worked for many years as a stockbroker.

Remembered in Illinois long after his departure for warmer climes, Krafft was inducted into the Illinois Basketball Coaches Association Hall of Fame in 1975.

Krafft died in 1984 at the age of 78.

GEORGE E. SULLIVAN wrote his "Put and Take" column for the *Woodstock Sentinel* until September 21, 1963. That afternoon, just three months after a community celebration in his honor, he collapsed and died in the press box during a football game between Woodstock and Palatine. He was 70 years old.

DON PEASLEY continues his work as a local photographer, reporter, and historian. In addition to projects of civic interest, Don has also covered the agriculture scene for many years. Of the thousands of photos he's taken, many are now located at the McHenry County Historical Society in Union, Illinois.

Still a well recognized face around the county, Don writes for the *Woodstock Independent* and also for the *Northwest Herald*, which publishes Don's reports in a weekly column called "On the Square."

Don and his wife, Fran, live in northern Illinois.

The Places

GEORGE HUFF GYMNASIUM was retired from the starting lineup in 1963 when the University of Illinois' Assembly Hall was completed. The gym served as an intramural facility until 1992, when the women's volleyball program claimed the historic facility and breathed new life into it. Renamed Huff Hall, it later became host to the women's basketball team as well.

Today the bleachers on the sides of the court are made of plastic and don't cover as much of the floor as the old wooden ones did. But all it takes is a little imagination. If you sit in the ancient seats in the balcony and picture two lights shining down from a big map of Illinois hung high on the wall, you can still get a sense of what it must have been like to play for the state championship in 1952.

THE WOODSTOCK TOWN SQUARE has seen few celebrations like the Hebron Caravan of March 23, 1952. The square is still paved in brick, and the downtown area remains a vital business center. If you'd like to see what the Town Square looks like today (or at least what it looked like in 1992), watch the movie *Groundhog Day.* Punxsutawney, Pennsylvania? Not on your life! That's Woodstock, Illinois.

Today there's a plaque on the spot, not far from where this photograph was taken, where Bill Murray's character stepped into the same puddle day after day after day. In honor of the filming, Woodstock now hosts its own Groundhog Day celebration every February 2.

ALDEN-HEBRON HIGH SCHOOL still occupies the same building on the south edge of Hebron. An addition in 1957 brought several new classrooms and a new gymnasium, later dedicated to Superintendent Paul Tigard. The windows of the old stage gym have been bricked in, the hardwood has been covered with tile, and the balcony has been turned into a storage room, but the basketball goals at the ends of the court are still vintage 1952.

If you make a pilgrimage to the school, stop at the display case inside the front door. There you'll find the center circle from the old gym floor, along with the championship trophy and other memorabilia from that once-in-a-lifetime season.

Linger awhile and let your imagination carry you back to a time when it was possible for a small team from a tiny town to set its sights on the biggest brass ring around and then work until it was within its grasp.

The Alden-Hebron basketball teams haven't won many trophies lately. That isn't really important.

As long as small-town kids still dream of winning a state championship against impossible odds, people will remember Hebron.

Notes

p. 7, IHSA: The Illinois High School Association (IHSA) was known as the Illinois High School Athletic Association (IHSAA) before it adopted a revised constitution in 1940.

p. 8, district tournaments: The description of the district-regional setup has been simplified here so as not to interfere with the story. The reality is considerably more convoluted.

Across the state the IHSA designated 60 district-regional groups of 11 to 15 teams each. When the district-regional setup was initiated in 1936, the teams relegated to the district stage were not the smallest schools in each group but the *lowest-ranked* ones, based on a poll of the coaches within the group. The system was put to the test immediately when Thornton Township of Harvey, a large school south of Chicago, was seeded by the coaches into the local district. Thornton had had a poor season, but in this instance reputation alone suggested that a higher seed might be deserved: Thornton had made it to the state championship game in each of the previous three years, finishing first, second, and second. In fact, the previous year Thornton had beaten Monee, 82-5, in one of the great first-round mismatches that led to the reorganization of the tournament. That Thornton was now entered in the special round designed to shield the smaller schools from such mismatches seemed a cruel irony, made even more aggravating by the fact that Thornton then won the district title. The system was changed in 1938 so that within each district-regional group the *smallest* schools, based on their enrollment, played in the district tournament. This system endured until the two-class system was introduced in 1972.

The unusual advancement of runners-up actually started in 1934, when the rules were changed to allow both the winner and runner-up of each old-style district tournament to advance to the sectional round automatically. In 1936, after the regional stage was inserted into the mix, it got even more confusing. Because the number of teams assigned to a district-regional group varied due to geographical factors, pains were taken to make sure that there were at least six teams to play for a district title *and* a full eight in regional competition. From 1936 to 1942, every district champion, most runners-up, and occasionally even a third-place team advanced to play in the regional. During the same time period, all regional champions and runners-up advanced to play in the sectional stage. It was therefore possible to lose two games (if the losses came in the right games) and continue advancing toward the state championship. This actually happened on five separate occasions. In 1940, both teams in the state championship game, Granite City and Herrin, were regional runners-up. The unwieldy system was finally eliminated in 1943 so that only winners continued advancing toward the state title.

It should also be noted that one of the reasons for the size and number of mismatches in 1935, which precipitated the introduction of the small-school district tournaments, was that there was still a center jump after every basket and free throw, which allowed good teams with a tall center to control the ball for virtually the entire game. The center jump was eliminated after successful free throws starting in the fall of 1935, and after field goals in the fall of 1937.

p. 10, 8 of 32 state championships: By contrast, Hebron's 1952 team beat three former champions: Elgin (2 previous state titles), Champaign (1), and Quincy (1).

p. 13, Lewistown had no particular reputation: Adding to the disappointment, this remains Lewistown's only state final appearance in the 94-year history of the tournament, through 2001.

p. 15, lost on their return trip: Several newspaper accounts from 1952 reported that the 1940 team arrived late at Huff Gym because one of the cars in the team's caravan went off the road. Apparently the first such story was based on someone's erroneous recollection and it was then repeated in print several times. The correct version is from contemporaneous newspaper accounts and information provided by Howie Judson and Keith Johnson.

p. 17, Henry V. Porter: Henry V. Porter rose from coach at Athens High School to assistant manager of the Illinois High School Association to executive secretary of the National Federation of State High School Associations. He also loved to write essays and poetry. Although his contributions to interscholastic athletics are innumerable, perhaps his most lasting legacy to the world of sport is the term "March Madness," now a trademark of the IHSA. His essay of the same name, published in 1939, and a later poem named "Basketball Ides of March," popularized the famous phrase within Illinois. The original and presumably only copy of "Hebron Humor" was found in Howie Judson's scrapbook, autographed by its author.

The complete list of players referred to in Porter's poem is (in order of their appearance): Russ Voltz, John Ryan, Keith Johnson, Gordon Burgett, John Kjellstrom (Kelly), Les Bigelow, Howie Judson (Juddy), Kenneth Rehorst, Harry Behrens, Erwin Norgard (Unc), Wally Tibbits, Howard Peterson (Pete), and Elwyn Behrens (Elly), along with Principal A.E. Marsh. We're not sure who Porter meant by "Jim."

p. 17, two waives in a row: The rules of the day allowed a team to waive a free throw near the end of the game and take possession of the ball out of bounds instead.

p. 37, Alden-Hebron High School: Although the school officially changed its name with the consolidation of 1948, it was not routinely called Alden-Hebron High School in the press until much later. In the entire catalog of 1952 newspaper clippings there are only a handful of such references, all of them in passing. To avoid confusing readers who never knew the 1952 team as anything but "Hebron," we've chosen, with apologies to the good people of Alden, to use the school's original name throughout this book, even though it is technically incorrect. We've used the same shortcut for a few other high schools that have since grown into their longer names: Richmond-Burton (in 1952 always referred to as "Richmond"), Bradley-Bourbonnais ("Bradley"), Oak Park and River Forest ("Oak Park"), Riverside-Brookfield ("Riverside"), Reed-Custer ("Braidwood"), and East Alton-Wood River ("Wood River").

It should be pointed out, however, that despite the fact that the high school's yearbook used the name "Alden-Hebron" in 1952, the letter in the center of the basketball floor and the letter awarded to athletes was a simple "H". Ironically, it was not until Ken Spooner coached at the school in 1972 that an "A" was finally added.

p. 48, wrote a letter to Doug Mills: This is Paul's version of the story. Phil doesn't think they wrote a letter but instead might have mentioned their plight to Howie, who then interceded with Mills.

p. 58, boarded the train: The train ride to Kankakee is one of the great mysteries of this story. The players were adamant that they never took a train to any game. And yet the telltale postcard from Bill Schulz to his parents, dated Dec. 27, 1950, cannot be refuted:

> *I am having a good time. It was a long trip down here. We got here at 2:30. The longest part was from Chicago to Kankakee. All I ate was a candy bar on the train, and we ate after practice, which was 6:00. I was hungry! It's a nice gym. We had to pay our way down on the train so I may run a little low on money, but don't worry.*

To which Phil Judson responded, "If Bill ate a candy bar, it wasn't when the coach was watching."

p. 59, hit the century mark: Several teams had actually scored 100 previously, but apparently none since the lopsided first-round games of 1935.

p. 59, Hal Bruno: He gained fame later as a political commentator for ABC News, but Hal Bruno's comments about basketball proved to be sage as well. After Russ Ahearn left Hebron, the Green Giants' basketball team won only one game in each of the next two seasons. The last piece of state tournament hardware won by the school is a district tournament plaque from 1957.

p. 61, Alex Saudargas: Alex Saudargas and his West Rockford team had their own success a few years later, winning back-to-back state championships in 1955 and 1956.

p. 62, his single free throw: Common (non-shooting) fouls were penalized by a single free throw in 1952 and the first bonus rule was still a year away.

p. 63, Cardunals: For those unfamiliar with nicknames of defunct Illinois high schools, this might appear to be a misprint. In fact, it's a combination of the names of the four communities that fed the school: *Car*pentersville, East and West *Dun*dee, and *Al*gonquin.

p. 71, Hebron's mayor: Technically Mark Spooner served as village president, but "mayor" is more often heard.

p. 93, Harv Schmidt: Schmidt's Kankakee team came on strong at the end of the 1951-52 season, and the next year was ranked No. 1 in the state for most of campaign. In a memorable showdown of unbeatens in the sectional tournament, the Kays fell to Lyons Township, which went on to win the state title. Schmidt starred at the University of Illinois and later served the school as head basketball coach.

p. 94, Danville's Maroons: Danville's teams are now known as the Vikings. In the early days of high school sport, many Illinois schools adopted maroon as one of their team colors and Maroons as their nickname, based on the success of the University of Chicago's early athletic programs. So many of the traditional powerhouses were known as Maroons that eventually some made bids for individuality. Danville High School and Peoria High School, among others, changed their nicknames but retained the color.

p. 101, Max Brady had been one of the officials: Many coaches (and also many sportswriters) supplemented their income by officiating high school contests. Ahearn himself officiated football games, but not basketball.

p. 116, the last quarterfinal game against the No. 4 seed: The regionals were seeded in an unusual pattern. Reading from the top of the bracket down, No. 1 played No. 5, then 3 versus 7, 2 versus 6, and 4 versus 8. As the district tournament winner, Hebron automatically received the No. 8 seed in the regional and was paired with the No. 4-seeded team in the quarterfinal round. The No. 8 seed would not meet the No. 1 seed until the championship game.

p. 119, Schulz dunks: Sportswriters in 1952 did not use the term "dunk" with the meaning it has today. Schulz never attempted a modern dunk in a game, although he sometimes dunked during warm-ups.

p. 132, Chicago Public League's entry: Younger readers may be surprised that the Chicago representative was not a factor in the tournament. In fact, the Public League's annual entry was usually dismissed out of hand, with Johnny Kerr's 1948 Tilden team being a rare exception. Not until the amazing DuSable Panthers came on the scene in 1953 and 1954 were Chicago teams finally taken seriously. Marshall High School won Chicago's first state championship in 1958 and the playing field changed forever.

p. 132, enrollment of 98 students: Hebron's actual enrollment at tournament time was variously reported, perhaps most often as 99, but Russ Ahearn, who as principal ought to have known, gave it as 98 (42 boys and 56 girls) in interviews printed just before and after the tournament.

p. 149, Jack Drees and Chick Hearn: Jack Drees had a long broadcasting career, and although he called Cubs and White Sox games for many years, he's best remembered as a horse-racing announcer par excellence. And Chick Hearn? He went on to become one of pro basketball's most famous broadcasters. He called every Los Angeles Lakers game for 36 years, a string of 3,338 straight games, until elective surgery finally knocked him out of the booth late in 2001.

p. 156, WENR: WENR is now WLS-TV.

p. 158, HEB-ron: Hebron was not named for the Biblical city in Palestine, but rather for a Scottish hymn. That being the case, it's not surprising that Hebron, Illinois, uses the traditional British pronunciation, "HEE-brin," though many people get it wrong.

p. 165, stationed in the first position: Originally, when a free throw was shot, a member of the shooting team occupied one of the lane positions closest to the basket, and a member of the opposing team occupied the position across the lane. The rule was changed in 1956 so that both of these positions were occupied by opponents of the shooter.

p. 173, Bob Novak: Now a noted political commentator, Bob Novak was a University of Illinois senior in 1952. He was in charge of the tournament coverage for the *Urbana Courier* the night Hebron won because his boss, Bert Bertine, chose instead to cover the college game in Chicago, a decision that no doubt left Bertine kicking himself for years to come.

p. 174, Jerome Holtzman: Jerome Holtzman went on to a long career in sports journalism and a berth in the Baseball Hall of Fame in Cooperstown, New York. He is now the official historian of Major League Baseball.

p. 197, on Illinois' list there is only one: Is Hebron the smallest school in Illinois to win a one-class basketball title? Be careful what you say. The tournament began in 1908, and in those days the enrollments of teams were never reported. When Hebron won its championship, Villa Grove's 1923 team was widely reported as the previous smallest champion, with an enrollment of 185. But a check of Illinois State Board of Education data shows three smaller champions: Batavia in 1912 (167 students), Hillsboro in 1914 (123 students), and Hinsdale in 1909 (100 students). Hinsdale is a large suburb now and an unlikely challenger to Hebron's claim to fame. Nevertheless, if Hinsdale Township High School's enrollment dropped after the enrollment survey was taken in the fall of 1908, it very well could have been the smallest school ever to win the one-class championship. We'll never know. Qualify the statement with the phrase "in the modern era" if you must, but in any case, Hebron certainly deserves the honor.

p. 198, supersectional: Illinois reduced its state final tournament from a "Sweet Sixteen" to an "Elite Eight" format in 1956 and has not changed it since. The eight first-round games that used to be played at Huff Gym are now held at eight separate supersectional sites, most of them on college campuses.

p. 219, center circle: The chunk of floor in the school's display case is marked by a simple circle outline with a straight line through the center. The photographs from 1952 clearly show a solid green circle with a white H and *two* center lines located a few feet on either side of the circle. Two lines were required since Hebron's gym was shorter than regulation length and a single line across the center of the floor would not have provided enough room for a full forecourt. So is this the real center circle? An article from the *Woodstock Sentinel* indicates that before the floor was tiled in 1982, the center circle was removed and then stripped, sanded, and refinished. Football coach Joe McGraw and Don Booker, head of maintenance for the school district, were credited with the idea of preserving the circle.

Acknowledgments

Although Hebron's moment of glory took place before either of us was born, the story has been with us for as long as we can remember, drifting through the recesses of our minds. *Little David. 98 students. "District school." Cinderella. Miracle team.* We knew little about the story beyond these general descriptions, but we knew we weren't the only ones who'd grown up with the legend. Every sports fan in Illinois knows something about Hebron. We got curious. It was time to find out more.

When we started this project we had no idea what we'd discover and whether it would be enough to fill a book. Now, at the end of the road, we consider ourselves incredibly fortunate. The surviving players from 1952 — Paul and Phil Judson, Bill Schulz, Ken Spooner, Jim Wilbrandt, Jim Bergin, Bill Thayer and Joe Schmidt — and "big brother" Howie Judson graciously allowed us to walk into their lives and rummage through their memories and their memorabilia, read their personal letters, ask probing questions, and analyze their actions. There would be no book without the players, and we thank them and their wives for sharing so much with us and for allowing us to tell their story.

We owe very special thanks to Judy Benda, daughter of Russ Ahearn, who helped us in every way we asked, from flying across the country to give us a tour of her parents' old haunts in Streator to spending nights in her attic digging for lost treasures. She and her husband, Pete, searched for days for her father's missing spiral notebooks, and when all hope of finding them seemed lost and it was time to give up, she prayed one last time for their recovery. Judy found them minutes later in a nearby box along with more of her parents' personal effects, including many she had never seen. She also located her father's college scrapbooks and many congratulatory telegrams and letters. Reuniting Judy with these lost items was the most beneficial side effect of the entire project. There were four notebooks in all, two that covered the end of the 1951-52 season and two that covered later seasons. The notebooks were the window through which we entered the coach's mind as the team made its way toward the championship.

All of the players had extensive material that they allowed us to examine. Phil Judson, in particular, has become a dedicated curator of Hebroniana over the years. From clippings to photos to signs to sweaters to a scale model of the Hebron water tower, Phil has faithfully collected it all. Phil provided valuable assistance in tracking down sources and arranging interviews, and reporting new information in a steady stream of e-mail. He also willingly took assignments, from drawing a map recreating the layout of downtown Hebron in 1952 to listing the diversions available to the youth of his era in small-town Illinois.

Two of the players' mothers also shared their memories and mementos. Helen Schulz and Florence Wilbrandt allowed us to browse and borrow whatever we needed from neatly organized collections that ranged from photographs to audio recordings to the torn halves of Helen's state final ticket, now digitally reunited, that graces our back cover.

Family members weren't the only ones who have kept the flame burning since 1952. In particular, the scrapbooks offered by superfans Cody LeBaron, who still works at Alden-Hebron High School, and Bobette Von Bergen, perennial reunion organizer, were invaluable to our effort.

All these items served as our guideposts, and we unashamedly admit that we engaged in "scrapbook journalism." The clippings lovingly compiled by the Hebron faithful provided an unanticipated jumpstart to our research and introduced us to many sources that we never would have stumbled across on our own.

Then as now, local sportswriters created colorful images of the players and games that go beyond a mere recitation of scores and statistics. We are indebted to these gentlemen for the stories they told in print. George Sullivan of the *Woodstock Sentinel* and Don Peasley of the *Community News* covered the Hebron story from start to finish and provided a cornucopia of details that have found their way into this book. Herb Jannusch of the *Kankakee Journal* provided interesting perspectives of the holiday tournament games played in that city. The columns written by Frank Reichstein of the *Beloit Daily News* gave unexpectedly detailed descriptions of the coach and players as well as a refreshing glimpse of the pageantry of the 1952 state tournament series in Illinois.

When the Chicago papers latched onto the story, esteemed writers such as Jerome Holtzman of the *Sun-Times*, David Condon of the *Tribune*, Tommy Kouzmanoff of the *Herald-American*, and Bud Nangle of the *Daily News* provided an interesting big-city perspective on the small-town doings. Once the team finally hit Champaign-Urbana, Jack Prowell and T.O. White of the *Champaign News-Gazette* and Bert Bertine, Bill Schroeder, Emil Hesse, George Henderson, and Bob Novak of the *Urbana Courier*, among others, offered insight into the state tournament experience from a local angle.

Dr. Louis Tobison's brief diary of his state final experiences with the Hebron team, which appeared in the *Harvard Herald*, yielded several interesting details that otherwise would have been lost forever. Other newspapers that covered the Hebron team regularly were the *Elgin Courier-News,* the *Rockford Register-Republic,* and the *Rockford Morning Star*. Across the state line in Wisconsin, the *Lake Geneva Regional News* and the *Sharon Reporter* also provided tangible evidence of Hebron's popularity. A few interesting items were gleaned from the *Streator Times-Press*, which kept close watch on its hometown hero, Russ Ahearn, as he coached Hebron to the championship.

From the many interviews conducted by all these reporters, we have borrowed quotes freely. Many of those interviewed in print have now passed away, and even among those participants still thriving none can be expected to reconstruct his own words fifty years after the fact. Thus the quotes preserved on newsprint allow the voices of the past to speak directly to the present. Other quotes used in this book are either attested to by one of the participants in the conversation or adapted from the comments in Coach Ahearn's notebooks. We were lucky that the coach went to considerable trouble to write out, in a conversational style, the remarks he intended to read to the players in his chalk talks.

We have attempted to identify the source of every photo used in this book. Many of the images that we included came from prints that were acquired by the players fifty years ago, and in a few cases the identification has been lost. Of those photos that could be identified, several came from the Associated Press and the *Champaign News-Gazette*, whose historic negatives are now stored in the University of Illinois Archives.

Don Peasley, in particular, needs to be recognized for his single-handed effort in providing such a rich photographic record of the Hebron team. Early on Don sensed a story in the making and on his own time took hundreds of photographs, providing them to the *Community News* free of charge. During the 1951-52 season his stories and photos appeared in the *Community News* without any attribution. Don's photographs are a major part of this book and we cannot thank him enough for allowing us to use them.

Then there are the *LIFE* Magazine photos. The players have always known that a photographer working for *LIFE* took pictures at the championship game and followed the team on their trip home. The pictures were never published. Russ Ahearn later obtained a few prints and distributed some of them to his players, who have kept them to this day. None of the players knew anything about the man who took the photos. Larry Burrows, who had just arrived in the United States from London and was witnessing his first basketball game, later became one of the world's most decorated war photojournalists, dying tragically while on assignment in Laos in 1971. His son, Russell Burrows, now oversees his photograph collection. Russell graciously produced new prints from the original negatives, many of which are included in this book.

Three recordings allowed us to recreate the championship game in its entirety. Although the first half of the historic television broadcast was lost in the studio, the second half remains priceless in evaluating the skills of the Hebron team and the look and feel of high school basketball in 1952. The second half, along with brief postgame interviews, is also preserved in a radio broadcast taped by WILL in Champaign and available in the University of Illinois Archives.

The entire championship game is preserved in a radio play-by-play recorded by WKRS in Waukegan and unearthed several years ago by Phil Judson. This broadcast, produced by the Public Service Company of Northern Illinois, was the last resort of the handful of homebound Hebron residents who could not find a friend with a television set. As an added bonus, the recording also includes interviews with the coaches and players after the caravan returned to Hebron the next day.

Dean Bentley, a 1977 Alden-Hebron graduate and basketball player, was partially responsible for our renewed interest in Hebron. His e-mail inquiring about an item on the IHSA Web site, which incorrectly listed the won-lost record of the championship team, prompted further investigation into the historic season, and one thing soon led to another. Subsequently Dean provided hours of microfilm research from the libraries in Woodstock and elsewhere in McHenry County.

Dean also looked over the manuscript prior to publication, as did a crack crew of researchers and writers — Bob Pruter, Dave Quinn, and Nelson Campbell — each of whom provided important feedback and encouragement.

In addition to those already mentioned, we would like to thank the following for their assistance.

- Family members of the 1952 players, coaches, and administration: Ruth Ann Judson Magnuson, Bill Ahearn, Daniel & Elinor Ahearn, Murry Ahearn, Tom Ahearn, Rosmary Ahearn, Irene Ahearn Cali, Craig Hadley, Shirley Schroeder Ihrke, Bob Schultz, and Marlene Tigard Peacock.
- Former Hebron basketball players: Lawrence Johnson ('36), Arthur "Red" Latham ('38) & wife Jeanette, Keith Johnson ('40), Wally Tibbits ('43), Tom Peacock ('47), Bob Nichols ('50), and Jim Judson ('51).
- Alden-Hebron High School administration: Delores Swanson, principal; Mary Ann Kahl, superintendent; Dr. Roger Damrow, retired superintendent.
- Other Hebron townspeople: John Lopeman, Tom Kuecker, Mary Nichols Holdeman, Jean Johnson, and Myra Vanderpal.
- Former players and coaches from other schools: George Latham (Quincy coach), Les Harman (Barrington coach), and Ron Weisner (Elgin '50).
- And others who provided assistance and information: Nancy Fike and Grace Moline of the McHenry County Historical Society, William Maher and Robert Chapel of the University of Illinois Archives, Chuck Rolinski of the Illinois Basketball

Coaches Association, Ken Mossman of Illinois State University, Jim O'Boye of KOST Broadcast Sales, Carter Crane and Woodrow Carroll of the *Fox Valley Labor News*, Bob Frisk of the *Daily Herald*, Corinne Smith of Elgin High School, Don Vogel of Oak Park and River Forest High School, Dick & Juanita Pilchard, William Maddux Sr., Dick Pierce, Harold Olson, Wayne Raguse, Doug Blair, and Brandon Burwell.

The final effort of turning our manuscript into a book fell to the IHSA's Desktop Publishing Department, Jackie Iverson and Kathy Casper, while Projects Manager Tina Brown helped coordinate the Hebron book and related activities. Together they and the rest of the staff make the IHSA a great place to work.

By coincidence, Tina's uncle played for Russ Ahearn (on the basketball team at Woodland High School). As it turns out, so did Scott's father (on the sophomore football team at Elgin). Previously undiscovered connections such as these popped up routinely in our conversations about Hebron and helped make the story very personal.

Scott's parents provided more than just moral support and guidance. Ben Johnson critiqued the manuscript while June and her husband Bob Burgess furnished overnight accommodations, not to mention provisions, during our frequent trips to Hebron.

Scott would be remiss if he did not mention the influence of his own mentor, E.C. Alft, Elgin High School economics teacher and historian extraordinaire, who started him on the path of research and writing in 1976 when Elgin approached its 1,000th basketball victory. Scott would also like to express his appreciation to Jim Flynn, IHSA Assistant Executive Director, who nurtured his interest in high school sports history until it eventually turned into a job.

Finally, we thank Dave Fry, IHSA Executive Director, for recognizing the special nature of Hebron's achievement and publishing the remarkable story of the 1952 Hebron Green Giants.

Scott Johnson & Julie Kistler
January, 2002

Appendix

Hebron's 1951-52 State Tournament Roster

No.	Name	Ht.	Wt.	Yr.	Pos.
4	Paul Judson	6-3	162	Sr.	G
6	Ken Spooner	5-11	172	Jr.	G
7	Joe Schmidt	6-0	165	Jr.	C
8	Don Wilbrandt	5-11	168	Sr.	F
9	Phil Judson	6-2	162	Sr.	F
10	Jim Bergin	5-10	141	Jr.	G
12	Bill Thayer	5-10	165	Sr.	G
17	Bill Schulz	6-10½	200	Jr.	C
21	Jim Wilbrandt	5-10	145	Soph.	F
22	Clayton Ihrke	5-10	148	Soph.	F

1951-52 Wire Service Polls

		Hebron		Quincy	
Date of Poll		AP	UP	AP	UP
Dec. 17	before McHenry County tournament	8	3	1	1
Dec. 24	before Kankakee Holiday Tournament	*	4	*	1
Dec. 31		1	1	4	5
Jan. 7		1	1	8	8
Jan. 14		1	1	7	6
Jan. 21	after loss to Crystal Lake	3	2	11	8
Jan. 28		1	2	9	4
Feb. 4		2	2	14	5
Feb. 11		2	2	12	7
Feb. 18		1	1	10	6
Feb. 25	before district tournament	1	1	8	3
Mar. 3	before regional tournament	1	*	5	*
Mar. 10	before sectional tournament (64 teams)	1	*	3	*
Mar. 17	before state final tournament (16 teams)	1	*	2	*

* — no poll taken

Hebron's Game-by-Game Record
(1948-52)

1948-49
Won 14, Lost 7

St. Mary's (Woodstock)	L	27	36
Barrington	L	35	43
St. Edward's (Elgin)	L	29	65
Genoa City, Wis.	W	46	45
McHenry	W	36	30
Huntley	W	34	32
Richmond	W	57	42
Harvard	W	49	38

McHenry County Tournament at Woodstock

• St. Mary's (Woodstock)	W	51	36
• Huntley	L	33	35
Genoa City, Wis.	W	60	53
Harvard	W	45	35
Huntley	W	30	27
Marengo	L	46	50
St. Edward's (Elgin)	L	44	70
McHenry	W	48	38
Wauconda	W	49	39
Woodstock	W	42	33
Richmond	W	71	31

District Tournament at Hebron

• Richmond	W	63	36
• St. Edward's (Elgin)	L	42	66

1949-50
Won 23, Lost 5

St. Edward's (Elgin)	W	53	26
Genoa City, Wis.	W	84	14
St. Mary's (Woodstock)	W	48	29
Woodstock	W	44	37
Huntley	W	49	27
Northwestern Military (Delafield, Wis.)	W	65	15
McHenry	W	64	36
Barrington	L	32	34
Richmond	W	62	26

McHenry County Tournament at Richmond

• Richmond	W	69	23
• St. Mary's (Woodstock)	W	59	25
• Crystal Lake	L	32	61

Holiday Tournament at Belvidere

• Belvidere	W	46	44
• St. Thomas (Rockford)	L	37	39
Genoa City, Wis.	W	85	19
Richmond	W	75	25
Wauconda	W	73	40
McHenry	W	71	42
Harvard	W	84	32
St. Mary's (Woodstock)	W	64	24
Wauconda	W	75	32
Huntley	W	65	41
Batavia	W	61	36
Marengo	L	44	47
Kirkland	W	79	45

District Tournament at St. Mary's

• St. Mary's (Woodstock)	W	44	27
• St. Edward's (Elgin)	W	39	35

Regional Tournament at Elgin

• Dundee	L	43	54

1950-51
Won 26, Lost 2

Dundee	W	35	30
St. Mary's (Woodstock)	W	79	26
Woodstock	W	40	24
Huntley	W	61	44
McHenry	W	56	31
Libertyville	W	67	52
McHenry County Tournament at McHenry			
• Woodstock	W	61	41
• Marengo	W	63	37
• Crystal Lake	W	55	36
Holiday Tournament at Kankakee			
• Bradley	L	53	56
• Urbana	W	64	28
• Kankakee	W	64	37
Huntley	W	71	24
Libertyville	W	74	36
Harvard	W	79	49
St. Edward's (Elgin)	W	46	42
Marengo	W	100	43
Kirkland	W	103	32
St. Mary's (Woodstock)	W	53	24
McHenry	W	63	24
Richmond	W	70	7
Batavia	W	71	53
West Rockford	W	57	56
District Tournament at Richmond			
• Huntley	W	69	32
• St. Edward's (Elgin)	W	61	36
Regional Tournament at Woodstock			
• Woodstock	W	68	56
• Dundee	W	63	56
• Elgin	L	51	54

1951-52
Won 35, Lost 1

Maple Park	W	63	37
McHenry	W	62	20
Joliet	W	51	43
St. Edward's (Elgin)	W	66	36
Lake Forest	W	81	55
McHenry County Tournament at Woodstock			
• Crystal Lake	W	56	39
• McHenry	W	85	47
• Woodstock	W	77	54
Holiday Tournament at Kankakee			
• South Shore (Chicago)	W	80	42
• Kankakee	W	69	54
• Danville	W	67	53
Oak Park	W	63	55
Harvard	W	96	34
St. Edward's (Elgin)	W	71	53
Marengo	W	77	32
Crystal Lake	L	68	71
Marmion	W	88	37
Woodstock	W	88	58
Riverside	W	71	54
Lake Forest	W	77	52
Marmion	W	60	55
DeKalb	W	70	40
Waukegan	W	61	46
Barrington	W	83	39
Belvidere	W	84	54
District Tournament at Richmond			
• St. Mary's	W	45	16
• St. Edward's (Elgin)	W	35	23
Regional Tournament at Elgin			
• Woodstock	W	95	45
• Crystal Lake	W	61	46
• Elgin	W	49	47
Sectional Tournament at Waukegan			
• Barrington	W	64	42
• DeKalb	W	68	46
State Tournament at Huff Gym, Champaign			
• Champaign	W	55	46
• Lawrenceville	W	65	55
• Rock Island	W	64	56
• Quincy	(OT) W	64	59

State Final Boxscores

First Round Game
Thursday, March 20, 1952

HEBRON (55)	FG	FGA	FT	FTA	Pts	PF
Paul Judson	5	12	7	13	17	2
Phil Judson	4	9	4	5	12	5
Bill Schulz	4	10	1	2	9	3
Ken Spooner	3	8	1	1	7	0
Bill Thayer	0	1	0	0	0	0
Don Wilbrandt	4	10	2	4	10	3
TOTAL	20	50	15	25	55	13

CHAMPAIGN (46)	FG	FGA	FT	FTA	Pts	PF
Clarence Burks	3	10	1	3	7	5
Stanley Butts	3	7	2	5	8	5
Larry Hopkins	2	10	0	0	4	0
Ken Kellerhals	0	3	0	0	0	3
Ronnie Koch	1	1	0	0	2	0
Loren Leach	8	20	2	3	18	5
Jerry McKinney	3	10	0	0	6	3
Tom Meeks	0	2	0	0	0	1
Dick Taylor	0	3	1	2	1	1
Raymond Wise	0	0	0	0	0	1
TOTAL	20	66	6	13	46	24

Hebron	16	20	11	8	—	55
Champaign	14	7	14	11	—	46

Semifinal Game
Saturday, March 22, 1952

HEBRON (64)	FG	FGA	FT	FTA	Pts	PF
Paul Judson	2	7	8	9	12	4
Phil Judson	5	18	2	4	12	1
Bill Schulz	7	11	6	6	20	3
Ken Spooner	2	8	2	3	6	0
Bill Thayer	0	0	0	0	0	2
Don Wilbrandt	5	15	4	6	14	2
TOTAL	21	59	22	28	64	12

ROCK ISLAND (56)	FG	FGA	FT	FTA	Pts	PF
Merrell Clark	8	27	2	4	18	2
Bill Geisler	1	5	0	0	2	1
Jerry Hansen	7	22	0	0	14	3
Albert Hanson	0	2	0	0	0	2
Dick Pewe	0	0	0	0	0	2
Milt Scheuerman	2	7	3	3	7	4
Chuck Thomas	2	3	1	1	5	5
Stuart Thoms	4	16	2	7	10	5
TOTAL	24	82	8	15	56	24

Hebron	15	17	13	19	—	64
Rock Island	12	14	20	10	—	56

Quarterfinal Game
Friday, March 21, 1952

HEBRON (65)	FG	FGA	FT	FTA	Pts	PF
Jim Bergin	0	0	0	0	0	0
Clayton Ihrke	0	0	0	0	0	0
Paul Judson	8	12	1	4	17	5
Phil Judson	3	9	4	5	10	4
Joe Schmidt	0	0	0	0	0	0
Bill Schulz	6	13	0	4	12	3
Ken Spooner	4	7	0	2	8	0
Bill Thayer	0	0	0	0	0	1
Don Wilbrandt	7	12	4	4	18	2
Jim Wilbrandt	0	0	0	0	0	0
TOTAL	28	53	9	19	65	15

LAWRENCEVILLE (55)	FG	FGA	FT	FTA	Pts	PF
Bill Albright	0	0	0	0	0	0
Larry Breyfogle	2	14	2	2	6	3
John Brooks	3	15	1	2	7	2
Kay Gosnell	1	10	3	5	5	5
Tom Kelly	7	23	6	8	20	3
Bill Woods	8	15	1	1	17	3
TOTAL	21	77	13	18	55	16

Hebron	20	18	13	14	—	65
Lawrenceville	12	9	19	15	—	55

Championship Game
Saturday, March 22, 1952

HEBRON (64)	FG	FGA	FT	FTA	Pts	PF
Paul Judson	6	12	1	4	13	3
Phil Judson	3	8	6	7	12	3
Bill Schulz	12	16	0	1	24	2
Ken Spooner	2	7	1	1	5	3
Don Wilbrandt	3	16	4	7	10	4
TOTAL	26	59	12	20	64	15

QUINCY (59)	FG	FGA	FT	FTA	Pts	PF
Bruce Brothers	8	12	4	6	20	5
Charley Fast	3	10	4	5	10	4
Jack Gower	5	10	1	2	11	2
Phil Harvey	2	12	4	4	8	2
Tom Payne	1	5	0	0	2	1
Dick Thompson	2	14	4	4	8	0
TOTAL	21	63	17	21	59	14

Hebron	14	20	14	10	6	— 64
Quincy	16	19	13	10	1	— 59

Source: IHSA press material

236

Index

"H.S." indicates "high school." Unless otherwise noted, all high schools are located in the Illinois town of the same name.

Permissions

UNPUBLISHED MATERIAL

Material from Russ Ahearn's notebooks and instructions is quoted with the permission of Judy Ahearn Benda.

NEWSPAPER ARTICLES

"Green Giants Become Team of Destiny," by Don Peasley. © Don Peasley. Used with permission. All rights reserved.

"Is It True What They Say About Hebron?" by Frank Reichstein. © *Beloit Daily News*. Used with permission. All rights reserved.

"Hebron Can Be Beaten," by Jack Prowell. © *Champaign News-Gazette*. Used with permission. All rights reserved.

PHOTOGRAPHS

Photos by Don Peasley: © Don Peasley. Used with permission. All rights reserved.

Photos by Larry Burrows: © 1952 Larry Burrows, © Larry Burrows Collection.

Photos by the *Elgin Courier-News*: © *Elgin Courier-News*. Used with permission. All rights reserved.

Photos by the *Rockford Morning Star* and the *Rockford Register-Republic*: © 2002 *Rockford Register-Star*. Used with permission. Cannot be used in any manner without permission from the *Rockford Register-Star*.

Photos by the *Champaign News-Gazette*: © *Champaign News-Gazette*. Used with permission. All rights reserved. Courtesy of the University of Illinois Archives.

Photos by the Associated Press: © Associated Press. Used with permission. All rights reserved.

About the Authors

DAVID LEE / PHOTOGRAPHY BY LEE

Scott Johnson and Julie Kistler are both graduates of Elgin High School and the University of Illinois at Urbana-Champaign. Although they have been married for 21 years, *Once There Were Giants* is their first literary collaboration. Johnson, an assistant executive director with the Illinois High School Association, has researched and written many articles and monographs on Illinois high school sports, while Kistler is a full-time writer with some 25 published novels and more than 600 theater reviews to her credit.

About the
Illinois High School
Activities Foundation

All proceeds from the sale of this edition go to the Illinois High School Activities Foundation. Established in 1994, the Illinois High School Activities Foundation (IHSAF) is a not-for-profit corporation that recognizes academic and interscholastic achievements by the young people who participate in the programs sponsored by the IHSA.

Every year, more than 350,000 young men and women represent their high schools in IHSA athletic and activity programs ranging from basketball to chess. Research shows that students who participate in high school athletic and activity programs achieve higher grade point averages, miss fewer days of school, score higher on standardized tests, and are more self-confident.

Through 2001, the IHSAF has awarded over $200,000 to deserving students across the state of Illinois through student recognition and award programs. With your support, the IHSAF will continue to pursue its mission.

For more information on the IHSAF, please contact:

Illinois High School Association
2715 McGraw Dr.
P.O. Box 2715
Bloomington, IL 61702-2715

Phone: (309) 663-6377
E-mail: ihsa@ihsa.org
World Wide Web: www.ihsa.org

247

Once There Were Giants

Order Form

<table>
<tr><td><u>Mail to:</u></td><td><u>Or fax to:</u></td></tr>
<tr><td>*Once There Were Giants*</td><td></td></tr>
<tr><td>**IHSA**</td><td>**IHSA**</td></tr>
<tr><td>**P.O. Box 2715**</td><td>**309-663-7479**</td></tr>
<tr><td>**Bloomington, IL 61702-2715**</td><td></td></tr>
</table>

Name _____

Address _____

City _____ State _____ ZIP _____

Telephone Number _____

Number of Copies _____ x $18 = Amount Due $ _____

($18 includes tax, shipping, and handling)

Paying by: _____ Check (payable to Illinois High School Assn.)

or Credit Card: ___Master Card ___Visa ___Discover

Credit Card No. _____Exp. Date ____/____

Authorized Signature_____

**All proceeds from the sale of this edition go to the
Illinois High School Activities Foundation.**

You may also call 309-663-6377 or visit
<u>www.ihsa.org/hebron</u> for more information.